Pritikin Success Stories Add Up—
As Weight *Goes Down*!

- The 56-year-old man who reduced his weight from 330 to 220, his waistline from 48 to 38 inches, and his dangerously high-blood pressure to the equivalent of a healthy *40*-year-old.

- The great-grandmother who trimmed down by forty pounds, put away her wheelchair, and today is happily rediscovering the joys of a vigorous outdoor life.

- Nathan Pritikin, founder of the Pritikin Program, who twenty years ago reversed a serious heart condition with a diet and exercise regimen that saved his life.

Since the first Pritikin Center was established five years ago, Nathan Pritikin has worked with thousands of overweight people, successfully introducing them to a permanent and pleasant new way of eating. Now, discover for yourself the exciting and proven treatment that's working scientific miracles. Prescribed by doctors across the country, it's adding glowing, vibrant years to the lives of their patients.

You've never dreamed dieting could be so easy or so effective—day after day, year after year. And *your* name to the growing list, and make yourself living proof to the phenomenal success of

The Pritikin Permanent
Weig

Bantam Books by Nathan Pritikin

THE PRITIKIN PERMANENT WEIGHT-LOSS MANUAL
THE PRITIKIN PROGRAM FOR DIET & EXERCISE
(with Patrick M. McGrady, Jr.)

QUANTITY PURCHASES

Companies, professional groups, churches, clubs, and other
organizations may qualify for special terms when ordering
24 or more copies of this title. For information, contact the
Special Sales Department, Bantam Books, 666 Fifth Avenue,
New York, NY 10103. Phone (800) 223-6834. New York State
residents call (212) 765-6500.

The Pritikin
Permanent Weight-Loss Manual

By Nathan Pritikin

Illustrated by Joann T. Rounds

BANTAM BOOKS
NEW YORK · TORONTO · LONDON · SYDNEY · AUCKLAND

THE PRITIKIN PERMANENT WEIGHT-LOSS MANUAL

*A Bantam Book / published by arrangement with
Grosset & Dunlap Inc.*

PRINTING HISTORY
*Grosset & Dunlap edition published April 1981
A Selection of Literary Guild August 1981
Serialized in* Good Housekeeping Magazine *and Syndication
L.A. Times Syndicate.
Bantam edition / April 1982*

To the overweight victims of modern cuisine, whose need for a healthful and livable approach to permanent weight control inspired this book.

BEFORE YOU START

The diets in this book are complete nutritionally so that the ordinary overweight person should be able to stay on them for whatever period is required for him or her to attain normal weight. However, anyone may have a special health problem, and it would be prudent to check with your physician before embarking on a new diet; similarly, if you are over thirty-five, first see your doctor. If you are on prescription drugs, your need for them may drop drastically. You should, therefore, be monitored by your physician during the weight-loss period. Your medication should be modified only by your physician.

Physicians, dietitians, and other health professionals with questions about starting or maintaining patients on these diets should address them to Pritikin Programs, P.O. Box 5335, Santa Barbara, California 93108.

AFTER YOU START

See "A Special Note to the Reader" on page 397.

Contents

PART II
RECIPES

APPENDIX

Preface

The insistent theme in my previous books, media appearances, and talks before medical professionals and lay audiences has been that Americans in large droves are eating themselves into degenerative diseases, including mass killers like heart disease and some cancers. The bright side of my message has been that with the proper dietary lifestyle these degenerative diseases need never occur, or, if symptoms have begun, are often reversible once the harmful foods are replaced by healthful ones.

Overweight is a problem that affects one out of two adults in our country and is very much related to the problem of degenerative diseases. Obesity provides the environment for the development of at least two degenerative diseases, adult-onset diabetes and hypertension. If millions of overweight people can be motivated to change to a healthy dietary lifestyle to achieve *permanent* weight loss, they will have removed themselves from the degenerative disease collision course. By solving their weight problem permanently, these people can also greatly reduce their risk of heart disease and other degenerative diseases, because the very dietary lifestyle that can return them to normal weight and keep them slim permanently will also stave off degenerative diseases.

Other approaches, if they are not based on a complete change in dietary lifestyle such as I have been recommending, do not achieve a permanent return to normal weight. Temporary diets, followed by a resumption of previous weight-accumulating eating patterns, are obviously guaranteed to fail. Episodes of weight loss consistently followed by return of the pounds lost are frustrating and demoralizing experiences. Though futile, these temporary diets may also be physically disastrous. Gout, kidney failure, diabetes, heart attacks, strokes, and even death have been caused by high-protein diets, the most popular form of reducing diet in use today.

Thirty years ago Dr. Walter Kempner, working at Duke University's Department of Medicine, demonstrated that a high-carbohydrate diet in which over 80 percent of calories ingested came from carbohydrates could reverse obesity as well as diabetes and hypertension in obese individuals. But somehow the myth that carbohydrate foods cause obesity has managed not only to survive but to flourish. The first line of defense for most people when they begin to put on weight is to cut back on carbohydrates. Man's natural diet—the diet that keeps people slim and free of degenerative diseases—is a diet that is high in whole natural carbohydrate foods. The Pritikin Diet, which has achieved such notable successes in restoring people sick with degenerative diseases to normal functioning, is a wide-ranging, highly palatable, and practical cuisine utilizing large amounts of whole natural carbohydrate foods combined with safe amounts of dairy and animal foods that are fat-free or low in fat.

In my work as director of the Pritikin Centers, the first of which I founded in January 1976, I have seen 7,000 people come through our program. About two-thirds of them were overweight. About half of these overweight people were obese, more than 20 percent over normal weight. Some of these individuals, veterans in the battle for normal weight, had already each lost (and subsequently regained) a total of 1,000 pounds. Many of these overweight individuals had already developed advanced degenerative disease symptoms, including angina. Others were unaware that degenerative disease symptoms had already begun and were mainly concerned with their impaired image because of their weight problem. At the Centers, following the weight-loss Pritikin Diet—a lower-calorie version of the regular Pritikin Diet—together with a walking program, they lost not only their excess pounds but also their diabetes and hypertension. Those with arthritis had a relief of symptoms. All experienced a reduction in risk factors leading to heart disease and other degenerative diseases. One of the most wonderful aspects of their Center experience, I was told repeatedly by many people, was that this was the first reducing diet they had been on which did not cause them to be hungry most of the time, and that it was a basic diet they could easily stay on the rest of their lives.

The American diet that makes many of us obese does so because natural whole carbohydrate foods are replaced in large amounts by high fat and fiber-depleted foods, the kinds of foods that also bring on degenerative diseases. The diet I advocate for all individuals, overweight or lean, restores the natural whole carbohydrate foods and drastically reduces the intake of other foods. Such a diet keeps people slim and healthy for life. During the period that excess weight needs to be shed, the diet is modified only in that the whole carbohydrate foods consumed are particularly low in calories; the more highly caloric whole carbohydrate foods are eaten in larger quantities after normal weight is achieved.

Many dietary programs are very expensive, requiring high-priced foods, supplements, pills, shots, or drugs. On the Pritikin Diet, your only expenditure will be ordinary foods that will very likely reduce your food budget. By choosing my dietary approach, you have nothing to lose but pounds and possibly some degenerative disease symptoms.

I am very proud of my successes in helping people achieve not only normal weight but improved health as well. I hope you will be motivated to try this approach so that you too may be successful in easily achieving and maintaining normal weight, as well as in improving your chances for a longer and more healthy life.

NATHAN PRITIKIN
April 1981

Acknowledgments

I am deeply indebted to two individuals in particular for invaluable assistance throughout the entire period of manuscript preparation. Ilene Pritikin, my wife, participated in many aspects involved and acted also as project coordinator. Nan Bronfen, nutritionist for the Pritikin Research Foundation, lent her considerable talents to research, writing, and editing. Their unfailing enthusiasm and support made the work of writing this book a joy.

Several staff members of the Pritikin Center in Santa Monica, California, were especially helpful. Jan Ostendorff, M.A., Exercise Physiologist, provided excellent reference material for Chapter 9. Janet Segall, R.D., Cristine Newport, Home Economist, and Barry Herman, Food Service Manager, were generous with suggestions, chapter reviews, and other forms of aid. I am grateful for the contributions of Cleaves Bennett, M.D., and Miles Robinson, M.D., for material in Chapter 11, "For the Health Professional," and for reviewing the finished chapter. Jana Trent devised the menu plans and supervised the recipe work, and Esther Taylor and Dorothy Diehl, R.D., tested all recipes. Nell Taylor, my capable secretary, did the indexing, and Donna Thiesen and Cathy Paradise assisted with recipe writing. Peter Lee of The Flower Drum, New York, provided the Chinese calligraphy. Last but certainly not least, my thanks to Nancy Brooks, our editor, for her unending care and exceptional competence in her work with this manuscript.

Part I
Mathematical

Part I
Why and How

1

Why Another Diet Book?

At your last birthday, was one of your "presents" another few pounds of unwanted padding? Chances are it was. Excess poundage afflicts most adults in our society, the pounds creeping up faster than the years. If you've been blaming yourself for it, don't. You and I are trapped in a crazy culture that worships slimness (Weight Watchers, TOPS, Overeaters Anonymous, and other such organizations enroll more members than do churches these days), yet seduces us at every turn with fattening foods.

It's the ultimate tease. "Stay slim," says our culture (or nobody will love you; you won't even love yourself). But it's practically impossible to stay slim on the kind of food most people have been taught to cook at home or that is served to us at dinner parties, in restaurants, even in hospitals. Pick up a woman's magazine and the contradictions hit you. You'll find fashions for the slender and glamorous next to fattening recipes for the family and for elegant entertaining. The medical consequences of obesity are grave, greatly increasing your chances of developing heart trouble and other degenerative diseases; and heart disease is the leading cause of death in our country, accounting for millions of lives, most of them men. So in the same magazine that offers dozens of recipes that contribute to obesity, you're likely to find an article on how to handle your sex life after your husband had had his first coronary. Insane, isn't it?

In response to the modern obesity epidemic, new diets and diet plans appear with boring regularity. In general, they fail because their adherents return in time to their former weight-accumulating lifestyle. Many of the diets are harmful; with some, the dieter even flirts with death. The liquid protein diets of recent years have gained notoriety because of at least 58 deaths attributed to their use. In desperation, the medical establishment

3

has evolved nondietary methods for treating the obese, especially the massively obese. The roster of bizarre and unnatural techniques is incredible, including procedures such as jaw-wiring and tying off part of the intestinal tract to curtail digestion. These are last-ditch measures that reflect the failure of medical science to deal with the problem in more rational ways.

My message in this book is that there is only one way out of the trap. The way out—that will make you slim permanently—will also protect you from a heart attack and other degenerative diseases like high blood pressure, adult-onset diabetes, gout, and other cheery conditions we're supposed to come down with as a "natural" consequence of aging. It doesn't have to be like this, and the style of eating I am going to introduce you to will keep you slim *and* healthy for the rest of your life. Unfortunately, until I began aggressively expounding these views, the idea had not caught on (except in limited circles) that a very simple approach to the problem of obesity and its medical consequences is to undo some of the evils of the modern diet, which is weight-accumulating by its very nature. Changing over to a diet based largely on foods as nature has grown them—nonfattening, nutritionally balanced whole carbohydrate foods—supplemented by optional and prudent amounts of low-fat animal foods, could trim billions of pounds of flab from overweight American figures.

The Pritikin Diet has gained growing respect and attention from both lay and medical communities because of the dramatic results it obtains with hypertensives, cardiac patients, adult-onset diabetics, and victims of other degenerative diseases. Over 7,000 people have come for rehabilitation to the two Pritikin Centers. For the one-third of these who are obese (20 percent or more over normal weight), we have found that our program can be very effective in weight control. While medication slowed the rate of weight loss for many, computer analysis of weight loss achieved by the first 893 Pritikin Center participants is impressive. Based on weights from day 2 to day 23, for a projected 30-day period weight loss for men was 15 to 27 pounds and for women 11 to 19 pounds (see chart, page 60).

When optimum weight is reached as a result of following the lower-calorie end of the Pritikin Diet, the formerly overweight individual merely graduates to the regular Pritikin Diet with its normal caloric intake, maintaining his or her slim new figure with no difficulties on the higher-calorie regimen. At this point

THE PRITIKIN DIET

Low-Calorie End   High-Calorie End

The Low-Calorie End of the Pritikin Diet Is the Pritikin Weight-Loss Diet

many graduates of the low-calorie end of the diet have to make a conscious effort to increase their caloric intake: they have become accustomed to and enjoy some of the low-calorie dishes, such as the salads and soups, and must be encouraged to eat higher-calorie meals. To help with this adjustment—a dream "problem" for most overweight people—Chapter 10 is devoted to the transition from low-calorie to maintenance diet to prevent continuing weight loss. Continuing to lose weight after optimum weight is reached actually becomes a concern for about one out of every six formerly overweight people who follow the weight-loss Pritikin Diet.

THE MECHANICS OF WEIGHT LOSS

The foods we eat are composed of protein, fats, and carbohydrates. Each of these major nutrients can be metabolized in the body to produce energy, which is measured in calories. Potentially, protein and carbohydrates contain 4 calories per gram; fat contains 9 calories per gram, more than twice as many. The ongoing normal body processes burn up a certain amount of calories, and physical activity expends more. All weight-reduction diets are based on the principle that if fewer calories are taken in than are expended, weight will be lost, but they differ in how the proportions of the basic nutrients—protein, fats, and carbohydrates—are manipulated. A safe diet needs to provide a proper balance in order to enable the dieter's body to function well without damage while shedding pounds. The Pritikin Diet, utilizing in the main low-calorie, whole carbohydrate foods supplemented by small amounts of animal-protein foods, is safe because it is balanced and therefore provides all the body's nutritional needs.

What's wrong with other diets and diet plans that are in use today? My main complaint about most of them is that they are harmful to the body. They are also ineffective, because sooner or later the dieter returns to his original weight-accumulating lifestyle. Even safe diet plans like the famous Kempner Diet developed by Dr. Walter Kempner at Duke University have this drawback. Unless patients leaving the Kempner facility make permanent changes in their eating habits, they gain back the weight they have lost. The Pritikin Diet, on the other hand, trains the dieter in a basic dietary lifestyle that is continued after optimum weight level is achieved with the sole modification of including greater amounts of higher-calorie carbohydrate foods that had been restricted during the weight-loss period.

HIGH-PROTEIN DIETS

These are the most popular diets in use today, followed by millions of people who have swallowed the widely accepted myths that 1. starchy foods are fattening and lacking in nutrients (about which more later); and 2. the higher the protein content in the diet, the better. These diets simply are not safe. The average American diet already contains excessive amounts of protein, and on the high-protein diets, which restrict carbohydrates and are correspondingly very high in fats (and cholesterol), the dieter develops health problems and doesn't even have permanent weight loss to show for it.

The best known high-protein diets of recent years are the Scarsdale Diet, the Atkins Diet, and the Stillman Diet, and there have been many others. Some of these diets gain prestige because they are written by a physician, and people are usually unaware that the high-protein diets have been vehemently criticized again and again by major medical organizations. Here's why.

Adherence to a high-protein diet usually results in initial weight loss, but the loss is not permanent. It is due primarily to large amounts of water lost from the tissues because the body is trying to eliminate the dangerous byproducts of the large amounts of protein ingested. The body dilutes these harmful substances by drawing water from the tissues. As the toxic materials together with the large amounts of water needed to dilute them are eliminated from the body, weight drops. The dieter is thrilled as the scale dips—but not for long. After the first week, when a certain amount of water is lost from the tissues, the dieter's weight tends to level off. When the high-protein diet is abandoned and the dieter returns to a normal diet containing less protein, there is no further weight loss. In fact, the body overreacts in an attempt to regain the water needed for the health

INITIAL WEIGHT LOSS ON HIGH-PROTEIN DIETS IS NOT PERMANENT

of the tissue cells, and weight soon increases toward prediet levels. Dr. R. C. Atkins bemoans this: "I concede that the worst feature about this diet is the rapidity with which you gain if you abandon it." When a person on a low-calorie diet that contains adequate carbohydrates goes to a moderate-calorie diet, weight loss continues. However, when you go from a low-calorie, high-protein diet that is correspondingly low in carbohydrates to one moderate in calories and carbohydrates, some of the lost weight is regained. Thus many followers of high-protein weight-loss diets develop a pattern of alternately bingeing on their regular diets, then doing penance and considerable damage to themselves by "doing time" on the high-protein regimens. This pingponging puts a strain on the heart and the various metabolic systems of the body.

Even in the opinion of their promulgators, high-protein diets are not safe to follow for long periods of time. Dr. Atkins admits that his diet acts as a diuretic resulting in the loss not only of tissue fluids but also of essential minerals. Dr. Herman Tarnower's Scarsdale Diet, which contains more than three times the protein in the average American diet, also contains a warning against following the plan for longer than two weeks. The dieter is advised as well that the regimen could be dangerous for pregnant women, alcoholics, and severe diabetics; and that if you feel ill while on the diet, you should go off it for a while.

Diets that are high in protein upset the body's chemistry in many ways—so much so that the urine of those on a high-protein diet tests like a diabetic's because of the presence of the highly toxic and acid substances known as ketones. In diabetics, ketones are produced because the patient cannot use carbohydrates properly. In the high-protein dieter, ketones are produced because the diet drastically restricts carbohydrate intake. Fat metabolism cannot take place without carbohydrates—the more fat in the diet, the more carbohydrate breakdown products are required. High-protein diets depend primarily upon animal foods, which contain no carbohydrates but which are high in fat and cholesterol. Plant foods, which contain carbohydrates along with their protein content, are highly restricted.

Unfortunately, the body reacts badly to this kind of dietary manipulation. The toxic breakdown products of protein metabolism must be eliminated, and they are flushed out of the body with large amounts of water. This frequent and copious elimination of water is a characteristic symptom of diabetics, along with the resulting excessive thirst. What's happening of course to the follower of the high-protein diet—who at this stage is "losing weight"—is that the body is dehydrating itself in order to avoid being poisoned! And poisoned is not too strong a word: kidney damage and even death could be the result.

In breaking down the "overdose" of protein, large amounts of ammonia are formed, which has adverse effects on the brain, liver, kidney, and spleen. The body odors associated with a high-protein diet result from both the ammonia and the ketone bodies, wich cause an unpleasant taste in the mouth and produce bad breath. For this, Dr. Atkins recommends chlorophyll tablets or Sen-Sen.

Toxins from protein breakdown also contribute to a sense of fatigue. Subjects on a high-protein diet who were studied experienced fatigue after two days, as well as a significant drop in blood pressure on rising from a sitting position.

So much for the ill effects of the excessive quantities of protein itself. The large amounts of fat and cholesterol consumed on the high-protein diets cause their own problems, particularly the formation of plaques, cholesterol-filled deposits that gradually build up on the inside of the artery walls, restricting blood flow to the heart and other organs and tissues. A group of physicians studying the effects of the Stillman Diet on healthy volunteers adhering to the diet for 3 to 17 days found that, on the average, blood cholesterol increased during this short period from 215 mg. % to 248 mg. %, putting the dieters into the high-risk category for developing heart disease. In addition, most of the subjects complained of fatigue, nausea, and diarrhea, and found it difficult to comply with the diet for more than a week. The average temporary weight loss was 6.8 pounds, due primarily to water loss. Contributing to weight loss was the fact that at first, when the dieters were growing accustomed to eating so much protein, they tended to eat less; when they became used to the diet and began consuming more calories, weight loss ceased.

The animal-source foods that dominate high-protein diets cause elevation of blood uric-acid levels. Dr. Atkins acknowledges that in people with a tendency to gout, an attack could be precipitated. To alleviate the problem he routinely recommends the use of a drug like Allopurinol. Of course, there is a risk of side effects from such a drug.

Since foods from animal products contain no fiber, malfunctions of the bowel, varicose veins, and thrombophlebitis may arise. For the constipation that often develops on high-protein diets, both the Atkins Diet and the Scarsdale Diet suggest laxatives. This is not a good idea, as laxatives can be harmful and habit-forming and should never be used on a regular basis. Constipation is rare in people whose diet, like the Pritikin Diet, contains adequate amounts of unrefined carbohydrate foods.

Because a diet that excludes or severely limits carbohydrates lacks vitamins and minerals present in natural carbohydrate foods, Dr. Atkins favors supplementing his high-protein diet from the start with very large amounts of vitamins and minerals. He explains that this will alleviate the "washed-out feeling" and other symptoms caused by the diet. Taking extracted vitamins and, especially, minerals can upset the delicate balance of these substances in the body and can do more harm than good. The best way to ensure getting all the vitamins and minerals your body requires to function properly is to take them the way nature has packaged them, in foods as grown.

Dr. Atkins admits that strenuous exercise is not feasible on his diet, acknowledging that the body is unable to convert fats to energy fast enough to sustain such exertion. People following the Atkins Diet who want to participate in any type of vigorous activity would probably be forced to include carbohydrates in the diet.

Some of the problems associated with high-protein diets don't show up right away. It takes years on such a diet to result in osteoporosis, or weakening of the bones. After protein has been metabolized, certain acid-forming substances remain in the body that cause minerals to be leached from the bones. The diet of the Eskimos, which is extremely high in protein, results in substantial bone loss by the age of thirty-five. There is also preliminary evidence that increasing dietary protein in experimental animals and possibly in human beings results in an increased amount of intestinal and liver cancer.

Dr. Atkins, who is well aware of the multiple and serious difficulties that can result from high-protein diets, recommends close medical supervision and constant laboratory testing for those following his regimen. In his response to the statement attacking his diet by members of the Council on Foods and

---

Adverse Effects of High-Protein Diets

- Diuresis and mineral imbalance
- Accumulation of toxic substances (ketones, uric acid, ammonia)
- Rapid weight gain after abandoning the diet
- Elevated blood cholesterol that narrows the arteries
- Increased risk of kidney malfunction
- Halitosis   • Fatigue   • Nausea   • Constipation
- Rapid lowering of the blood pressure on rising
- Possible increased risk of colon disease
- Vitamin and mineral depletion

Nutrition of the American Medical Association, he prided himself that "they were able to cite no more than three areas of danger potential—impaired kidney function, elevation of uric-acid levels, and elevation of serum lipid [blood fats]." We concur that these are indeed serious consequences of following his or any high-protein diet, and there are other problems as well. For a summation, see the chart on page 10.

If high-protein diets are bad for you, a version of these diets in which the nutrients are given in liquid form is even worse.

LIQUID PROTEIN DIETS

For a while, dieting with predigested protein liquids was the rage. As of the summer of 1978, these nutritionally incomplete diets had caused 58 deaths and many severe illnesses. Sudden deaths were caused by irregular heartbeat in people with no history of heart disease, who died either while they were on the diet or shortly after discontinuing it. These diets can cause nutritional deficiencies, dehydration, rapid lowering of the blood pressure on standing, dizziness, fainting, muscle weakness and cramps, nausea and vomiting, dry skin, and loss of hair. They also create insulin deficiency, fatty deposits in the liver, and stress on the kidneys. People are in most danger from these diets when they first start on them and when they return to solid food. It's a good thing that the dieters are hungry most of the time, as the fact that many people do not adhere to the diet strictly but nibble on the side prevents the loss of an even greater number of lives.

These diets have recently emerged again in a new wave of popularity in supervised medical settings, under the name PSMF or protein-sparing modified fast. The assumption is that with careful medical supervision such as exists in a large university hospital, medical schools, or physicians' offices, patients will not be in danger. The tragic fallacy of this assumption was brought out in a recent study that exposed the dangers of PSMF and called for a ban on liquid protein diets while further investigations are made.

There is nothing good that can be said for high-protein diets, whether liquid or solid. I am against them because of their inherent dangers, because they discourage people from adopting healthy and satisfying eating habits, and because they are of dubious effectiveness even in the short term. High-protein diets don't even have economy to recommend them, since a diet relying heavily on food from animal sources is more costly than one using large amounts of foods as grown.

FASTING

While some people pingpong back and forth between their regular diet and a high-protein diet in an effort to fight obesity, others play the weight-control game by going on occasional fasts. Fasting, in the misguided view of many, is a healthy way to shed pounds and also to detoxify the system. Nothing could be further from the truth. Fasting, especially prolonged fasting, can be dangerous. Even if fasting were safe, it is questionable whether the additional loss of approximately 6 pounds per month over the weight loss that can be achieved on the lowest calorie level (700 calories daily intake) of the Pritikin Diet justifies the physical and emotional trauma of fasting.

SOURCES OF WEIGHT LOSS IN A TWO-WEEK PERIOD ON TWO WEIGHT-LOSS REGIMENS				
	Pounds Lost on Liquid Protein Diet		Pounds Lost Fasting	
	Week 1	*Week 2*	*Week 1*	*Week 2*
Emptying of digestive tract	3–9	0	4–10	0
Dehydration	4	0	2	0
Water loss due to breakdown of muscle	0	0	3	1.5
Tissue loss (fat + muscle)	3	3	4	4
Total loss	10–16	3	13–19	5.5
Loss after deducting weight loss due to water and emptying of digestive tract	3	3	4	4

People on fasts and high-protein diets are fooled about the amount of weight they have really lost. Our 25-foot-long intestinal tract normally holds about 4 to 10 pounds of food contents in various states of digestion. On fasts lasting several days, the tract is emptied. When normal eating is resumed, the tract fills up again within a week—and back come 4 to 10 pounds. The absence of bulk in the high-protein diet produces a similar although lesser effect of illusory weight loss due to decrease in the intestinal contents. The water loss that accompanies the breakdown of body protein during fasting, or of dietary protein on high-protein diets, promotes the illusion of dramatic weight loss.

The excessive breakdown of protein in the lean body tissue is the main problem with fasting. The body's most essential requirement is, of course, energy. In the absence of food to supply energy, the body quickly depletes its glucose stores and then begins to break down the protein in the body tissues. Lean body mass—muscle tissue and the tissue of vital organs—is broken down to release protein to be burned for the energy necessary for life. On prolonged fasts, a very large amount of muscle, including heart muscle, is lost, especially during the first month. During this time, half of the weight loss comes from lean body mass rather than from adipose (fat) tissue, and muscle cells shrink to half their normal size. After the first month, a fourth to a third of the weight loss is due to loss of muscle tissue.

Metabolism takes place largely in the lean tissue cells; the main function of the fat cells in adipose tissue is to store energy in the form of fat. When the proportion of lean tissue cells to fat cells is lowered because of the loss of lean tissue mass, after the fast is broken the body is less efficient in converting food to energy and a larger proportion of the food eaten goes to fat. Thus it actually becomes harder to lose weight after you have fasted, especially after an extended fast.

It is undesirable to lose body protein; it is the excess fat that has accumulated in the cells of adipose tissue that needs to be depleted. You need to lose weight in a manner that causes the greatest loss of fat and the smallest loss of protein. A recent study compared protein lost in fasting and on two 800-calorie diets, one of which was high in protein, while the other included more carbohydrates. The protein-wasting propensity of fasting showed up clearly in the number of grams of protein lost on each of the three regimens over a five-day period:

Regimen	Carbohydrate	Grams of Protein Lost Per Day
Fasting	0	50.4
800-calorie ketogenic (high-protein) diet	10 gm (~5%)	17.9
800-calorie mixed (moderate-carbohydrate) diet	90 gm (~45%)	9.5

The 5 percent and 45 percent carbohydrate diets contain the same number of calories. However, there is a much greater loss of body protein on the high protein diet, because it contains so little protein-sparing carbohydrate. As the carbohydrate in the diet is increased to 45 percent, the loss of body protein is decreased. A regimen high in carbohydrate, such as the weight-loss Pritikin Diet, which is about 70 percent carbohydrate, spares body protein to a greater degree than other hypocaloric regimens. Fasting results in the greatest loss of lean body tissue because no carbohydrate is taken in.

Fasting presents other problems, too. Though body tissue is broken down, the amount of glucose thus released for energy will still be below normal levels. Because glucose is essential for brain cells—the brain cannot normally use other energy sources—fasting can result in sluggishness, nausea, blackouts, confusion, inability to concentrate, lack of coordination, dizziness, behavior changes, sudden drop of blood pressure on standing, even coma or death.

The cardiovascular system does not take kindly to fasting. In addition to the wasting of heart muscle, depletion and imbalance of minerals involved with heart contraction and hormonal changes will impair the reflexes of the cardiovascular system. Such impairments can and do result in the deaths of people undergoing prolonged fasts even when under medical supervision.

Ketosis in fasting is even more severe than on a high-protein diet, so that the dehydration, loss of essential minerals, and strain on the kidneys associated with this condition can be especially serious. The excessive amount of body protein broken down during fasting results, too, in elevated levels of oxalates and uric acid in the blood, which can cause kidney or bladder stones and, in those susceptible, can precipitate attacks of gout. Alteration in liver function, decreased blood volume, vitamin deficiency, and anemia can also result. You still think fasting is healthy?

It is especially dangerous to engage in strenuous exercise during a prolonged fast, though the lethargy it causes will discourage all but the most fanatic. You'd be inviting further depletion of several essential minerals, which can lead to severe, possibly lethal, electrolyte imbalance. And in a fasting body there is a lack of protein and other nutrients necessary for the repair of tissues torn during exercise.

Prolonged fasts are harmful for everyone. For people with heart, kidney, or other medical problems, even fasts that last no longer than a day or two can be dangerous. As a weight-control method, fasting certainly is not helpful and can even be counterproductive. As with the high-protein diet, when the fast is broken there is a regaining of weight because water-starved tissues are rehydrated, and many people then exceed their prefast weight.

SKIPPING MEALS

Many people fast for part of the day by skipping meals in the belief that they can achieve considerable weight loss. This rarely works. In addition to decreasing your blood-sugar level and making you irritable, missing a meal usually only serves to make you hungrier at the next one, and you'll eat more. Dieters should also know that people gain less weight from a given amount of food when it is consumed in numerous small meals than when it is eaten in a few large ones; this is because the body becomes more efficient in absorbing nutrients when meals are far apart.

QUACKERY

In their despair, dieters fall prey to many futile approaches. Almost as numerous as the fat people in our country are the gimmicks they have tried, which enjoy popularity because they promise quick and easy methods of losing weight. People soon realize that the promises are seldom kept—at least in the long and often not even in the short run. Then a new plan or gimmick becomes available, is tried, and found worthless if not harmful. Quackery abounds in the weight-loss field, feeding on the desperation of the obese. One program recently advertised consisted of nothing more than bathing in water to which a "miracle" liquid was added. It was claimed that 60 pounds could be lost by taking five 15-minute baths. The liquid was said to clean out the pores, opening the way for fat to be dissolved and expelled through the skin. The plan sounds not only easy but fun. I'll bet lots of people tried it.

DRUGS

For those of you who may not think this method of reducing by bathing away one's fat sounds very scientific, there are many drugs on the market that lure prospective buyers with claims of a sound physiological basis. Over $100 million of such medicinal aids are sold each year in the form of gums, candies, capsules, liquids, and powders. These drugs are used mainly by women between the ages of eighteen and fifty, and are taken to suppress the appetite. They are undesirable because they are based on stimulation of the nervous system; irregular beating of the heart, sometimes fatal, can result. Some of these drugs are addicting. All of them lose their effectiveness in curbing the appetite after a month or so, as the body becomes accustomed to them, but the harmful side effects continue.

Hormone injections in combination with a 500-calorie diet have been used in the treatment of obesity. This potentially dangerous therapy, however, has proved to be no more effective than the 500-calorie diet alone.

The use of diuretics is another harmful method too often employed in weight-loss programs. "Water pills" do not cause a loss of body fat. They cause temporary weight loss only because they deplete the tissues of water—water that is needed for the normal functioning of all the cells of the body. When diuretics are discontinued, weight usually increases to more than what it was before taking the pills. This kind of drug is especially dangerous if combined with a high-protein diet that itself causes dehydration.

A dramatic and regrettable example of the ill effects than can result from this combined dehydrating drug-diet therapy is the case of F.P., a beautiful woman in her early forties. She persisted in her attempts to lose weight as a patient of Dr. Atkins for ten years, not realizing that the diet and diuretics were themselves responsible for her many physical symptoms. These included headache, constant fatigue, depression, low blood sugar, and bloating due to water retention despite the many water pills she was taking (as many as thirty 40-mg. Lasix tablets per day). Through years of acclimation, her body had adapted to the dehydrating effects of the diet and the water pills and held water in her tissues tenaciously. When she left the Pritikin Center in the summer of 1980, she was thrilled by her response to the high-carbohydrate weight-loss diet. In a six-week period she had been slowly reduced to 2½ water pills each day and was within 10 pounds of her desired weight. Her physical symptoms had completely disappeared as well.

Still, the search for drugs continues. It was recently reported that researchers are developing a drug that coats the intestines, causing less food to be absorbed. This drug may be effective in causing weight loss, but it will lead to deficiencies in vitamins, minerals, and other nutrients.

SURGERY

There is a way you can eat all you want of anything you want and still lose weight. By surgical procedure, part of the intestines can be bypassed so that less food is absorbed. While the operation will result in weight reduction, there are a few disadvantages to consider. A group of doctors performed this surgery on 55 patients between 1970 and 1975. Four of them died. All but two of the patients had an increased amount of oxalates in the blood and two of them developed urinary stones as a result. Two patients became deficient in calcium and magnesium and developed tetany—prolonged muscular spasms.

Among the more serious complications of bypass surgery are kidney stones, kidney disease, arthritis, bone disease, and sometimes fatal liver disease. Severe and foul-smelling diarrhea, hemorrhoids, and rectal irritation commonly occur after the bypass operation. Anemia, low amounts of potassium and carotene in the blood, and protein malnutrition result from the surgery. All postoperative patients must receive vitamin B_{12} injections.

Other effects of this procedure are the development of gastric

STOMACH-STAPLING

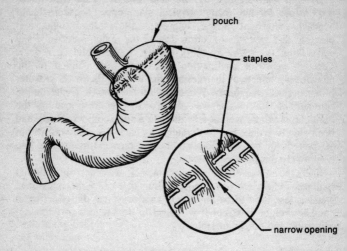

ulcers and low blood pressuure on standing. Drug therapy must be employed in the treatment of many of these conditions, and frequently the surgery must be reversed. Almost none of the patients who subject themselves to this operation reach ideal weight; those who are 100 pounds overweight lose only about 16 pounds the first year.

Is it worth it? Some people don't think so, and choose another operation. They have their stomachs stapled. The upper part of the stomach is partitioned off, forming a small pouch that holds the food. A very narrow opening, about the width of a pencil, is left between the staples. After a time the stomach walls grow together along the line of the staples. Food trickles very slowly from the pouch into the lower portion of the stomach. Needless to say, the amount of food the person can eat is limited to the volume of about half a sandwich. Overeating a little causes pain, and excessive overeating causes vomiting. As with the intestinal bypass surgery, patients who subject themselves to stomach stapling seldom reach their ideal weight. In case you are not satisfied with the stapling job, the surgeons who perform the operation say that although the procedure is permanent they might be able to use a dilator to widen the opening between the pouch and the lower portion of the stomach. Surgical intervention may be necessary in any case because scar tissue sometimes closes off the opening completely.

JAW-WIRING

For those opposed to a surgical solution to their weight problem, there is yet another option that some have chosen—having their jaws wired shut. During the time you are wired, you adhere to a low-calorie liquid diet consisting of tomato juice, unsweetened orange juice, and milk. Replacement of the wires is sometimes necessary because of the patient's discomfort or because they have been damaged by sneezing or coughing. If vomiting occurs, asphyxiation could result. It's not very pleasant, and not very effective. Of one group of patients who had this done, 1 of 17 reached ideal weight. It is possible not to lose any weight at all if high-calorie liquids are consumed when the jaws are wired. Of course, any weight lost is regained when the wires are removed. And by the way, some people require physiotherapy in order to restore complete jaw movement.

JAW-WIRING

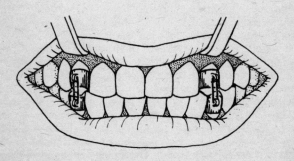

Why another diet book? Because millions of overweight and obese individuals need to know the truth about the no-win game they are playing on the American diet, which puts pounds on most of us in time; and because the present solutions offered them in or out of the medical establishment are no solutions at all. The nondietary ones are shocking, or make a mockery of the consumer; the dietary ones are ineffectual if not harmful. In the light of widely held dietary beliefs, the popularity and constant reappearance of the high-protein diets, each time under a new name, is perhaps inevitable. The hapless individuals who have been brainwashed by the protein myth that "more is better" predictably succumb to the allure of high-protein diets, even in the face of their dismal record for only transient results and serious medical consequences.

Now let's see how our modern diet has led inexorably to the obesity epidemic, and why and how the weight-loss program I am proposing is effective, safe, and an introduction to a lifestyle that will keep you slim and healthy for the rest of your life.

2

Why We Become Obese

I've called obesity a modern epidemic, and so it is: modern because in the last century our food supply has been radically altered to predispose to obesity, and epidemic because over 60 percent of all American adults are overweight (among middle-aged Americans the figure is considerably higher).

In our day, animal products are the backbone of the American diet. Bacon and eggs for breakfast, hamburgers for lunch, steak (generally from fatty feed-lot beef) for dinner, all accompanied by quantities of dairy products high in butterfat, are everyday fare for millions of Americans. These foods are high in fat, which has twice as many calories as proteins or carbohydrates. At the same time, technology, always a mixed blessing, has had largely undesirable effects on the rest of our food supply. In their original state, foods as grown are nutritionally balanced, providing ample carbohydrate, protein, fat, vitamins, and minerals. Because they are high in bulk, they are not high in calories. But when they are stripped of their low-calorie fiber and the most caloric parts of the plant are extracted for use as foods, what remains is a nutritionally unbalanced, depleted, and calorie-condensed food substance.

The result has been an upsurge in our population in the incidence of obesity and of many degenerative diseases as well. The trend toward obesity is often well established by the teen years, particularly in certain population subgroups. Low-income adolescents (who may not get much steak but eat other highly caloric foods) have an especially high rate of obesity, and many from affluent circumstances fill posh summer camps designed to whittle them down before the next school term.

The explanation for the prevalence of obesity in our society is the basic character of our modern food supply. This is a truth perhaps too obvious, or too unacceptable, to be generally acknowledged. Instead, most people, including some considered to be experts, prefer to flounder in a sea of physiological, psychological, and nutritional myths.

One physiological explanation blames underactive thyroid glands. People with this condition do in fact have a low metabolism, and thus tend to gain more weight from a given amount of food than do people with normally functioning thyroid glands. But hypothyroidism is uncommon, and when it does occur it is easily diagnosed and readily treated. Chances are that hypothyroidism is no excuse for you.

Another blames too many fat cells. In fact, most overweight people, including people who have been overweight from childhood, have a normal number of fat cells but an abnormal amount of fat in those cells. These people can easily achieve normal weight. There is one type of childhood obesity, however, in which the child does have a greater number of fat cells as well as more than the normal amount of fat stored in them. These children are massively obese. Although it isn't possible to decrease the number of fat cells in the adult who suffers this rare kind of juvenile-onset obesity, the amount of fat in the cells can be, and should be, reduced to normal levels. When this is accomplished, some of these people may still tend to weigh somewhat more than other people with the normal number of fat cells. But they certainly will be thinner than they were, and the metabolic disturbances caused by having too much fat in the cells will have been corrected.

An intriguing but unfounded theory for obesity asserts that obese people have too little or defective brown fat. Brown fat is found in bears and other hibernating animals and, to a lesser degree, in pigs, rodents, and newborn human infants. But brown fat, sometimes called the hibernating gland, has not been found in human beings in older age groups, so its involvement in obesity is extremely unlikely.

The concept of specialized stores of fat tissue popularly called cellulite that allegedly are extremely refractory to conventional dieting has received attention in the lay press in recent years. There is little scientific evidence that "cellulite" differs in any way from ordinary adipose tissue, although it is possible that this tissue is a manifestation of a phenomenon in animals in which excessive fat stores may occur even when caloric intake is restricted. The most effective treatment for this form of obesity is diet and exercise; specific local physical therapy measures have not been proved effective.

Psychological explanations for obesity usually implicate the overweight individual's personality as the cause of the problem. Generally it's the other way round. Extremely low energy, often perceived as "laziness," is more likely a consequence of overweight rather than its cause. While a sedentary lifestyle may accelerate the process of piling on unwanted pounds, most often hypoactivity develops as people start to become overweight. It takes more effort for fat people to move; they feel clumsy, they look clumsy, and they are more apt to look for solace in a hot fudge sundae or its caloric equivalent than to find pleasure in taking a brisk walk. Feelings of low self-esteem similarly often *result* from overweight, and here too a damaging cycle is quickly established. There are rare cases of severe personality disorders that manifest themselves in exaggerated and pathological food compulsions, but this is a behavioral extreme.

Of all the myths concerning the causes of obesity, the one that is almost universally believed—and the most counterproductive— alleges that starches are fattening. How often have you heard these words exchanged over a dinner table:

"Potatoes?"

"No, thank you. I'm trying to lose weight."

The poor maligned potato, unless it's been doused with fattening toppings or fried in oil, has in fact the same number of calories as a large apple. Potatoes, bread, and other starchy foods are, realtively speaking, among the lower-calorie foods. If you were to eat a diet only of bread, which is higher in calories than potatoes, it would be difficult to keep your weight from falling. The reason the Pritikin Diet works so well in preventing hunger while contributing relatively few calories is that it is composed mainly of foods like bread, potatoes, and other foods high in natural starch and fiber.

For most of us, the causes of overweight do not lie in abnormal physiology or abnormal psychology. We can't even blame genetic inheritance. Fat people have fat spouses, fat children (natural *or* adopted), and they frequently have fat pets, too. It has been often observed that when people make changes in their lifestyle and lose weight, the physical, chemical, and even the psychological effects of obesity are reversed.

What *is* responsible for overweight in most people is the

abnormal diet that most of us consume day after day, a diet high in caloric density.

CALORIC DENSITY

Food is our body's fuel. Some of this fuel is converted to energy, the rest is converted to fat. Fat is stored in fat cells, which have an almost unlimited ability to enlarge to contain this reserve. So the solution to the problem of obesity lies in depleting some of your excessive stores of potential energy (fat), taking in fewer calories than you expend until you reach your desired weight. Does this mean you must starve yourself? Certainly not. Hunger is not a component of the Pritikin Diet. But it does mean you must eat the right kinds of foods.

Foods that make people fat are foods that are high in calories in proportion to their volume; in other words, they have high caloric density. Though capable of some stretching, the capacity of the stomach is finite, holding on the average about 4 cups. Calories are not a measure of quantity, and your stomach doesn't put limits on the number of calories you consume. It is the

STOMACH HOLDS LIMITED VOLUME
BUT UNLIMITED CALORIES

large amounts of fiber in food   little or no fiber in food

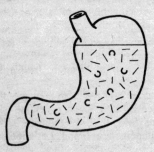
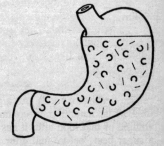

Stomach Filled with Food of   Stomach Filled with Food of
Low Caloric Density   High Caloric Density

C = Calories   / = Fiber

volume of the food you have eaten, filling the space in the stomach, that causes you to feel full and signals you to stop eating. Indigestible fiber and water content provide bulk, increasing food volume. By choosing foods with maximum bulk, so as to give you the greatest feeling of fullness, *and* minimum calories, so as to expedite your weight loss, you won't suffer hunger pangs and you'll be able to adhere to your weight-loss program until you have reached your optimum weight.

Foods vary naturally in their caloric density. Some foods are high in fiber or water; some contain more fats or oils than others. Our intervention with foods as grown by refining or processing, either commercially or in our kitchens at home, has a further and direct effect on caloric density.

Caloric Density Is Affected By

- Natural composition—amounts of fiber, water, fat, protein, carbohydrate

- Processing—juicing, puréeing, drying, etc.

- Refining—extraction of food constituents

REFINED FOODS

Refining extracts part of the whole food for human consumption while the rest, usually the coarser and more nutritious part, is either discarded or used as animal fodder. Many people are opposed to refined foods because valuable vitamins, minerals, and fiber are thus lost. This is a very good reason to reject refined foods, and there is another as well: refining increases the caloric density of foods. As a general rule, a given volume of a food in its natural state contains fewer calories than the same volume of that food after it has undergone refining. Let's look at a sugar beet, before and after.

Almost all the potential calories in sugar beets come from sugar. The sugar in the whole beet is not concentrated, but diluted by natural fiber and water. Refining extracts the sugar in a very pure and compact form. The whole sugar beet is actually a low-calorie food: the average beet weighs 2 pounds and contains 500 calories. But the sugar extracted from that beet, containing virtually the same number of calories, weighs only 4¾ ounces. Or, if you prefer, compare 2 pounds of sugar beet (500 calories) with 2 pounds of beet sugar (3500 calories!).

REFINING INCREASES CALORIC DENSITY
OF SUGAR BEETS

500 calories   3500 calories

It's no wonder that most refined foods are fattening—they are so much more highly concentrated in calories. When you fill your stomach with this kind of food, you take in many more calories than you would if you ate the food in its natural state.

PROCESSED FOODS

Sugar, highly dense calorically, is one of the chief culprits responsible for obesity. If you're like most people, you're probably eating considerably larger quantities than you realize, much of it hidden in processed foods. Many people think of Jell-O as a nonfattening dessert. Jell-O is 83 percent sugar. Other supposedly nonfattening food items are Coffee-mate (65 percent sugar), Cremora (57 percent sugar), and Quaker 100% Natural Cereal (24 percent sugar). Shake 'n Bake (Barbeque Style) is 51 percent sugar, Wish-Bone Russian Dressing 30 percent, Hamburger Helper 23 percent, Cool Whip 21 percent, Libby's Canned Peach Halves 18 percent, Wyler's Beef Flavor Bouillon Cubes 15 percent, Ritz Crackers 12 percent, and Skippy Creamy Peanut Butter 9 percent.

Sometimes the label will indicate the presence of sugar, but not always—not if it's "sugar once removed." For instance, a manufacturer who added catsup (30 percent sugar) to his product would need only to list "catsup" on his label, not the sugar it contains. Even when sugar is listed among the ingredients given on a label, you may not always recognize it as such. Look for the suffix "ose": glucose or dextrose, fructose, lactose, sucrose, maltose, etc. Corn syrup or malted barley or other malted grains are also sources of hidden sugar. Ingredients are listed in decreasing order of the amounts present, so if the different forms of sugar appear individually, they fall toward the end of the list, and it is not always obvious that sugar is a main ingredient.

Processed foods also contain enormous amounts of fats and oils, which have even more calories than sugar. Corn oil is a good example. Most of the calories in corn come from starch, but corn also contains water, fiber, and oil. It takes hundreds of ears of corn to produce one cup of corn oil! When extracted oils are used in foods, their caloric density is greatly increased.

Foods are processed commercially to retard spoilage, reduce preparation time, and enhance eye appeal or "mouth feel." Terrific. So they usually contain coloring and flavoring agents, emulsifiers, humectants, stabilizers, buffers, surfactants, thick-

IT TAKES SEVERAL HUNDRED EARS OF CORN
TO MAKE ONE CUP OF OIL

eners, extenders, maturing, drying, and chelating agents, deodorants, antioxidants, fungicides, and any number of other additives. Not so terrific. Unfortunately, most of modern America's food budget goes for processed foods: ready-to-eat cereals, canned soups, luncheon meats, and convenience foods like ready-to-heat French fries and TV dinners. And of course you're paying extra for the processing that is making your foods nutritionally depleted and denser in calories.

PROCESSED FOODS ARE MUCH MORE EXPENSIVE

We process foods at home, too. A common technique is juicing. It's quite satisfying to eat an orange, which is not highly caloric; an orange contains only about 39 calories. On the other hand, 1/3 of a cup of orange juice, the yield from that orange, would hardly give you the same sense of fullness. An 8-ounce glass of orange juice, requiring three oranges, provides 112 calories, or nearly three times as many as a single, satisfying whole orange. Similarly, a cup of apple slices contains only 73 calories; a cup of apple juice contains 117. It's obvious that you're much better off eating whole fruits with their natural fiber than drinking the extracted juice: you'll have a greater feeling of satiety and you'll take in far fewer calories. Experiments have shown that eating two apples can cause the recurrence of hunger to be delayed at least two hours, partly because it takes more than ten times longer to eat the fruit than to drink its extracted juice, and chewing has been found to stimulate the satiety center in the brain. The main reason for the delay of hunger is that the whole

THREE ORANGES ARE THE CALORIC EQUIVALENT OF AN 8-OUNCE GLASS OF JUICE

fruit contains fiber that contributes bulk. There is a chemical factor as well: when the whole fruit with its fiber is eaten, the sugar is released slowly as digestion proceeds, delaying hunger. Eating puréed apples will also delay hunger but to a lesser extent, because the fiber though still present has been disrupted and intact fiber is more effective than fiber that's been broken up. But when you drink apple juice, the chemical response of the body is quite different. In a sense, apple juice is "predigested," as the natural sugar from the fruit is immediately available when the fiber is not present, causing dramatic changes in the blood levels of glucose and insulin. These blood changes cause sensations of hunger—which is why "having a little something," if

WHOLE APPLES
(fiber intact)
Prolonged Delayal
of Hunger

PURÉED APPLES
(fiber disrupted)
Moderate Delayal
of Hunger

APPLE JUICE
(fiber-free)
Rapid Return
of Hunger

it's the wrong kind of something, can make you hungrier than you were before.

Some methods of food preparation, especially frying, also greatly increase the caloric density of foods. Look what happens to the caloric density of potatoes prepared in different ways:

WHITE POTATO
Boiled or Baked: 1 cup = 118 calories
French-fried: 1 cup = 456 calories

SWEET POTATO
Boiled or Baked: 1 cup = 291 calories
Candied: 1 cup = 409 calories

Drying, too, increases caloric concentration. The caloric density of raisins, for instance, is more than 600 percent greater than that of an equal weight of grapes.

In their natural state, the foods lowest in caloric density are generally vegetables because of the high percentage of fiber and water they contain. Fruits are somewhat higher in calories because of their sugar content, and grains are more caloric than fruits or vegetables because they contain less water and somewhat more fat. The foods of greatest caloric density are mainly animal products, sugar, oils, nuts and processed foods. At the end of this book there is a table showing the relative caloric densities of some eighty common foods. These foods are listed in ascending order of number of calories in an eight-ounce cup. The table is divided into four sections: foods you may eat freely, foods to be eaten in moderation, foods to be restricted, and foods you should avoid because of their extremely high caloric density. For your convenience, the data in this table are repeated in two following tables, which list the same foods by food group and alphabetically.

3
Why a High-Carbohydrate Diet for Weight Control

Much-maligned carbohydrates turn out to be not only the healthiest kinds of foods we eat, but also the kinds that keep people slim. The source of the confusion derives from the fact that there are two kinds of carbohydrates: simple carbohydrates (sugars) and complex carbohydrates (starches). Simple carbohydrates, glucose for example, are small molecules that are rapidly absorbed. Complex carbohydrates, although essentially thousands of sugar units strung together, have far different effects on the body than sugar alone, since they take much longer to metabolize.

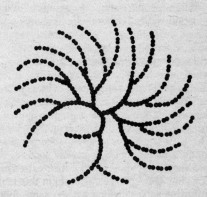

SIMPLE
CARBOHYDRATE:
GLUCOSE

COMPLEX
CARBOHYDRATE: STARCH

STARCHES (COMPLEX CARBOHYDRATES)

It takes time for the body to break down starches, so they are absorbed more slowly and delay the return of hunger. Even more important to weight control, starchy plant foods also contain large amounts of fiber. The fiber in our food can't be broken down by the enzymes we produce, and it passes through our systems without being absorbed. Since it absorbs large quantities of water, thereby providing a good deal of bulk, the caloric density of the food is greatly diluted. *A diet high in whole, natural complex-carbohydrate foods is the best possible diet for weight control*. The reason so many people in our country and in other industrialized societies are overweight, contrary to conventional wisdom, is that we don't eat enough such carbohydrates. As we've seen, carbohydrate foods that are high in bulk and low in calories are replaced in our diets with foods of much greater caloric density: refined and processed foods as well as excessive amounts of foods from animal sources.

Unfortunately, most Americans are averse to carbohydrate foods, and ironically they are avoided most diligently by overweight people who are trying to reduce. Not realizing that carbohydrates contain only 4 calories per gram, these earnest but

FOODS THAT CAN KEEP YOU THIN

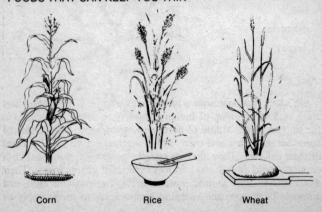

Corn   Rice   Wheat

misled individuals pass them up for cheeses, meat, and other high-fat foods, which have 9 calories for every gram of fat they contain. And of course the highly caloric fat in foods from animal sources is devoid of calorie-diluting fiber that is found in unprocessed carbohydrate foods.

People in societies less developed technologically than ours do not have our problem with obesity. In two typical undeveloped Asian countries, East Pakistan and Malaya, a large proportion of the calories consumed comes from carbohydrates, principally rice, and the people are lean. These Asian populations were recently compared with those of two South American countries. The diet of Uruguay, which is very similar to the American diet, is high in food from animal sources and contains only a small amount of carbohydrates. The incidence of obesity is much greater than in the Asian countries. In Venezuela, the amount of carbohydrates in the diet is less than in the Asian countries and more than in Uruguay; the percentage of obesity in the population is also intermediate.

Percentages of Carbohydrate Consumption and Obesity in Four Countries		
COUNTRY	% CALORIES FROM CARBOHYDRATES	% OF OBESITY IN POPULATION
East Pakistan	83	0
Malaya	77	0
Venezuela	62	14.8
Uruguay	53	34.4

Let's look at a population a little closer to home. The Tarahumaras are a very large group of Indians who live in cabins and caves in the rugged Sierra Madre of northwestern Mexico. The staples of their diet are beans and corn, which account for up to 90 percent of their calories. They also eat squash, pumpkins, potatoes, chili peppers, wild plants, and fruits, especially citrus fruits. Their diet contains little animal protein or fat, but contains sufficient amounts of protein and essential amino acids to meet amply or surpass the recommendations of the World Health Organization; it also provides adequate or more than adequate amounts of vitamins and minerals. Strenuous work is necessary for the Tarahumaras to sustain life, and their play is strenuous, too. Their favorite pastime is participating in kickball races. During competitions, which last up to two days, the contestants run as far as 200 miles day and night kicking a small oak ball the size of a baseball while other runners carry torches to light their way. They stop for a few minutes only every dozen miles or so for food and water. These Indians are strong and lean—but not underweight—because most of their diet is composed of natural carbohydrate foods. We would do well to emulate their diet, though their national sport may be somewhat impractical for us.

SUGARS (SIMPLE CARBOHYDRATES)

While large amounts of complex carbohydrates in the diet are very beneficial, the opposite is true of simple carbohydrates. Because sugar is absorbed very rapidly and at a higher site in the gastrointestinal tract than other foods, it causes the body to secrete large amounts of insulin. Insulin works with speed in lowering the sugar level in the blood, but since so much of the hormone is secreted, and since it takes a while for the system to rid itself of the excess, the result can be a drop in blood sugar to below normal levels. This condition of hypoglycemia, or low blood sugar, causes us to feel hungry as the body seeks to restore the level of blood sugar by additional food intake.

Sugar also increases the level of triglycerides, or fats in the blood. One of the ways the body works to reduce the level of sugar in the blood is to convert it to fats. This is not a happy solution, especially in people who already have symptoms of arterial disease. In the past, doctors have been opposed to high-carbohydrate diets, wrongly believing that *all* carbohydrates caused an increase of blood fats. Actually, only simple sugars lead to this condition. Complex-carbohydrate foods containing starches and fiber serve to lower the amount of fats in the blood. In the United States, as people approach middle age they usually get fatter, their blood pressure rises, and the levels of fats, cholesterol, and frequently sugar and insulin in the blood increase. These are not inevitable consequences of the aging process. They occur as a result of years of eating too much rich food and too few starches, the lower-octane fuel on which the body prefers to run.

CRAVING FOR SWEETS

People who are in the habit of eating a lot of sweets are caught in a truly vicious cycle. Their bodies have become accustomed to extreme variations in insulin and blood-sugar levels, rather than the fairly even levels in the healthy person. During the period of low blood sugar caused by the action of insulin, they crave sweets. People caught in this pattern are used to feeling their best only when their sugar level is quite high. And so it goes. The cycle can be broken only by giving up sweets and letting the body become accustomed to the type of fuel—the complex carbohydrates—that produces energy at a slower, more even rate. When the body adjusts, the troublesome sweet tooth will have been extracted.

The best way to cope with the problem during this period of adjustment is not to allow it to get out of hand. Don't let yourself get hungry, because that's when you'll crave the stimulant effect of sugar. Eat some raw vegetable sticks or a big salad. Try to get used to eating more often, choosing foods of low caloric density to keep down your total intake of calories. In this way your blood sugar won't fall too low and you'll have energy all through the day.

In addition to avoiding sugar, you should avoid alcohol and caffeine beverages, which also affect blood-sugar levels. Coffee, even when decaffeinated, contains substances called caffeols, which cause you to feel hungry.

REFINED SUGARS

These sugars have been extracted from inside the cells of plants. The refined sugar with which we're most familiar is sucrose, or table sugar, extracted commercially from sugar cane or sugar beets. It is pure, containing none of the substances with which it was associated before refining: no fiber, no water, no vitamins, no minerals. That's why its effect on the body is so potent.

NATURAL SUGARS

Most people realize that they should cut down on the amount of sugar they use, but they are under the mistaken impression that "natural" sugars are innocuous; some even think they are beneficial. Well, we'll see.

Sucrose (table sugar) is composed of two simpler sugars, glucose and fructose. When sucrose is broken down in the body, these two sugars are liberated. Glucose is the sugar that is found in the blood; it is the only form of sugar the body can use, and all other kinds of sugar, including fructose, must first be converted to glucose.

Fructose occurs naturally in many fruits, and health store owners attribute special qualities to it. Actually, fructose has only one point in its favor: it is sweeter than most sugars, and therefore you can use a little less of it. Like all sugars, however, it raises blood triglycerides.

What about honey? Magical qualities have been attributed to the nectar of the bees since the time of the ancient Egyptians. Honey tastes sweeter than table sugar because it contains only a small amount of sucrose; most of the sugar in honey is in the form of glucose and fructose, and the large amount of free fructose present accounts for its sweetness. Although nutrients are not removed from honey, they occur only in trace amounts.

Blackstrap molasses, which sounds pretty "natural," is in fact a byproduct of the refining of sucrose. It contains the minerals of sugar cane or beets in concentrated form, and thus is significantly higher in iron. Fine. But the nutrients in molasses can be more easily obtained from other foods that don't affect your blood sugar levels.

Brown sugar is simply table sugar with a little molasses or caramel added for flavoring and color. Turbinado sugar is the same as table sugar except that the granules are larger and it has not undergone bleaching, the final step in the processing of ordinary table sugar.

USE OF THE HIGH COMPLEX-CARBOHYDRATE DIET IN THE TREATMENT OF OBESITY

Normal weight can usually be maintained by eating as much as you like if the diet is composed mainly of unrefined carbohydrate foods. Once overweight, however, it is necessary to adhere to a diet low in calories until your desired weight is attained.

While animal studies are not always applicable, recent evidence from the University of Virginia suggests that there may be a substantial difference in the deposition of fat depending upon whether the low calorie diet is high in protein or in carbohydrates. One group of adult rats was fed a high-protein diet in which 25 percent of the calories derived from protein and another group a high-carbohydrate diet in which only 5 percent were from protein. Fat contributed 10 percent of total calories in both diets. After 8 weeks on these diets, the 25 percent protein group weighed 22 percent more and had 23.9 percent of their body weight in fat. The 5 percent protein group only had 15.6 percent of their body weight as fat. The researchers noted that the average protein intake on the U.S. diet is 16.1 percent, twice the amount necessary for good health. They suggested that the best way to lose weight is to follow a diet high in complex carbohydrate foods such as grains, vegetables and fruits, and low in fat and protein.

More than thirty years ago, the high-carbohydrate diet was found effective in reducing body fat in humans when Dr. Walter Kempner prescribed a low-calorie, almost pure (90-95 percent) carbohydrate diet for his patients with high blood pressure. The diet is well known in the medical profession because it was so successful. Its principal constituent was rice, and it included sugar, fruit, fruit juices, and supplements of vitamins and iron. After the first month on the diet, vegetables were also included, and subsequently small amounts of poultry or lean meat were added. Dr. Kempner later found that the diet could be successfully used in the treatment of diabetics. More recently he developed a modified version of the rice diet, in which 80 percent of the calories come from carbohydrates, that proved to be safe and effective in the treatment of his obese patients.

The Pritikin Diet is like the rice diet in that it is high in carbohydrates and effective in causing weight loss. It differs from Dr. Kempner's regimen on four important counts: it doesn't necessitate going hungry; it is nutritionally balanced; it is not monotonous, but rather quite varied; and it trains the dieter in the principles of a permanent dietary lifestyle.

VARIETY AND SATIETY ON THE PRITIKIN DIET

Healthful diets can be built around the use of many different foods as long as their nutritional composition fulfills our needs. In many nutritionally successful "prmitive" societies, rice, corn, wheat, or sweet potatoes are used as the principal source of calories. But while such diets are well balanced nutritionally, it would be difficult for most Americans to adopt the eating habits of, say, the Tarahumaras, which would seem too limited to us. The Pritikin Diet is based on a wide variety of foods prepared as much as possible to conform to American tastes. You want to be slim the rest of your life, but you don't want to go through life feeling hungry and deprived. Our way of eating works so well because the food tastes good, because it fills you up (but not out!) and because there is a great deal of variety available. There are a multitude of foods from plant sources and they can be prepared in many ways, which solves the problem of monotony inherent in so many reducing diets. In fact, the weight-loss Pritikin Diet actually offers more variety than the normal—and fattening—fare of the average American.

NUTRITIONAL ADEQUACY OF THE PRITIKIN DIET

In evaluating a weight-loss diet it is necessary not only to determine whether it is effective in causing weight loss, but also whether it is nutritionally adequate.

The first thing most Americans worry about is whether they're getting enough protein. What they don't know is that the amount of protein required is related to the amount of carbohydrate in the diet. Carbohydrates have a protein-sparing effect, that is, the carbohydrate in the diet can be used to provide energy, sparing the protein for essential purposes. If the diet contains a small amount of carbohydrates, the requirement for protein is increased. This is because protein is utilized to supply calories (energy) and the body is less efficient in obtaining energy from protein than from carbohydrate foods. Because the Pritikin Diet is high in carbohydrate, less protein is required than is recommended by the Food and Nutrition Board in their RDAs (Recommended Dietary Allowances). Still, the amount of protein provided on all four caloric levels of the weight-loss Pritikin Diet meets the RDAs, and you will be consuming a good deal more protein than you require.

It is important in weight-loss diets to limit severely the intake of fats, as they contain more than twice as many calories as carbohydrates or protein. Most people are aware that we require some fat in the diet; most people are not aware that we require very little. Fats are composed of fatty acids, and the body can make the fatty acids it needs as long as an adequate amount of the essential fatty acid—linoleic acid—is present. This fatty acid is considered essential because it can't be made in the body. The requirement for it—2 grams a day—is amply met on the Pritikin Diet. There is no added benefit to be derived from obtaining more than this amount. (Some researchers believe that linolenic acid is also essential; both linoleic acid and linolenic acid are obtained in ample amounts when the diet contains adequate amounts of unrefined carbohydrate foods.)

On most reducing diets, including the Kempner Diet, vitamin and mineral supplements are taken. However, it is always better to obtain the necessary nutrients from the food you eat without relying on supplements. When your diet includes ample amounts of a variety of fresh fruits and yellow and dark green vegetables, you will be getting large amounts of minerals, vitamin C, and carotene (the precursor of vitamin A). Some of the dark green vegetables are an especially good source of iron and calcium. Your grain allotment will provide you with a rich source of amino acids (protein), minerals, fatty acids, vitamin E, and the B vitamins. Skimmed milk dairy products in suitable amounts can augment protein and some mineral requirements.

There is no way of knowing with certainty that supplements will replace in the proper amounts all the nutrients naturally present in a good diet. On the Pritikin Diet it is not necessary to take supplements, and we advise against it.

Studies following patients up to 51 months on this type of high-carbohydrate diet have found no evidence suggesting mineral or vitamin deficiency. Absorption of calcium and phosphorus is especially high on the Pritikin Diet as compared with the ordinary American diet. In fact, whereas intake of these nutrients on the weight-loss Pritikin regimen meets the RDA guidelines, calcium and iron intakes on the average American diet do not, even though caloric intake is high. A recent national survey of food consumption conducted by the U.S. Department of Agriculture revealed that intakes of calcium for both men and women age 23 and over, and of iron in women age 25 to 50, were below the RDAs. Many people worry about iron absorption from vegetable sources, but in a study comparing iron absorption from plant and animal sources, there was equally high absorption from lettuce as from liver in iron-deficient subjects. In addition, iron absorption is enhanced on our diet because of its high vitamin C content.

The weight-loss diets in this book are designed to provide a minimum of 10 milligrams of iron daily, which meets the RDA guidelines for all groups except menstruating women. The average amount of iron supplied daily on our menu plans is approximately 14 milligrams; we consider this amount more than adequate for menstruating women and do not advocate supplementation. However, if you wish your iron intake to meet the RDA recommendation of 18 milligrams, add 1 or 2 cups of lettuce, especially butterhead varieties, or cooked greens, especially mustard greens (see the recipe for Herbed Greens) to bring it to this level on days when the amount provided by the day's menu plan falls below this value; or, you can choose to use only those menu plans that do provide 18 milligrams of iron for the day (18 milligrams or more of iron are provided at all calorie levels by menu plans 6, 11, and 13; at calorie levels 1000 and up, by menus 4, 5, 6, 11, 13, and 14; and at the 1200 calorie level by menus 1, 3, 4, 5, 6, 7, 8, 9, 12, 13, and 14).

For a more technical discussion of the nutritional adequacy of the Pritikin Diet, including charts enabling comparison of the nutrient intake of the weight-loss Pritikin regimens with the most recent RDAs and average American nutrient intakes, see pages 176–183 in Chapter 11, "For the Health Professional," and pages 363–371 in the Appendix.

4

Why a High-Carbohydrate Diet for Health

Wouldn't it be wonderful if the same diet that can make you slim forever could also make you healthy all your life? Well, the Pritikin Diet can do just that.

The degenerative diseases—heart disease, atherosclerosis, high blood pressure, adult-onset diabetes (which accounts for 90 percent of all diabetes), gout, some forms of arthritis, and most kinds of cancer—are all products of our calorie-dense diet. The medical profession in this country is beginning to recognize this, and a diet high in complex carbohydrates, similar to the Pritikin Diet, is being used more and more frequently in the treatment of these diseases. At the Pritikin Centers, thousands of documented cases show remarkable results in returning to normal function people who suffered from angina, or who were on insulin or hypertension medication for years.* In England, largely as a result of the work of Dr. Denis P. Burkitt and Dr. Hugh Trowell, the treatment of choice for digestive tract disorders, including ulcers and diverticulitis, is now a diet high in natural carbohydrate foods. These two researchers, working in Africa over a period of years, had observed that the local populations were free of such diseases, while resident Europeans who continued to follow a Western diet were prey to them.

Undeveloped societies lack the medical technology to prevent and treat infectious diseases, which claim the lives of many of their people, especially infants and young children. They are, however, virtually free of degenerative diseases. Let's look at two examples.

---

*If you wish, your physician may request specific data by writing to me at P.O. Box 5335, Santa Barbara, California 93108. Information about our live-in Centers and classes may also be obtained by writing to this address.

The lean, muscular people of New Guinea are sometimes called the sweet potato eaters, as this plant is the staple of their diet. Carbohydrates account for 94 percent of their caloric intake. Unlike people in industrialized societies, as New Guineans grow older they don't become fat, and the levels of cholesterol and fats in the blood don't increase. It will be interesting to see if the incidence of degenerative diseases increases in the next few years. It is almost inevitable that it will. Lucrative mineral deposits have recently been discovered in New Guinea, and as undeveloped societies become wealthier and adopt Western ways, the amount of fats and protein in the diet goes up, and the amount of starches declines. Time and time again it has been seen that such dietary changes are followed a few years later by a decline in the health of the people. For example, the Jews living in the Yemen eat very little sugar and only modest amounts of fat. When they immigrate to Israel, they eat a lot more sugar and fat and fewer complex carbohydrates. After 20 years they suffer the same rate of heart disease as the native Israelis.

In Japan, the incidence of colon cancer is much lower than that in the United States. When Japanese immigrate to our country, their consumption of rice (a complex-carbohydrate food) goes down while the consumption of fats goes up, and there is a corresponding increase in their incidence of large-bowel cancer. Among the Japanese who settle in Hawaii, where the amounts of fat and carbohydrate in the diet are intermediate between the levels found in the mainland United States and in Japan, the incidence of colon cancer is correspondingly intermediate. In Japan itself, as the country has increased in wealth, the incidence of colon cancer and other degenerative diseases has been increasing in recent years. The Japanese can now afford to replace a large amount of the healthful starches in their traditional diet with meat and other foods rich in fats and cholesterol, and American fast-food restaurants are springing up in the larger cities throughout the country. As these dietary changes have occurred, they have been followed by a decline in the health of the Japanese people.

When too much of the protective carbohydrates are removed from the diet, the workings of the body go awry. Impaired functioning may lead in time to any number of conditions of varying degrees of seriousness.

CONSTIPATION

Americans spend millions of dollars every year on laxatives. When I toured and spoke in Australia in 1980, I was advised to address myself less to the beneficial effects of the Pritikin Diet in protecting against heart disease, and more to its usefulness in preventing constipation, apparently a national curse!

Constipation is usually considered annoying but fairly harmless, but if uncontrolled it can lead to more serious conditions: hemorrhoids, varicose veins, thrombophlebitis, diverticulitis, and other intestinal diseases. Constipation is a common problem in industrialized countries because of the foods consumed, and a particularly frequent complaint of people on most reducing diets, especially on those that recommend large amounts of animal protein because of the lack of fiber in foods from animal sources. Because the Pritikin Diet is high in bulk, it may prevent constipation even in people for whom it has been a problem for many years.

CANCER

In October 1979 Dr. Arthur Upton, then director of the National Cancer Institute, issued that organization's first dietary recommendations for protection against cancers of many types. These called for changing the average American's diet to include far greater amounts of whole natural carbohydrate foods and far smaller amounts of meat and other high-fat and high-cholesterol animal-source foods. Dr. Upton recommended that oils and fats of all kinds, including polyunsaturates, be restricted. For years the American Heart Association has advocated the polyunsaturates to prevent and control heart disease, but in many large-scale tests there has been no significant improvement in death rates with their use. Research has shown, however, that a diet high in fat, especially the polyunsaturated fats, is instrumental in increasing the incidence of many kinds of cancer.

A diet high in fat and cholesterol that is deficient in fiber because of insufficient whole carbohydrate foods acts in several different ways to make us vulnerable to various kinds of cancers; conversely, a diet high in whole natural carbohydrate foods protects against them. Colon cancer is directly diet related. On the high-fat American diet, bacteria in the large intestine break down bile and cholesterol into potent cancer-causing agents. The more fat and cholesterol in the diet, the more such agents are present in the bowel. Fiber, however, acts as a protection against colon cancer because it retains water in the intestines, forming bulk which serves to dilute the toxins that come into contact with the intestinal cells. Transit time—the time from ingestion of food to its evacuation as a bowel movement—is also a factor. Transit time on a diet high in animal foods and low in natural whole carbohydrate foods is 85 hours; on a diet high in natural carbohydrate foods it is 20 to 35 hours. This reduced transit time means that cancer-causing toxins are in contact with the walls of the bowels for a shorter period.

Increased production by intestinal bacteria of certain sex hormones results from a diet high in fat and cholesterol, and diet is thus also related to the incidence of breast, ovarian, uterine, and prostate cancer. In countries that, like ours, are on a high-fat diet, breast cancer rates are high. These rates are very low in countries consuming a diet high in whole natural carbohydrate foods and correspondingly low in fat content. Extensive epidemiological studies have revealed virtually no other factors that correlate with the incidence of breast cancer. On the Pritikin Diet, a harmless population of bacteria predominates in the large intestine. These bacteria do not break down bile and so do not produce the cancer-causing substances and hormones involved in bile breakdown.

LIVER, GALL BLADDER, AND KIDNEY DISTURBANCES

Cirrhosis—fatty degeneration of the liver characterized by fibrous scarring and reduced liver function—is two and a half times more common in obese people. Obesity is also linked with gall bladder disease. In the developed nations, most gallstones are 85 percent cholesterol, and are formed when concentrations of blood cholesterol are so high as to lead to its deposition in tissues and organs.

Obesity puts a strain on the kidneys and can result in a malfunction of these organs known as the nephrotic syndrome. Among the symptoms are fatigue, the presence of protein in the urine, and edema (swelling of the tissues due to an accumulation of fluids). Treatment is a low-protein, low-calorie diet. The Pritikin Diet, which is not excessive in protein content, avoids such stress on the kidneys.

URIC-ACID ELEVATION

People who are obese often have elevated levels of uric acid, which is related to gout, kidney disease, and high blood pressure. On the Pritikin Diet, weight loss is accompanied by a lowering of uric-acid level. A diet high in whole carbohydrate foods and relatively low in protein, such as the Pritikin Diet, is effective in lowering uric-acid level because most protein foods contain purine and nucleic acids, substances that are converted to uric acid in the body. A high-protein diet can double uric-acid level, precipitating attacks of gout.

OSTEOPOROSIS

The large amount of meat and other protein foods in our diet has been implicated as the most important factor leading to osteoporosis (weakening of the bones). In time the bones become brittle and break easily, a frequent occurrence among the elderly in our country.

Proteins in large quantities again are the culprit, because the mineral ash remaining in the body after proteins have been metabolized tends to form acids that must be neutralized in order for the body to maintain the optimum balance between acidity and alkalinity. The minerals of bone tissues serve as one of the body's buffering, or neutralizing, systems. The average American diet, too high in protein foods, results over the years in a gradual loss of bone minerals. High-protein weight-loss diets are especially harmful in this regard: they are the best way to accelerate aging of the skeletal system. The Pritikin Diet contains optimum amounts of protein, enough for tissue maintenance but not so much as to contribute to osteoporosis.

PREMATURE AGING

The skeletal system is not the only part of the body that ages prematurely on diets that are too high in protein. Animal studies first alerted researchers to the dramatic acceleration in signs of aging and decreased life span resulting from high-protein diets, and there is much evidence that this is the case with people, too. You may now be convinced that the protein myth has done us all a disservice, but wonder whether living longer with a younger-looking body will be much fun if the skin on your face is dry and wrinkled due to fat deficiencies. Skin wrinkles are not due to lack of fat in your diet; they are due largely to the action of sunlight on skin and to the oxygen-deficient circulation associated with smoking. In any case, the fat content of the Pritikin Diet provides more than four times the body's fat requirements even though it is less than 10 percent of total calories compared with the average fat intake of 40 percent or more.

HEADACHES

Headaches, too, are diet related, which is not surprising when you consider that most headaches, including migraines, are caused by abnormal circulation. After following the Pritikin Diet at our Centers for a month or two, people who had had histories of migraines for as long as 25 years obtained relief. We have tracked many of these people for a number of years and find their freedom from headaches continues. Recently I received a letter from a follower of the Pritikin Diet who chided me for failing to emphasize the fact that migraine-sufferers could virtually eliminate their misery by following my diet. He had experienced this benefit and wanted to share it with fellow sufferers. Well, now the word is out.

BLOOD-CLOTTING DISTURBANCES

Without the ability to form clots, we would bleed to death from minor wounds. But if clots occur spontaneously in the bloodstream, they can travel to the lungs and cause death. To avoid spontaneous clotting in the blood vessels, the body produces clot-dissolving material—which becomes less effective when a high-fat diet is consumed.

The rate at which clot-dissolving (fibrinolysis) occurs in people who eat a high carbohydrate diet is faster than in individuals who eat a great deal of meat and far fewer carbohydrates. Such a relationship between a diet high in unrefined starchy foods and a good fibrinolysis rate has been demonstrated in many studies.

BLOOD-SUGAR-LEVEL DISTURBANCES

Excessive amounts of sugar in the blood—hyperglycemia or diabetes—is usually the consequence of a high-fat diet deficient in whole natural carbohydrate foods. Insulin is the hormone that enables sugar to leave the bloodstream and enter the cells, where it is broken down to provide energy. When the diet is high in fat, some of the cell receptor sites for insulin become coated with an impermeable layer of fat, rendering the insulin less effective. Then blood sugar begins to accumulate, leading to hyperglycemia or diabetes. Insulin is taken by the diabetic in an attempt to overcome this decrease in effectiveness of the body's insulin.

Hypoglycemia, or low blood sugar, results from too much simple carbohydrate (such as sugar, honey, and molasses) in the diet. The simple sugars cause the pancreas to overreact and put out too much insulin. Hypoglycemia develops because the excessive insulin causes the blood-sugar level to drop precipitately. When the diet is also high in fat, the condition can develop into diabetes.

Diabetes is a serious body disturbance, accounting for 17 percent of all new blindness and 80 percent of all amputated gangrenous legs. Numerous nerve disturbances that develop in diabetics cause derangement of a diversity of functions, including smell, taste, hearing, and sexual performance. Dr. Kelly M. West, Professor of Medicine at the University of Oklahoma, believes that much of such functional failing is unnecessary and diet related. Referring to the low-fat diet high in whole natural carbohydrate foods used by Dr. James Anderson, Chief of Endocrinology at the University of Kentucky Medical Center, Dr. West was quoted in the McGovern Hearings on Nutrition and Human Needs in February 1977, stating that Dr. Anderson's work was "one of the most exciting research programs going on in the world today" and that 2½ million (or 62 percent) of the 4 million known adult diabetics in the United States now on drugs "could be safely freed from them entirely by using this diet." I introduced my dietary approach to Dr. Anderson in 1974–1975 and since then he has been using it as a model with excellent results.

BLOOD-PRESSURE ELEVATION

Fat people tend to have high blood pressure, and losing weight will result in a lowering of blood pressure in many whose blood pressure is too high. The Pritikin Diet is especially effective in this respect because it is so low in salt and fat. The relationship between high blood pressure and salt has been well established, and preliminary evidence implicates fat as well. In fact, dietary experiments in which the salt content was unchanged but fat was lowered and then raised showed that blood pressure varied as fat content changed: lowering fat content reduced blood pressure; raising fat content raised it again. This study and work at the Pritikin Centers suggest that fat may actually be more important than salt as a cause of high blood pressure. Fat, absorbed into the blood from the intestines, causes the red cells and platelets in the blood to become sticky and adhere to each other, forming clumps of cells that can't pass through the smaller blood vessels and resulting in increased pressure within them.

This clumping of red blood cells has another effect. Not only does it increase blood pressure, it also prevents the red blood cells, which carry osygen to all the cells of the body's tissues, from carrying out this essential task. The capillaries are tiny indeed, half the diameter of a red blood cell. The red blood cells must distort themselves and squeeze through the capillaries one at a time. When the cells are stuck together, passage is impossible. The nutrients—the fuel—in the body's tissue cells must be oxidized (that is, burned) for energy to be produced. When sufficient oxygen is not available for this combustion, substances that should have become energy are instead converted to fats and stored in adipose tissue.

HEART AND BLOOD-VESSEL DAMAGE

Heart disease is responsible for a million deaths a year in this country. It is the biggest single cause of death in the adult population. Unfortunately, for half the victims, first attacks are fatal. The symptoms that tell you there is something wrong with the circulation to your heart—the pains of angina—don't appear until the arteries supplying the heart are 90 percent blocked by plaques, the cholesterol-bearing boil-like deposits on the interior walls of the vessels. The cholesterol level in the blood has been shown to be related to the degree of plaque development, and lowering cholesterol levels is one of the main goals in taking people out of the risk classification for heart disease.

Once you have lost weight, your blood cholesterol will be lower. The weight-loss Pritikin Diet causes a greater lowering of blood cholesterol than do other reducing diets. This is partly because the Pritikin Diet is much lower in fats and ten times lower in cholesterol, and partly because it is high in fiber. Cholesterol, unlike fats, proteins, and carbohydrates, is not broken down in the body but is retained for long periods of time. Some cholesterol leaves the body in the feces. Cholesterol is used by the liver to make bile acids, which are secreted into the intestines to aid in digestion. In the absence of fiber in the diet, the bile acids are reabsorbed from the lower end of the small intestine. When adequate fiber is present it binds some of the bile acids, preventing them from being absorbed and allowing them to be excreted from the body. The liver must then draw on the body's reserves of cholesterol to replenish the bile acids. Thus the fiber in our diet helps rid the body of unwanted cholesterol and serves to protect against the buildup of cholesterol-laden plaques in the arteries.

As you can see, getting slim on the Pritikin Diet will give you important benefits in improved health. While you begin to look better on the outside with your new streamlined body, you'll be doing yourself a world of good on the inside. Your entire body will be healthier and better able to fend off the degenerative diseases that start to develop early in life for most Americans.

5

Planning Your
Weight-Loss Timetable

By now you have undoubtedly been sold on the merits of the Pritikin Diet as an approach that will slim you quickly and permanently and provide important health benefits. All right. Now we need your active participation. *You* need to decide what rate of weight loss is right for you, given your daily activities, your adaptability to a lower-calorie diet, your unique home situation, and other individual factors that may influence the picture.

While some people may be content with a weight loss of 1½ to 2 pounds per week, others may want a faster drop (and are ready to accept the extra restrictions that go with it). To accommodate different weight-loss goals, we offer four different diet plans based on varying daily caloric intakes. For those uncomfortable with the discipline of plans requiring that they use specific recipes and daily menus, we also have an effective approach for the "free-form" dieter, described on pages 108–111. Following these guidelines will also produce continuous and gratifying weight loss, but the rate of that weight loss will be less predictable and controlled.

For either approach, structured or free-form, you should start by determining with reasonable accuracy what your ideal weight is, so you have a definite and realistic goal.

DETERMINING YOUR IDEAL BODY WEIGHT

To estimate ideal body weight, you need first to determine whether your frame size is large, medium, or small. The best way to do this is by measuring your wrist. Although in a few overweight people fat around the wrists may distort the mea-

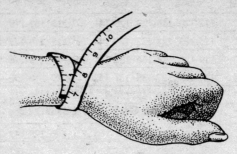

surement, wrist size usually correlates well with skeletal frame size. Find your frame size in the chart below:

	SMALL FRAME	MEDIUM FRAME	LARGE FRAME
WRIST MEASUREMENT, ADULT MALES	less than 6¼"	6¼"–7"	more than 7"
WRIST MEASUREMENT, ADULT FEMALES	less than 5¼"	5¼"–6"	more than 6"

A height-weight table may then be used to determine ideal weight based on frame size.

	Weight in Pounds (in indoor clothing)					
	Men			Women*		
Height (in shoes)**	Small Frame	Medium Frame	Large Frame	Small Frame	Medium Frame	Large Frame
4'10"	—	—	—	92-98	96-107	104-119
11"	—	—	—	94-101	98-110	106-122
5' 0"	—	—	—	96-104	101-113	109-125
1"	—	—	—	99-107	104-116	112-128

2"	112-120	118-129	126-141	102-110	107-119	115-131
3"	115-123	121-133	129-144	105-113	110-122	118-134
4"	118-126	124-136	132-148	108-116	113-126	121-138
5"	121-129	127-139	135-152	111-119	116-130	125-142
6"	124-133	130-143	138-156	114-123	120-135	129-146
7"	128-137	134-147	142-161	118-127	124-139	133-150
8"	132-141	138-152	147-166	122-131	128-143	137-154
9"	136-145	142-156	151-170	126-135	132-147	141-158
10"	140-150	146-160	155-174	130-140	136-151	145-163
11"	144-154	150-165	159-179	134-144	140-155	149-168
6' 0"	148-158	154-170	164-184	138-148	144-159	153-173
1"	152-162	158-175	168-189	—	—	—
2"	156-167	162-180	173-194	—	—	—
3"	160-171	167-185	178-199	—	—	—
4"	164-175	172-190	182-204	—	—	—

Courtesy of Metropolitan Life Insurance Company

*Women between 18 and 25 should subtract 1 pound for each year under 25.
**Assuming a one-inch heel height for men and a two-inch heel height for women.

Various formulas may also be used to determine optimum weight, but we prefer the use of an accurate height-weight table, such as the one above, in which desirable weights are given as ranges of figures. Using a formula gives a single figure for "ideal" weight, which does not take into account variations because of differences among individuals.

One important such difference has to do with the amounts of muscle tissue present in different people. Muscle tissue weighs more than fat tissue, which means that two people can be the same height and weight but one may be noticeably thinner if he or she has more muscle tissue than the other. There may even be a size or two difference in the clothes they wear.

Of course, you'd need a laboratory to determine absolutely your proportion of muscle tissue to fat tissue, but you can still

MORE
MUSCLE
TISSUE

5'4"
120 pounds

LESS
MUSCLE
TISSUE

5'4"
120 pounds

pinpoint the right weight for yourself in the privacy of your own home. Take a good hard look at yourself in a full-length mirror dressed only in your birthday suit. If you see lots of bulges and bumps and flab, chances are you still need to lose some weight, even if the reading on your bathroom scale is within the proper range for your height and frame. Or, use the "pinch test." Take hold of the flesh at the side of your chest at the bottom of the rib cage. If it's more than an inch thick, you can afford to lose weight.

Incidentally, many overweight people assume they have a large frame and so can accommodate extra weight; actually, they generally have medium frames with an abundance of adipose padding. Using your wrist measurement to determine frame size in combination with the height-weight table, the "take-a-good-hard-look-at-yourself-in-a-mirror" test, and the "pinch" test, you should be able to make a good determination of what your ideal weight should be.

FACTORS AFFECTING WEIGHT-LOSS RATE

You and your spouse may be following the same diet equally faithfully, and one of you will probably lose weight faster than the other. Some of the factors responsible for this variation are sex, age, level of physical activity, body composition, water changes, and medication.

Physical activity is the greatest variable in energy expenditure and plays a big role in how fast you can lose weight. Both job-related and leisure-time activities can greatly increase the number of calories you burn. A secretary who trades in her manual typewriter for an electric model, making no other changes in her diet or level of activity, will in time put on a small amount of weight. How far you park your car from your place of work, whether you climb the stairs or take the elevator, whether you rock in a rocker or slouch on a couch, all influence your calorie expenditure.

People who exercise a great deal are burning additional calories. They are also building muscle tissue, which is more active metabolically than fat tissue. Therefore a muscular person uses more calories, even when at rest, then a person of the same weight with less muscle and more fat. As you build muscles through exercise, you can afford (and will in fact need) to take in more calories.

Your sex plays a role in rate of weight loss. Men have more muscle tissue in proportion to the amount of adipose or fat tissue in their bodies, while in women sex hormones cause more fat to be deposited in relation to the amount of muscle. Since muscle tissue uses more energy than fat tissue, a man will lose weight more quickly than a woman when both adhere to the same diet. Also, of course, the fact that men are usually taller than women means that they require more calories to maintain their weight.

In most people in our country the metabolic rate declines with age. This is partly because there is generally a decrease in muscle tissue in older people. It used to be thought that such loss of muscle was a natural consequence of the aging process. It is now realized, however, that the reason for most of the shrinking of muscle cells is that the level of physical activity usually goes down as a person gets older. This does not have to happen. In less technologically developed countries, it is necessary for both the old and the young to engage in strenuous activity, and older people in these societies retain their youthful physiques.

Changes in weight-loss rate because of changing muscle/fat ratio are apparent only over a period of time. Water retention or loss, however, has an immediate weight-influencing effect, causing rapid fluctuation, sometimes even in the course of a single day. There is an optimum amount of water that should be retained by the body in order for it to function properly. The kinds of food we eat and the medications we take affect the amount of water in the tissues.

MUSCLE MASS NEED NOT DECLINE WITH AGE IF ACTIVITY CONTINUES

Painting by Robert Giusti
© 1979 Champion International Corporation
Reprinted by permission

Most Americans consume extremely large amounts of salt. Much of it is already in the processed foods we eat, even before we reach for the salt shaker. Such quantities of salt cause too much water to be retained. Other substances—the caffeine in coffee, cola beverages and other soft drinks, and in various teas, and the theobromine in tea, cocoa, and chocolate—act as diuretics and cause water to be lost from the body. If you stop consuming these beverages, your body will replace the lost fluids and you will regain the "water weight." Don't worry, though—it's fat and not water you need to lose.

If you have been on a high-protein diet that has caused water to be drawn from your tissues, your body will become rehydrated when you change to the high-carbohydrate Pritikin Diet. There will be an initial gain in weight, representing the water that should never have left your body in the first place. If in your first week on the Pritikin Diet you lose 3 pounds of fat, that weight loss will be masked by the gain of water weight (possibly 2 to 5 pounds over that week) as your tissues become rehydrated. Once your body has regained the water it requires, the weight registered on your scale will reflect more accurately the actual loss of fat.

Certain drugs affect the amount of water in the tissues: diuretics, frequently prescribed for high blood pressure, will cause loss of water weight. Others affect the rate of weight loss directly by influencing metabolism. Thyroid extract temporarily increases the metabolic rate; in time, however, the body adjusts by producing less of its own thyroid, and weight returns to the premedication level.

Temporary fluctuations in body weight are caused by variations in the contents in the intestinal tract (which can hold 4 to 10 pounds of food) as well as in the bladder, and in the amount of water being held in the tissues. Because of these ups and downs, we recommend against daily weighing. It is better to weigh yourself no more than twice weekly, always at the same time in the morning after voiding, wearing either no clothes or the same amount of clothing at each weighing.

THE CALORIC-INTAKE PLANS

To accommodate people with different caloric needs and goals for weight loss, we have worked out four different plans based on daily intakes of approximately 700, 850, 1000, and 1200 calories. To choose the right one for you, first you must know how many calories per day you need to maintain your ideal weight for your level of activity. Multiply the ideal weight you have determined for yourself by the factor shown in the following table:

LEVEL OF ACTIVITY	MULTIPLY IDEAL WEIGHT BY
Sedentary	13
Moderately active	15
Strenuously active for large part of day	20

For example: If your ideal weight is 120 pounds and you are moderately active, your calculation would be 120 × 15 = 1800 calories. To maintain your ideal weight of 120 pounds, then, you would need to take in 1800 calories per day.

But until you reach your ideal weight, you would have to follow a lower-calorie diet plan. If you were to choose the 1000-calories-per-day plan, your daily calorie deficit would be 800 calories. Since it takes a deficit of approximately 3500 calories to lose a pound of fat, devide 3500 by 800 to calculate how many days this would take. In this example, it would take a little over four days to lose one pound of pure fat.

Your actual weight loss would be somewhat greater. There may be some water loss, because the Pritikin Diet uses no added salt. Other factors involved in the greater actual weight loss may be (these possibilities are still theoretical) the loss of extra muscle tissue, capillaries, and blood volume previously needed to support and supply the fat cells now being reduced as fat content is burned.

If you want a faster weight loss, you could choose to follow a lower-calorie diet plan. In most instances, however, the 1000- or 1200-calorie diet is appropriate for men; many women function happily on a lower plan.

It can be a good idea to follow a lower caloric intake plan during the week, then on weekends to permit yourself the luxury of more calories. As long as you don't exceed a daily intake of

1200 calories, you will continue good weight loss, though of course at a less rapid rate. In any case, don't feel you absolutely must adhere to a low caloric intake on a particular day or even at a particular meal, if you feel you simply must have something more to eat. It is self-defeating to make the diet difficult for yourself. The key to success is being able to diet without feeling unduly deprived. The Pritikin Diet, because it is based on foods of high bulk and low caloric intake, is easy to follow. You can eat a lot of food—even on the lower-calorie-intake plans—and avoid the hunger that most people come to associate with weight-loss diets.

The table on p. 60 shows the amounts of weight lost in a group of 893 individuals who participated in a residential Pritikin Center program. Data on this group were analyzed by the Department of Epidemiology and Biostatistics of Loma Linda University. Some of the people in this group were on medication that slowed down their rate of weight loss. Most were primarily concerned with degenerative disease symptoms, such as angina, rather than with overweight, and some of these people very often ate the higher-calorie food at the Center meant for people of normal weight. Despite these considerations, average weight losses achieved by the overweight groups on the high-carbohydrate diet are impressive.

Your rate of weight loss will probably be as good or better as that shown on this table. A more technical treatment of the data can be found on page 174 in Chapter 11, "For the Health Professional."

In formulating your weight-loss goals, remember that you must always take in enough calories to meet the body's minimal fuel needs. If you don't, you'll be burning body protein—muscle mass and organs. Six hundred calories per day is a minimum for most adults.

Don't be impatient about the progress you are making. Remember, if you require 1800 calories per day to maintain your ideal weight and you were on a total fast consuming no calories at all, it would still take about two days to burn a single pound of fat. Remember that on a total fast you would lose only six pounds per month more than you would on the 700-calorie diet plan (most people are genuinely surprised to learn that). Remember, too, that illusory weight loss due to dehydration or emptying of the intestinal tract is not your aim. You are after permanent weight loss.

WEIGHT CHANGES IN 21-DAY PERIOD DURING PRITIKIN CENTER PROGRAM

WOMEN

Percent above Ideal Weight	Initial Weight in Pounds	Ending Weight in Pounds	Total Lost in Pounds	Projected Weight Loss in Pounds for 30-Day Period
10–19	143.57	135.55	8.02	11.47
20–29	156.36	148.23	8.13	11.63
30–39	167.54	157.08	10.46	14.96
40 or more	201.67	188.15	13.52	19.33

MEN

Percent above Ideal Weight	Initial Weight in Pounds	Ending Weight in Pounds	Total Lost in Pounds	Projected Weight Loss in Pounds for 30-Day Period
10–19	177.56	166.74	10.82	15.47
20–29	195.29	181.67	13.62	19.48
30–39	206.65	191.30	15.35	21.95
40 or more	242.04	222.86	19.18	27.43

6

Success Stories

The cold statistics reported in the preceding chapter may be convincing, but personal stories are far more likely to get you going. I have selected a few representative case histories presented in letters sent to me by the individuals concerned. They will give you some idea of the kinds of successes that can be achieved by people with weight problems who elect to follow the Pritikin Diet.

Some of the people who wrote these and other such letters had come to the Pritikin Centers; others simply went on the diet at home, of their own accord or on the recommendation of their physician. Those who followed the diet on their own used as a guide my book *The Pritikin Program for Diet and Exercise,* in which there is a chapter about losing weight by using the low-calorie end of the Pritikin Diet.

A number of the letters were sent to me as "birthday letters" for my sixty-fifth birthday in August 1980, which coincided with the 100th session of the Pritikin Center in Santa Monica. My wife had written to graduates of the Pritikin Centers suggesting that a letter about their present state of health would be a wonderful way to say "Happy Birthday" to me. She was right!

CASE HISTORY 1

Mr. Lankford, grossly overweight at the time, went on the Pritikin Diet on his physician's recommendation. Though I am not a physician, he addressed me as though I were.

DIXIE PLANT COMPANY
H A LANKFORD, JR OWNER
Growers and Shippers of
FIELD CROWN HIGH GRADE VEGETABLE PLANTS
CABBAGE, TOMATO, PEPPERS
And All Kinds of Vegetable Plants
P O Box 327 — TELEPHONE 562-5276
Franklin, Virginia 23851

This Plant Company gives no warranty, express or implied, as to description, quality, productiveness or any other matter of any seeds and plants it sends out, and will be in no way responsible for the crop. If the purchaser does not accept the seeds and plants on these terms they are at once to be returned. Seller is not obligated to deliver if prevented from doing so by wars, strikes, fires, or acts of Providence, weather conditions or crop shortage.

December 5, 1979

Dr. Nathan Pritikin
Longevity Institute
Santa Barbara, California

Dear Dr. Pritikin,

When one man is responsible for saving another man's life
it seems only fitting that he should know about it. You have
been responsible for the formula that my physician, Dr. Salvatore
Amari, Loudoun County Hospital, Leesburg, Virginia tells me has
accomplished this.

In February, 1979, I entered the hospital at Leesburg,
Virginia. I weighed 320 pounds and my blood pressure was
$\frac{170}{80-90}$ $\frac{180}{80-90}$. During the stress test my blood pressure went

to 243 and they had to cut off the machine before I finished
the test. At this time it took 6 minutes to return to normal.

This is where you came into the picture. Dr. Salvatore
Amari recommended your diet and cookbook to my wife and me and
that started the rebuilding of my life. I have lost one third
of my original weight, 110 pounds and went from suit size 54
to size 46, shirt size 19 to 15½, waist line 48 to 38. My
blood pressure now runs $\frac{110}{60}$ to $\frac{120}{60}$. These are mere statistics

for I feel years younger and have taken a new lease on life.
In fact, Dr. Amari told me in October when I went back for a
check-up, stress test and all that I had gained 10-15 years
on my life. My blood pressure returned to normal in 3 minutes
after I finished the test. He said with my blood pressure now
$\frac{110}{60} - \frac{120}{60}$ that my heart and physical condition was equivalent

of a 40 year old man. I was 56 years of age in November.

We, I say we for my wife has done all the meal planning and cooking.

Needless to say, I am not drinking but in addition to that I have learned new eating habits. I must confess that part of this success must be accredited to my wife's support and interest. For not only is she a professionally trained dietitian but she is also a gourmet cook. However, the formula for this miracle is yours and it seems only fitting that I should express my heart felt appreciation for your research. If there is anyway in which I might help others by testifying to the effectiveness of your work, I shall be eager and happy to do so.

The first 90 days I had the support of Chlorthalidone-50mg. tablets, Inderal-40mg. tablets, Slow K tablets prescribed by the physican. However, from there on (June) it was the Live Longer Diet alone.

I can truthfully say that I feel better than I have in 30 years. I work 10-14 hours a day and don't seem to get tired anymore. When I start out mornings I feel as if I've been on vacation and feel great. Lots of people tell me I look 10-15 years younger.

Sincerely Yours,

Harvey A. Lankford, Jr.

CASE HISTORY 2

Sidney R. Silverman was recommended to the Pritikin Center by Dr. Fred Kasch of San Diego State University, an exercise physiologist.

SIDNEY R. SILVERMAN
4835 VERBA SANTA DRIVE
SAN DIEGO, CALIFORNIA 92115

SEP 10 1980

September 8, 1980

Nathan Pritikin, Director
Longevity Center
1910 Ocean Front Walk
Santa Monica, California 90405

Dear Nathan,

Belated Birthday Greetings and Congratulations on reaching
your 65th year! You are your own best walking advertise-
ment for the "Pritikin way of life."

As you know, ever since attending the Santa Monica Pritikin
Longevity Center's 41st Session in 1978, I am a staunch
believer and supporter of the Pritikin way of life. Prior
to that time I was constantly tired, generally lacked energy,
depressed and overweight. In the fall of 1977 had a medical
examination with an abnormal treadmill reading which fright-
ened me enough to seek help. Your program was recommended
to me by Dr. Fred Kasch of San Diego State University.

After following your program I lost 18 pounds in 30 days
and then an additional 12 pounds, and have kept this excess
weight off to date. Further, I could barely walk a mile,
but after just 6 days was doing 10 miles a day and now
continue to walk an average of 5 miles each day.

Since changing my dietary habits I no longer suffer from
depression, do not require as much rest and have better
endurance and thought processes. Also, my family, friends
and employees notice an improvement in attitude - more
tolerance. And, as an added bonus, when I went to take a
physical in May of this year for an application of life
insurance, was able to take 13½ minutes on the treadmill
with heartrate of 167! Dr. John Mazur, Chief Cardiologist
of Mercy Hospital in San Diego, conducted the test and was
duly impressed. My personal physician did not think I
would ever have a normal treadmill reading. Even though you were
rather reluctant in promising any change. So you see, we
both conquered, and I was able to apply for and receive a
large amount of life insurance at the <u>standard</u> rate. I
attribute all this to following your program of exercise
and proper diet.

God Bless You Nathan. I wish you continued success in
furthering the cause.

Sincerely yours,

/mtl
Encl.

Sidney R. Silverman

CASE HISTORY 3

Mrs. Lattin, who describes herself as a "trim 120-pound great-grandmother," followed the Pritikin Diet on her own.

Denver, Colo.
10 January, 1980

Dear Mr. Pritikin:

A Happy New Year to you and your loved ones and to all of your wonderful associates in the Live Longer tradition. And a great big Thank You for my transformation from a 162 pound cocoon in April 1979 to a trim 120 pound great grandmother in September which I can hardly believe myself, but it's true! I had never realized my potentialities until I learned of the special way to bring them about by following the tried and true logic in your compelling book The Pritikin Diet and Exercise Program.

My son-in-law Captain Jack Leffler, U.A.L., Seattle, also benefitted a lot on your program at your Longevity Center in Maui in Mid-1979 and told me about it. His wife (my daughter Helen) accompanied him to Maui and they sent me some of your tapes and I became more convinced to continue the program. The discipline becomes built-in once the program is undertaken and makes the goal not only earned - but yearned because one knows they are 'right-on' the trail. I really enjoy the Program and have made it my perma- nent way of life and find it easy to follow now, and I have grown to rediscover and LOVE the great outdoors. And how much nicer to be sitting in this stenographer's chair instead of a wheel chair which might have been my fate had I not started eating correctly and getting the kinks out! (Jack gave me the typewriter and chair for Christmas.) How sweet it is!

My Doctor says I'm "terribly healthy," and I passed the tread- mill test in flying colors and have overcome a slight fibrillation. Keep busy typing, roving, shopping for the right foods, do my own housework, etc. but since my debut into the Pritikin Program, note an additional spark to all of this and every day is now a holiday.

I just thought that you should be more adulated for helping so many people in their own homes by reading and absorbing the for- mulas in your exciting book, as well as those who come to your Lon- gevity Centers. So again, thank you Mr. Wonderful for your gener- osity and compassion in contributing and sharing the harvest of many years of research at big expense, and of putting your own self on the line to prove that man's physique can be figuratively changed and greatly enhanced psychologically through proper approach to a sound program for a more active and exciting life style, even the second time around. It's been fun for me!

Gratefully yours

Fay F Lattin
FAY F. LATTIN
Rover in the Rockies

CASE HISTORIES 4 AND 5

The Spurgeons seem happy enough, even with their clothing problem.

GALLERY
William and Elizabeth Spurgeon
IMPORT

August -- 1980

Dear Nathan Pritikin,

When my wife and I attended Session #88 (March 1980), we were given a hooded exercise jacket with the Longevity Center decal on the back.

During our 26 day stay we never wore the jackets, but brought them home with us as a pleasant reminder of our California stay and a practical covering for our outside walking in our Connecticut spring.

Now, four months later, those same jackets have never been worn for two reasons: first, we walk inside with our recently purchased treadmill. Second and most important, both jackets are much too big for us! Strict adherence to the Maxi Diet has resulted in 40 pounds weight loss for Elizabeth, and for me, sixty pounds.

We are planning to return our unworn jackets to the Center so that they in turn may be given to new participants who hopefully in five months will find they cannot wear them!

Thank you for your <u>many</u> gifts.

Happy birthday!

Wm and Elizabeth Spurgeon

Montgomery Street, Lakeville, Connecticut 06039, USA   203 435-9277

CASE HISTORY 6

I'm still not sure what "humma-hummas" are, but you get the point.

PCC FINANCIAL SERVICES COMPANY

A DIVISION OF PACIFIC CONSULTING CORPORATION

JAMES C. BARKS, CLU

5700 STOCKDALE HIGHWAY, SUITE 100
BAKERSFIELD, CALIFORNIA 93309
TELEPHONE (805) 327-7101

August 5, 1980

AUG 2 2 1980

Ilene Pritikin
P.O. Box 5335
Santa Barbara, CA 93108

Dear Nathan:

Happy Birthday! I just want you to know that you look a lot better than Dr. Atkins! (That's not saying much because of his fat Humma-Humma's. However, considering he is 20 year younger, it needs to be communicated.)

Nathan, before I came to the Center I was a 38 year old who had the body of a 58 year old. I weighed 220, smoked 3 packs a day, did not exercise, was taking 11 pills per day for B.P., Gout, Uric Acid, ect, ect. I felt lousy, looked lousy and acted lousy. The inderal effected my productivity and energy levels. I had trouble walking a mile, let alone walking up stairs. With Children only 9 and 11 and a great wife, I decided that all the money in the world along with a great family would be no good dead. I wanted to change, but, How? There was so much to do--your center was the answer.

I'm jogging 3 to 4 miles per day. I've lost 30 pounds, quit smoking and the greatest of all--I'm off of all medication. To be sure my life has changed.

I can't say I'm happier because of the pressure of business and of the world's economic and social problems. I can say, however, that I can handle it better because I feel better. Certainly I like myself better.

Please know your Center has been a great Joy and positive adventure in my life. Instead of worrying about dieting I can now worry about positive things--such as--will humma humma's really increase in size with the same diet as the Tyamara Indian?

My warmest regards to you, a person I love and respect.

Happy Birthday!

James C. Barks, CLU

JCB/jph

A PACIFIC MUTUAL COMPANY

I could go on and on with more examples of permanent weight loss and health improvements achieved on the Pritikin Diet by people who went on the regimen themselves at home or who came to a Center. But now it's your turn: why don't you write the next case history yourself? Fill it in as you lose weight on the Pritikin Diet.

Please send me a copy when you are ready to share your success story with me. I enjoy keeping track of all the people who have been helped on the Pritikin Diet. When you send your case history, be sure you've included health improvements you've noticed and improvements in your emotional well-being that have resulted. Good luck—I know you'll make it!

PERSONAL CASE HISTORY

Name _____

Street Address _____

City/State/Zip _____ M F Age_____

Date starting Pritikin Diet _____

Weight when starting Pritikin Diet _____ pounds

Ideal weight _____ pounds

Diet followed before starting Pritikin Diet _____

Monthly Weight Loss Record

(Record on same date each month;
if necessary, add more months.)

Date	My Weight	Total Weight Loss Since Starting Diet
MONTH 1 _____	_____ pounds	_____ pounds
MONTH 2 _____	_____ pounds	_____ pounds
MONTH 3 _____	_____ pounds	_____ pounds
MONTH 4 _____	_____ pounds	_____ pounds

General health improvements and improvements in emotional
well-being resulting from my successful weight-loss program:

7

The Four Diet Menu Plans

Ready—set—*GO!* In this chapter you will be provided with the road maps for your weight-loss trip, which will give you a choice of four routes. The fastest is the 700-calorie-per-day plan; the most leisurely and least taxing permits approximately 1200 calories per day. There are two intermediate routes, allowing in the vicinity of 850 and 1000 calories per day.

While it is generally a good idea to stick closely to the plan you have selected as the best for you, it may be helpful for you occasionally to change to another for a meal or even for one or two days' meals. It's easier to adhere to a program if a certain

mount of flexibility is built into it. You might choose to stay on
e 700-calorie diet during the week and let go over the weekend
y using the 1200-calorie plan on Saturday and Sunday. If you
id, you would lose only one less pound for the month. If you
xceeded your planned caloric intake for the day by 100 calories
ach day, in a month the difference would also be just one
ound. In other words, while you need to be disciplined when
ou are dieting, you don't need to be fanatical about meeting
our target caloric intake each day.

To facilitate crossovers from one plan to another, the diets are
lanned so that in many cases the recipes for any one day for all
our diets are the same; the menu differences are either in serving
ize or in the choice of foods accompanying the main dish. The
igher-calorie plans may have noodles along with the dinner
ntrée, while the lower-calorie plans will substitute a low-
alorie vegetable. Or, instead of bread the lower-calorie plans
ay offer raw vegetable relishes.

Menu plans for the four diets are provided for fourteen days.
hey are interchangeable, so that if you especially like the
cipes on one day's menu plan you can use that day's plan as
ften as you wish, substituting it for daily plans for which you
on't have the ingredients on hand or perhaps you don't find so
ppealing. You may want to substitute recipes from the Recipe
ection, particularly if you have been following the menu plans
or a while and need a change. To ensure that your nutritional
quirements are still being met, check the Guidelines for Free-
orm Dieters on page 110. Also, be sure to adjust serving sizes
substitute recipes so that your caloric intake remains approxi-
ately the same.

Most of the recipes make four or more servings. Plan to use
e recipes for family meals; you'll be delighted to find that they
e consumed with gusto. Just make sure that nondieters get the
alories they need by letting them help themselves to larger
rvings or augmenting the meal with other foods. Leftovers can
ften be refrigerated or frozen for use another day, or you may
ish to halve some recipes to produce a smaller yield.

There is an additional special menu plan included for the
dividual who lacks the time, interest, or talent for cooking, and
r others who at least on certain days would prefer a no-fuss
enu plan. This plan, which requires almost no cooking, follows
e 14 regular menu plans.

BREAKFAST

Most of the breakfast menus contain some grain food. Grain are limited on the diet because they are higher in calories than most other plant foods, but you need some to meet important nutritional requirements. Because they tend to be filling, they also give you a more substantial start for the day.

Hot cereal, made from cracked wheat, rolled oats, or corn meal, is offered on most days. Cornmeal, which is low in calories compared with other cereal grains, is not common as a breakfast cereal in this country, except in the South as hominy grits. Known to Italians as polenta, hot cornmeal is a delicious cereal. Choose a cornmeal that hasn't been stripped of valuable nutrients. Bolted cornmeal, which has had only the hull removed, or ground whole-grain cornmeal, is preferable to degerminated cornmeal, which is minus both germ and bran.

If you don't like hot cereal every day, you may prefer the alternate suggestion offered on some days, or you may substitute a suitable bread, lightly toasted if you wish. Shredded Wheat or Grape-Nuts, in small servings, though not as nutritious or filling as the hot cereals suggested, can be used in special situations. Unfortunately, most convenient packaged dry cereals are nutritionally inferior and are laden with sweeteners, additives and other ingredients it's best to sidestep.

Some Pritikin dieters like to have hot soup or hot cooked vegetables in the morning, reserving their grain intake for later in the day, in the form of whole-wheat pasta, brown rice, or other whole-grain foods.

LUNCH AND DINNER

You'll find that these interesting, diversified menus can be very successfully adapted for family meals, too, if you choose. Use them in the way that best meets your needs. Many luncheon entrées are suitable for dinner, and you may prefer to use them in the evening instead of at lunch. Perhaps for lunch you'll find a bowl of hot soup and a green salad most convenient to prepare and perfectly satisfactory. If so, you could use the soup of the day or another soup in the Recipe Section as the basis for your luncheon meal. If as a consequence your caloric intake is less than it would be on the regular menu plan lunch, you'll be free calories ahead.

SNACKS

Snacking between meals is definitely approved on the Pritikin Diet. At the Centers, food is offered at eight different times during the day. The body functions best when food is taken at closer rather than more spaced-out intervals. Low-calorie between-meal snacks will add somewhat to your day's caloric intake, but may help you to get through each day feeling better. If you are following the menu plans and are able to, you can avoid additional caloric intake by reserving a part of your mealtime menu to have as a snack between meals. If you need the entire meal to satisfy you, choose low-calorie foods for your snack supplement. Keep some leftover soups and salads and some cut-up vegetable sticks in the refrigerator for this purpose. Raw vegetables are ideal for snacking, as the additional chewing required stimulates greater secretion of digestive juices, resulting in more of a feeling of fullness.

BEVERAGES

Beverages are not specified on the diet plans, so a few comments are in order. It is not necessary for health reasons to drink anything at all beyond what your thirst dictates since the diet provides ample fluids in the water naturally present in abundant quantities in vegetables or added to soups; still, many people enjoy drinking beverages during the day, especially with meals.

Fluids drunk right before or during meals will make you feel fuller. Of course, you will want to avoid beverages that add to your caloric intake. Alcoholic beverages are highly caloric (your average martini contains 140 calories), so should be avoided from this standpoint alone. Even skim milk (88 calories in 8 ounces) as a beverage, in excess of a cup a day, adds unnecessary calories, since the diet provides adequate amounts of protein and other nutrients contained in milk. Fruit juices, too, are discouraged because they are much less filling, calorie for calorie, than whole fruits.

Caffeine drinks, such as coffee and tea, are a problem for the dieter even if no milk, cream, or sugar is added, because they stimulate the appetite. Decaffeination of coffee removes the caffeine, but caffeols that cause appetite stimulation remain.

Soft drinks contain very large amounts of sugar. Many of them—colas, Dr. Pepper, and Mountain Dew—also contain caffeine. The "diet" colas, although virtually calorie-free, still contain caffeine, and we don't know the ultimate results of consuming over a period of time large amounts of the noncaloric artificial sweeteners they contain. Be wary also of sodium chloride (salt) or other sodium compounds in "diet" soft drinks (and in club soda); sodium compounds tend to make you retain water.

That leaves little but herb teas and beverages made with roasted grains, like Postum or Roastaroma, which contain very few if any calories. At the Pritikin Centers we serve herb teas (red bush and linden flower), or just plain hot water and lemon, which many find surprisingly pleasant. Carbonated mineral waters (choose those low in sodium) are refreshing when served with a slice of lime or other fruit. They make a good substitute for alcoholic beverages and have become quite acceptable choices even on the cocktail party circuit.

DESSERTS

Most people have grown to love rich desserts, sugary, calorie-dense concoctions that promote weight gain and low blood-sugar levels. You will find Pritikin-style desserts that are low in fat in the Recipe Section. But because many of them do contain generous amounts of sweeteners in the form of fruit juices, they should be restricted and reserved for use, if desired, on special occasions. A few have been included in the menu plans. If you wish, you can try the others over a priod of time, when entertaining, celebrating birthdays, or at other occasions when you feel the need for a special dessert. Your best dessert, of course, is fresh fruit.

BRAN

To increase their feeling of fullness, some people find it helpful to take a small amount of unprocessed miller's bran twice a day until they reach their desired weight. You could add two tablespoons to your breakfast cereal and another two tablespoons as a topping for your soup, hot vegetables, or other luncheon dish.

The menu plans don't make a calorie allowance for the bran, but the small number of calories contributed are probably offset by the effect of bran in causing a somewhat faster transit time of food through the intestines. This faster transit time reduces the total number of calories absorbed from a given amount of food. Even without this effect, the intake of four tablespoons of bran per day would only decrease your total weight loss by half a pound per month.

Bran is often very helpful in treating constipation. The high-fiber content of the Pritikin Diet usually prevents the constipation that occurs on most reducing diets, but taking bran will help to insure spontaneous bowel movements. If constipation continues to be a problem even with the bran, try taking a glass of water within an hour after ingesting each intake of bran.

Although bran is often useful in the treatment of gastrointestinal disorders, it can't be used by everyone. If you have an intestinal problem other than ordinary constipation, check with your physician before adding bran to your diet.

The 14 different daily menu plans that follow not only will give you good nutrition, they will also keep you well satisfied. They have been carefully structured to provide good nutrition for your weight-loss regimen. Many recipes utilize certain specific ingredients because of their special nutritional composition. Later, when you have reached your weight-loss goals and begin to follow a higher-calorie maintenance diet, your menu planning can be more casual. As calories increase, intake of particular nutrients becomes less critical. The menu plans and many of the recipes have been worked out in my own home kitchen by a team that includes Esther Taylor, the talented head cook at the Pritikin Center in California in its first years, a dietitian, and two able supervisors in the persons of Jana Trent and my wife, Ilene. Some of the recipes have been used at the Pritikin Center in

Santa Monica; others have been suggested to us by people who have been following the Pritikin Diet (and we are very grateful to them); still others are original for this book or adaptations of standard recipes. All recipes may be found in the Recipe Section and are separately indexed at the end of this book.

HOW TO USE THE DAILY MENU PLANS

You can use the menu plans in many ways. Here are a few suggestions.

1. You can use the menu plans as given in sequence (or in any other sequence you prefer) for 14 days, then repeat them over and over as often as necessary until you reach your desired weight.

2. You can use some of the menu plans, repeating those that you like as often as you wish and eliminating those you like less.

3. To cut down on cooking time, you can prepare each recipe in double or triple quantities, then use them on alternate days (or in any sequence you desire). Many of the recipes are suitable for freezing.

4. You can vary any day's menu by substituting recipes from the Recipe Section. When making substitutions, your calorie intake should be equivalent. If a recipe has too many calories, use a smaller serving. To make sure your nutritional requirements are met when you substitute recipes, check the Guidelines for Free-Form Dieters on page 110.

5. On days when you are less inclined to be bound by rules or have less time for food preparation (or will be eating out), you may decide to ignore the menu plans entirely and instead choose free-form dieting (described on pages 108–111). You'll get good weight loss on this approach, but the rate of loss may be somewhat less predictable.

Good luck, and good eating!

DAY 1

	700	**850**
BREAKFAST	¾ cup *HOT CRACKED WHEAT* ¼ medium banana, sliced ½ cup nonfat milk, hot or cold ½ medium grapefruit	1 cup *HOT CRACKED WHEAT* ½ medium banana, sliced ½ cup nonfat milk, hot or cold ½ medium grapefruit
LUNCH	1 cup *TOMATO BOUILLON* garnished with 1 lemon slice *RAW VEGETABLE SALAD* No. 2 (¼ recipe) ¼ cup *CREAMY ARTICHOKE DRESSING* 1½ cups steamed chopped broccoli	1½ cups *TOMATO BOUILLON* garnished with 1 lemon slice *RAW VEGETABLE SALAD* No. 2 (¼ recipe) ¼ cup *CREAMY ARTICHOKE DRESSING* 1½ cups steamed chopped broccoli 2 triple rye crackers (Ry-Krisp brand)
DINNER	*STIR-FRIED STEAK AND GREEN PEPPERS* (¹/₅ recipe) *CHINESE STIR-FRIED VEGE-TABLES* (⅓ recipe) *CUCUMBER SUNOMONO SALAD* (¹/₆ recipe)	*STIR-FRIED STEAK AND GREEN PEPPERS* (¹/₅ recipe) *CHINESE STIR-FRIED VEGE-TABLES* (⅓ recipe) *CUCUMBER SUNOMONO SALAD* (¼ recipe)

1000	1200
1 cup *HOT CRACKED WHEAT*	1 cup *HOT CRACKED WHEAT*
½ large banana, sliced	½ large banana, sliced
½ cup nonfat milk, hot or cold	½ cup nonfat milk, hot or cold
½ medium grapefruit	½ medium grapefruit
	1½ slices whole-wheat bread, toasted
2 cups *TOMATO BOUILLON* garnished with 1 lemon slice	2 cups *TOMATO BOUILLON* garnished with 1 lemon slice
RAW VEGETABLE SALAD No. 2 (¼ recipe)	*RAW VEGETABLE SALAD* No. 2 (¼ recipe)
¼ cup *CREAMY ARTICHOKE DRESSING*	¼ cup *CREAMY ARTICHOKE DRESSING*
1½ cups steamed chopped broccoli	1½ cups steamed chopped broccoli
2 triple rye crackers (Ry-Krisp brand)	2 triple rye crackers (Ry-Krisp brand)
STIR-FRIED STEAK AND GREEN PEPPERS (¹/₅ recipe)	*STIR-FRIED STEAK AND GREEN PEPPERS* (¼ recipe)
CHINESE STIR-FRIED VEGE-TABLES (⅓ recipe)	*CHINESE STIR-FRIED VEGE-TABLES* (⅓ recipe)
CUCUMBER SUNOMONO SALAD (¼ recipe)	*CUCUMBER SUNOMONO SALAD* (¼ recipe)
½ cup *BROWN RICE*	¾ cup *BROWN RICE*

DAY 2

	700	850
BREAKFAST	¾ cup *HOT CRACKED WHEAT* ¼ medium banana, sliced ¾ cup nonfat milk, hot or cold	1 cup *HOT CRACKED WHEAT* ½ medium banana, sliced ¾ cup nonfat milk, hot or cold
LUNCH	*VEGETABLE COMBINATION* No. 5 (¼ recipe) *RAW VEGETABLE SALAD* No. 2 (¼ recipe) ¼ cup *CANTONESE DRESSING*	*VEGETABLE COMBINATION* No. 5 (¼ recipe) *RAW VEGETABLE SALAD* No. 2 (¼ recipe) ¼ cup *CANTONESE DRESSING*
DINNER	*STUFFED BREAST OF CHICKEN* *WITH LEMON-WINE SAUCE* ($^1/_6$ recipe) *ORANGE, ONION, AND BUTTER* *LETTUCE SALAD* ($^1/_6$ recipe) 8 spears steamed asparagus ¾ cup steamed sliced carrots	1 cup *BROCCOLI BISQUE* *STUFFED BREAST OF CHICKEN* *WITH LEMON-WINE SAUCE* ($^1/_6$ recipe) *ORANGE, ONION, AND BUTTER* *LETTUCE SALAD* ($^1/_6$ recipe) 8 spears steamed asparagus 1 cup steamed sliced carrots

1000	1200
1 cup *HOT CRACKED WHEAT*	1 cup *HOT CRACKED WHEAT*
1 small banana, sliced	1 small banana, sliced
¾ cup nonfat milk, hot or cold	¾ cup nonfat milk, hot or cold
	2 *BLUEBERRY MUFFINS* *or* 2 slices whole-wheat bread, toasted
VEGETABLE COMBINATION No. 5 (¼ recipe)	*VEGETABLE COMBINATION* No. 5 (¼ recipe)
RAW VEGETABLE SALAD No. 2 (¼ recipe)	*RAW VEGETABLE SALAD* No. 2 (¼ recipe)
¼ cup *CANTONESE DRESSING*	¼ cup *CANTONESE DRESSING*
1½ cups *BROCCOLI BISQUE*	1½ cups *BROCCOLI BISQUE*
CHICKEN BREASTS AUX CHAMPIGNONS (¼ recipe) ½ cup *MUSHROOM CREAM SAUCE* *or* *STUFFED BREAST OF CHICKEN WITH LEMON-WINE SAUCE* (¹⁄₆ recipe) served over ⅓ cup hot whole-wheat noodles	*CHICKEN BREASTS AUX CHAMPIGNONS* (¼ recipe) ½ cup *MUSHROOM CREAM SAUCE* *or* *STUFFED BREAST OF CHICKEN WITH LEMON-WINE SAUCE* (¹⁄₆ recipe) served over ⅓ cup hot whole-wheat noodles
ORANGE, ONION, AND BUTTER LETTUCE SALAD (¹⁄₆ recipe)	*ORANGE, ONION, AND BUTTER LETTUCE SALAD* (¹⁄₆ recipe)
8 spears steamed asparagus	8 spears steamed asparagus
1 cup steamed sliced carrots	1 cup steamed sliced carrots
	PUMPKIN MOUSSE PIE (¹⁄₆ recipe) *or* 1 small apple

DAY 3

	700	850
BREAKFAST	¾ cup *HOT CORNMEAL* ¼ cup blueberries (fresh or unsweetened frozen) *or* ¼ medium banana, sliced ¾ cup nonfat milk, hot or cold ½ medium grapefruit	1 cup *HOT CORNMEAL* ¼ cup blueberries (fresh or unsweetened frozen) *or* ¼ medium banana, sliced ¾ cup nonfat milk, hot or cold *or* 3 pieces *VANILLA-SESAME FRENCH TOAST* topped with 2 Tbsp. *STRAWBERRY PRESERVES* and ⅓ cup nonfat yogurt ½ medium grapefruit
LUNCH	*RATATOUILLE* No. 1 (⅓ recipe) *RAW VEGETABLE SALAD* No. 2 (¼ recipe) ¼ cup *WINE-VINEGAR DRESSING*	*RATATOUILLE* No. 1 (⅓ recipe) *RAW VEGETABLE SALAD* No. 2 (¼ recipe) ¼ cup *WINE-VINEGAR DRESSING*
DINNER	*BREADED FISH* (halibut preferred, ⅛ recipe) with 2 Tbsp. *YOGURT-HORSERADISH DRESSING* *RAW VEGETABLE SALAD* No. 4 (¼ recipe) ¼ cup *SPICY TOMATO DRESSING* *HERBED GREENS* (mustard or turnip) (½ recipe)	*BREADED FISH*, (halibut preferred, ⅛ recipe) with ¼ cup *YOGURT-HORSERADISH DRESSING* *or* ¼ cup *EGG-MUSTARD SAUCE* *RAW VEGETABLE SALAD* No. 4 (¼ recipe) ¼ cup *SPICY TOMATO DRESSING* *HERBED GREENS* (mustard or turnip) (½ recipe) *SQUASH SOUFFLÉ* (¼ recipe)

1000	1200
1 cup *HOT CORNMEAL*	1½ cups *HOT CORNMEAL*
½ cup blueberries (fresh or unsweetened frozen) *or* ½ medium banana, sliced	½ cup blueberries (fresh or unsweetened frozen) *or* ½ medium banana, sliced
¾ cup nonfat milk, hot or cold	¾ cup nonfat milk, hot or cold
or	*or*
4 pieces *VANILLA-SESAME FRENCH TOAST* topped with 2 Tbsp. *STRAWBERRY PRE-SERVES* and ⅓ cup nonfat yogurt	6 pieces *VANILLA-SESAME FRENCH TOAST* topped with ¼ cup *STRAWBERRY PRE-SERVES* and ⅓ cup nonfat yogurt
½ medium grapefruit	½ medium grapefruit
EGGPLANT STEAKS (¼ recipe)	*EGGPLANT STEAKS* (⅓ recipe)
or	*or*
RATATOUILLE No. 1 (½ recipe)	*RATATOUILLE* No. 1 (½ recipe) with 1 slice whole-wheat bread
RAW VEGETABLE SALAD No. 2 (¼ recipe)	
¼ cup *WINE-VINEGAR DRESSING*	*RAW VEGETABLE SALAD* No. 2 (¼ recipe)
	¼ cup *WINE-VINEGAR DRESSING*
BREADED FISH (⅙ recipe) with	*BREADED FISH* (⅙ recipe) with
¼ cup *YOGURT-HORSERADISH DRESSING*	¼ cup *YOGURT-HORSERADISH DRESSING*
or	*or*
¼ cup *EGG-MUSTARD SAUCE*	¼ cup *EGG-MUSTARD SAUCE*
RAW VEGETABLE SALAD No. 4 (¼ recipe)	*RAW VEGETABLE SALAD* No. 4 (¼ recipe)
¼ cup *SPICY TOMATO DRESSING*	¼ cup *SPICY TOMATO DRESSING*
VEGETABLE COMBINATION No. 5 (⅕ recipe)	*VEGETABLE COMBINATION* No. 5 (¼ recipe)
SQUASH SOUFFLÉ (¼ recipe)	*SQUASH SOUFFLÉ* (¼ recipe)

DAY 4

	700	850
BREAKFAST	¾ cup *HOT CRACKED WHEAT* ¼ medium banana, sliced ½ cup nonfat milk, hot or cold ½ medium grapefruit	1 cup *HOT CRACKED WHEAT* ½ small banana, sliced ½ cup nonfat milk, hot or cold ½ medium grapefruit
LUNCH	1½ cups *CHINESE TOMATO-VEGETABLE SOUP* *EGG WHITE SCRAMBLE* (1 recipe)	1¾ cups *CHINESE-TOMATO-VEGETABLE SOUP* *EGG WHITE SCRAMBLE* (1 recipe) 2 rye crackers (Kavli brand, thin)
DINNER	1 *CHICKEN OR TURKEY ENCHILADA*, with 2 Tbsp. *GREEN GODDESS TOPPING*, on 2 cups shredded romaine lettuce 1½ cups steamed summer squash	1 *CHICKEN OR TURKEY ENCHILADA*, with 2 Tbsp. *GREEN GODDESS TOPPING*, on 2 cups shredded romaine lettuce *VEGETABLE COMBINATION* No. 4 (¹/₅ recipe) *or* 3 cups steamed summer squash

1000	1200
1 cup *HOT CRACKED WHEAT*	1 cup *HOT CRACKED WHEAT*
½ small banana, sliced	½ small banana, sliced
½ cup nonfat milk, hot or cold	½ cup nonfat milk, hot or cold
½ medium grapefruit	½ medium grapefruit
1¾ cups *CHINESE TOMATO-VEGETABLE SOUP*	1¾ cups *CHINESE TOMATO-VEGETABLE SOUP*
EGG WHITE SCRAMBLE (1 recipe)	*EGG WHITE SCRAMBLE* (1 recipe)
2 rye crackers (Kavli brand, thin)	2 rye crackers (Kavli brand, thin)
1 *CHICKEN OR TURKEY ENCHILADA*, with 2 Tbsp. *GREEN GODDESS TOPPING*, on 2 cups shredded romaine lettuce	2 *CHICKEN OR TURKEY ENCHILADAS*, with ¼ cup *GREEN GODDESS TOPPING*, on 2 cups shredded romaine lettuce
VEGETABLE COMBINATION No. 4 (¹/₅ recipe) *or* 3 cups steamed summer squash	*VEGETABLE COMBINATION* No. 4 (¹/₅ recipe) *or* 3 cups steamed summer squash
⅔ cup *SPANISH RICE* *or* ⅔ cup *REFRIED BEANS*	⅔ cup *SPANISH RICE* *or* ⅔ cup *REFRIED BEANS*

DAY 5

	700	850
BREAKFAST	¾ cup *HOT OATMEAL*	1 cup *HOT OATMEAL*
	½ cup whole strawberries (fresh or unsweetened frozen), sliced	½ cup whole strawberries (fresh or unsweetened frozen), sliced
	¼ cup nonfat milk, hot or cold	½ cup nonfat milk, hot or cold
	½ medium grapefruit	½ medium grapefruit
LUNCH	1½ cups *CREAM OF MUSHROOM SOUP*	1½ cups *CREAM OF MUSHROOM SOUP*
	RAW VEGETABLE SALAD No. 4 (¼ recipe)	*RAW VEGETABLE SALAD* No. 4 (¼ recipe)
	¼ cup *SWEET–AND–SOUR VINEGAR DRESSING*	¼ cup *SWEET–AND–SOUR VINEGAR DRESSING*
		1 triple rye cracker (Ry-Krisp brand)
DINNER	*SALMON SOUFFLÉ* (¼ recipe)	*SALMON SOUFFLÉ* (¼ recipe)
	CUCUMBER-TOMATO SALAD (⅓ recipe)	*CUCUMBER-TOMATO SALAD* (½ recipe)
	BAKED BANANA SQUASH (¹/₆ recipe)	*BAKED BANANA SQUASH* (¼ recipe)
	VEGETABLE COMBINATION No. 1 (¼ recipe)	*VEGETABLE COMBINATION* No. 1 (½ recipe)

1000	1200
1 cup *HOT OATMEAL*	1 cup *HOT OATMEAL*
½ cup whole strawberries (fresh or unsweetened frozen), sliced	½ cup whole strawberries (fresh or unsweetened frozen), sliced
½ cup nonfat milk, hot or cold	½ cup nonfat milk, hot or cold
1 medium orange *or* ½ large grapefruit	1 medium orange *or* ½ large grapefruit
1½ cups *CREAM OF MUSHROOM SOUP*	1½ cups *CREAM OF MUSHROOM SOUP*
RAW VEGETABLE SALAD No. 4 (¼ recipe)	*RAW VEGETABLE SALAD* No. 4 (¼ recipe)
¼ cup *YOGURT-CHEESE DRESSING*	¼ cup *YOGURT-CHEESE DRESSING*
1 slice whole-wheat bread	1 slice whole-wheat bread
SALMON SOUFFLÉ (¼ recipe)	*SALMON SOUFFLÉ* (¼ recipe)
⅓ cup *WHITE SAUCE* No. 2	⅓ cup *WHITE SAUCE* No.2
CUCUMBER-TOMATO SALAD (½ recipe)	*CUCUMBER-TOMATO SALAD* (½ recipe)
BAKED BANANA SQUASH (¼ recipe)	*PARSLIED POTATOES* (¹/₆ recipe) *or* *BAKED BANANA SQUASH* (½ recipe)
VEGETABLE COMBINATION No. 1 (⅓ recipe)	*VEGETABLE COMBINATION* No. 1 (⅓ recipe)
	¾ cup *CAROB-MINT MOUSSE* *or* 1 small pear and 2 cups hot air-popped popcorn

DAY 6

	700	**850**
BREAKFAST	¾ cup *HOT CORNMEAL* ¼ medium banana, sliced ¾ cup nonfat milk, hot or cold ½ medium grapefruit	1 cup *HOT CORNMEAL* ½ small banana, sliced ¾ cup nonfat milk, hot or cold ½ medium grapefruit
LUNCH	*COUNTRY CLUB SALAD* (¼ recipe)	*COUNTRY CLUB SALAD* (¼ recipe) with ¼ cup additional *TANGY FRENCH DRESSING* on the side
DINNER	1¾ cups *VEGETABLE STEW* *RAW VEGETABLE SALAD* No. 1 (¼ recipe) ¼ cup *WINE-VINEGAR DRESSING*	2½ cups *VEGETABLE STEW* *RAW VEGETABLE SALAD* No. 1 (¼ recipe) ¼ cup *ITALIAN DRESSING*

1000	**1200**
1 cup *HOT CORNMEAL*	1 cup *HOT CORNMEAL*
½ small banana, sliced	½ small banana, sliced
¾ cup nonfat milk, hot or cold	¾ cup nonfat milk, hot or cold
½ medium grapefruit	½ medium grapefruit
1¼ cups *CARROT BISQUE*	1½ cups *CARROT BISQUE*
TROPICAL PINEAPPLE-CHICKEN SALAD (¼ recipe) 6 steamed chilled asparagus spears with 1 lemon slice on a bed of ½ head butter lettuce *or* *COUNTRY CLUB SALAD* (¼ recipe) with ⅓ cup additional *TANGY FRENCH DRESSING* on the side	*TROPICAL PINEAPPLE-CHICKEN SALAD* (⅓ recipe) 6 steamed chilled asparagus spears with 1 lemon slice on a bed of ½ head butter lettuce *or* *COUNTRY CLUB SALAD* (⅓ recipe) with ⅓ cup additional *TANGY FRENCH DRESSING* on the side
3 cups *VEGETABLE STEW*	3 cups *VEGETABLE STEW*
RAW VEGETABLE SALAD No. 1 (¼ recipe)	*RAW VEGETABLE SALAD* No. 1 (¼ recipe)
¼ cup *ITALIAN DRESSING*	¼ cup *ITALIAN DRESSING*
	1 medium apple

DAY 7

	700	850
BREAKFAST	*OMELET* (¼ recipe) ½ medium grapefruit	*BUTTERMILK PANCAKES* (⅓ recipe) 3 Tbsp. *BLUEBERRY SYRUP* ¼ cup nonfat yogurt *or* *OMELET* (⅓ recipe) 1½ slices whole-wheat bread, toasted ½ medium grapefruit
LUNCH	*BOUQUET OF GARDEN VEGETABLES* (¼ recipe) *RAW VEGETABLE SALAD* No. 1 (¼ recipe) ¼ cup TANGY FRENCH *DRESSING*	*BOUQUET OF GARDEN VEGETABLES* (¼ recipe) *RAW VEGETABLE SALAD* No. 1 (¼ recipe) ¼ cup *TANGY FRENCH DRESSING*
DINNER	*HALIBUT CREOLE* (1/5 recipe) *CONFETTI STRIP COLESLAW* (1/10 recipe) 1 medium stalk broccoli, steamed	*HALIBUT CREOLE* (1/5 recipe) *CONFETTI STRIP COLESLAW* (⅛ recipe) 1 medium stalk broccoli, steamed

1000	1200
BUTTERMILK PANCAKES (⅓ recipe) 3 Tbsp. *BLUEBERRY SYRUP* ¼ cup nonfat yogurt *or* *OMELET* (⅓ recipe) 1½ slices whole-wheat bread, toasted ½ medium grapefruit	*BUTTERMILK PANCAKES* (½ recipe) 3 Tbsp. *BLUEBERRY SYRUP* ¼ cup nonfat yogurt *or* *OMELET* (½ recipe) 1½ slices whole-wheat bread, toasted ½ medium grapefruit
BOUQUET OF GARDEN VEGETABLES (¼ recipe) *RAW VEGETABLE SALAD* No. 1 (¼ recipe) ¼ cup *TANGY FRENCH DRESSING*	*BOUQUET OF GARDEN VEGETABLES* (¼ recipe) *RAW VEGETABLE SALAD* No. 1 (¼ recipe) ¼ cup *TANGY FRENCH DRESSING*
HALIBUT CREOLE (¹/₅ recipe) *CONFETTI STRIP COLESLAW* (⅛ recipe) 1 medium stalk broccoli, steamed 1 cup *HERBED RICE PILAF*	*HALIBUT CREOLE* (¹/₅ recipe) *CONFETTI STRIP COLESLAW* (⅛ recipe) 1 medium stalk broccoli, steamed 1 cup *HERBED RICE PILAF* *BANANA WHIP* (¹/₅ recipe) *or* 1 large banana

DAY 8

	700	850
BREAKFAST	¾ cup *HOT CRACKED WHEAT* ¼ medium banana, sliced ¼ cup nonfat milk, hot or cold ½ medium grapefruit	¾ cup *HOT CRACKED WHEAT* ½ small banana, sliced ¼ cup nonfat milk, hot or cold ½ medium grapefruit
LUNCH	1 cup *CHINESE TOMATO-VEGETABLE SOUP* *RAW VEGETABLE SALAD* No. 2 (¼ recipe) ¼ cup *CREAMY CAULIFLOWER DRESSING* ½ baked potato with 1 Tbsp. chopped chives	⌐1½ cups *CHINESE TOMATO-VEGETABLE SOUP* *or* 1⅓ cups *FRENCH ONION SOUP*⌐ *RAW VEGETABLE SALAD* No. 2 (¼ recipe) ¼ cup *CREAMY CAULIFLOWER DRESSING* ½ baked potato with 2 Tbsp. *MOCK SOUR CREAM* and 1 Tbsp. chopped chives
DINNER	1½ *CRAB OR CHICKEN CRÊPES WITH WHITE SAUCE* *RAW VEGETABLE SALAD* No. 1 (¼ recipe) ¼ cup *"CAESAR" DRESSING* 8 spears asparagus and ⅔ cup mushroom halves, steamed together	2 *CRAB OR CHICKEN CRÊPES WITH WHITE SAUCE* *RAW VEGETABLE SALAD* No. 1 (¼ recipe) ¼ cup *"CAESAR" DRESSING* 8 spears asparagus and ⅔ cup mushroom halves, steamed together

1000	1200
1 cup *HOT CRACKED WHEAT* ½ small banana, sliced ¼ cup nonfat milk, hot or cold ½ medium grapefruit	1 cup *HOT CRACKED WHEAT* ½ large banana, sliced ½ cup nonfat milk, hot or cold ½ medium grapefruit
[1½ cups *CHINESE TOMATO-VEGETABLE SOUP* *or* 1⅓ cups *FRENCH ONION SOUP*] *RAW VEGETABLE SALAD* No. 2 (¼ recipe) ¼ cup *CREAMY CAULIFLOWER DRESSING* 1 baked potato with ¼ cup *MOCK SOUR CREAM* and 2 Tbsp. chopped chives	[1⅔ cups *CHINESE TOMATO-VEGETABLE SOUP* *or* 1½ cups *FRENCH ONION SOUP*] *RAW VEGETABLE SALAD* No. 2 (¼ recipe) ¼ cup *CREAMY CAULIFLOWER DRESSING* 1 baked potato with ¼ cup *MOCK SOUR CREAM* and 2 Tbsp. chopped chives
2 *CRAB OR CHICKEN CRÊPES WITH WHITE SAUCE* *RAW VEGETABLE SALAD* No. 1 (¼ recipe) ¼ cup *"CAESAR" DRESSING* 8 spears asparagus and ⅔ cup mushroom halves, steamed together 1 cup steamed cubed turnips	2 *CRAB OR CHICKEN CRÊPES WITH WHITE SAUCE* *RAW VEGETABLE SALAD* No. 1 (¼ recipe) ¼ cup *"CAESAR" DRESSING* 8 spears asparagus and ⅔ cup mushroom halves, steamed together 1 cup steamed cubed turnips [*PINEAPPLE-LEMON CHEESE-CAKE* (⅛ recipe) *or* 1 medium apple and 2 cups hot air-popped popcorn]

DAY 9

	700	**850**
BREAKFAST	¾ cup *HOT CORNMEAL* ¼ medium banana, sliced *or* ¼ cup blueberries (fresh or unsweetened frozen) ¾ cup nonfat milk, hot or cold ½ medium grapefruit	1 cup *HOT CORNMEAL* ½ medium banana, sliced *or* ½ cup blueberries (fresh or unsweetened frozen) ¾ cup nonfat milk, hot or cold ½ medium grapefruit
LUNCH	*HONG KONG EGG WHITE SCRAMBLE* (⅔ recipe) *RAW VEGETABLE SALAD* No. 3 (¼ recipe) ¼ cup *ORANGE VINAIGRETTE DRESSING*	*HONG KONG EGG WHITE SCRAMBLE* (1 recipe) *or* *OMELET* (⅓ recipe) with ½ cup *SPANISH SAUCE* *RAW VEGETABLE SALAD* No. 3 (¼ recipe) ¼ cup *ORANGE VINAIGRETTE DRESSING*
DINNER	*STUFFED EGGPLANT* (½ recipe) *RAW VEGETABLE SALAD* No. 2 (¼ recipe) ¼ cup *CREAMY ARTICHOKE DRESSING*	*STUFFED EGGPLANT* (½ recipe) *RAW VEGETABLE SALAD* No. 2 (¼ recipe) ¼ cup *CREAMY ARTICHOKE DRESSING*

1000	1200
1 cup *HOT CORNMEAL*	1 cup *HOT CORNMEAL*
½ medium banana, sliced	½ medium banana, sliced
or	or
½ cup blueberries (fresh or unsweetened frozen)	½ cup blueberries (fresh or unsweetened frozen)
¾ cup nonfat milk, hot or cold	¾ cup nonfat milk, hot or cold
½ medium grapefruit	½ medium grapefruit
HONG KONG EGG WHITE SCRAMBLE (1 recipe)	*HONG KONG EGG WHITE SCRAMBLE* (1 recipe)
or	or
OMELET (⅓ recipe) with ½ cup *SPANISH SAUCE*	*OMELET* (⅓ recipe) with ½ cup *SPANISH SAUCE*
RAW VEGETABLE SALAD No. 3 (¼ recipe)	*RAW VEGETABLE SALAD* No. 3 (¼ recipe)
¼ cup *ORANGE VINAIGRETTE DRESSING*	¼ cup *ORANGE VINAIGRETTE DRESSING*
½ slice whole-wheat bread	½ slice whole-wheat bread
STUFFED EGGPLANT (½ recipe)	*STUFFED EGGPLANT* (½ recipe)
RAW VEGETABLE SALAD No. 2 (¼ recipe)	*RAW VEGETABLE SALAD* No. 2 (¼ recipe)
¼ cup *CREAMY ARTICHOKE DRESSING*	¼ cup *CREAMY ARTICHOKE DRESSING*
BAKED BANANA SQUASH with *BURGUNDY SAUCE* (⅓ recipe)	*BAKED BANANA SQUASH* with *BURGUNDY SAUCE* (⅓ recipe)
	1 baked potato with ⅓ cup *MOCK SOUR CREAM* and 1 green onion, chopped

DAY 10

	700	850
BREAKFAST	¾ cup *HOT OATMEAL* ¼ medium banana, sliced 1 cup nonfat milk, hot or cold ½ medium grapefruit	¾ cup *HOT OATMEAL* ¼ medium banana, sliced 1 cup nonfat milk, hot or cold ½ medium grapefruit

LUNCH	*POACHED FISH* (halibut preferred, ¼ recipe), hot or chilled, with ¼ cup *FISH DRESSING*, on a bed of 3½ cups shredded romaine or butter lettuce, with:
	   ¼ cucumber, sliced
	   1 tomato slice
	   1 pickle slice
	   1 lemon slice
		POACHED FISH (halibut preferred, ¼ recipe), hot or chilled, with ¼ cup *FISH DRESSING*, on a bed of 3½ cups shredded romaine or butter lettuce, with:
		   ¼ cucumber, sliced
		   2 tomato slices
		   1 pickle slice
		   1 lemon slice

DINNER	1½ cups *WATERCRESS AND WATER CHESTNUT SOUP* 1 *CHINESE EGG ROLL* *or* 4 *BOK CHOY CAKES* *CHINESE STIR-FRIED VEGE-TABLES* (¼ recipe)	1½ cups *WATERCRESS AND WATER CHESTNUT SOUP* 2 *CHINESE EGG ROLLS* *or* 8 *BOK CHOY CAKES* *CHINESE STIR-FRIED VEGE-TABLES* (¼ recipe)

1000	1200
¾ cup *HOT OATMEAL*	1 cup *HOT OATMEAL*
½ medium banana, sliced	¾ medium banana, sliced
1 cup nonfat milk, hot or cold	1 cup nonfat milk, hot or cold
½ medium grapefruit	½ medium grapefruit
POACHED FISH (¼ recipe), hot or chilled, with ½ cup *FISH DRESSING*, on a bed of 3½ cups shredded romaine or butter lettuce, with: ¼ cucumber, sliced 2 tomato slices 1 pickle slice 1 lemon slice 1 slice whole-wheat bread	*POACHED FISH* (¼ recipe), hot or chilled, with ½ cup *FISH DRESSING*, on a bed of 3½ cups shredded romaine or butter lettuce, with: ¼ cucumber, sliced 2 tomato slices 1 pickle slice 1 lemon slice 2 slices whole-wheat bread
1½ cups *WATERCRESS AND WATER CHESTNUT SOUP* ⌐ 2 *CHINESE EGG ROLLS* *or* 8 *BOK CHOY CAKES* ⌐ *CHINESE STIR-FRIED VEGETABLES* (⅓ recipe)	1½ cups *WATERCRESS AND WATER CHESTNUT SOUP* ⌐ 2 *CHINESE EGG ROLLS* *or* 8 *BOK CHOY CAKES* ⌐ *CHINESE STIR-FRIED VEGETABLES* (⅓ recipe) ⌐ *PINEAPPLE MERINGUE* (¹/₆ recipe) *or* 1 cup fresh diced pineapple *or* ⅔ cup unsweetened crushed pineapple (juice packed) ⌐

DAY 11

	700	850
BREAKFAST	¾ cup *HOT CRACKED WHEAT* ¼ medium banana, sliced ¾ cup nonfat milk, hot or cold	1 cup *HOT CRACKED WHEAT* ½ small banana, sliced ¾ cup nonfat milk, hot or cold
LUNCH	1 cup *SNOW PEA SOUP* *ORIENTAL SALAD BOWL* (⅓ recipe) ½ medium grapefruit	1½ cups *SNOW PEA SOUP* *ORIENTAL SALAD BOWL* (⅓ recipe) ½ medium grapefruit
DINNER	*MALAYSIAN CHICKEN* (with variation) (¹/₆ recipe) *RAW VEGETABLE SALAD* No. 3 (¼ recipe) ¼ cup *BUTTERMILK DRESSING* 1½ cups steamed chopped broccoli	*MALAYSIAN CHICKEN* (with variation) (¹/₆ recipe) *RAW VEGETABLE SALAD* No. 3 (¼ recipe) ¼ cup *BUTTERMILK DRESSING* 1½ cups steamed chopped broccoli ⌈ *OVEN-ROASTED POTATOES* (¹/₉ recipe) *or* ½ cup *CURRIED RICE PILAF* ⌋

1000	1200
1 cup *HOT CRACKED WHEAT*	1 cup *HOT CRACKED WHEAT*
1 small banana, sliced	1 small banana, sliced
¾ cup nonfat milk, hot or cold	¾ cup nonfat milk, hot or cold
1⅓ cups *SNOW PEA SOUP*	1⅓ cups *SNOW PEA SOUP*
ORIENTAL SALAD BOWL (⅓ recipe)	*ORIENTAL SALAD BOWL* (⅓ recipe)
3 wheat crackers (Hol-Grain brand, unsalted)	4 wheat crackers (Hol-Grain brand, unsalted)
½ medium grapefruit	½ medium grapefruit
MALAYSIAN CHICKEN (with variation) (⅙ recipe)	*MALAYSIAN CHICKEN* (with variation) (⅙ recipe)
RAW VEGETABLE SALAD No. 3 (¼ recipe)	*RAW VEGETABLE SALAD* No. 3 (¼ recipe)
¼ cup *BUTTERMILK-MUSTARD DRESSING*	¼ cup *BUTTERMILK-MUSTARD DRESSING*
1½ cups steamed chopped broccoli	1½ cups steamed chopped broccoli
OVEN-ROASTED POTATOES (⅑ recipe) *or* ½ cup *CURRIED RICE PILAF*	*OVEN-ROASTED POTATOES* (⅙ recipe) *or* ⅔ cup *CURRIED RICE PILAF*
YOGURT WITH CUCUMBER AND MINT (¼ recipe)	*YOGURT WITH CUCUMBER AND MINT* (¼ recipe)
	3 *CHAPATIS or* 1½ slices whole-wheat bread
	1¼ cups diced melon or melon balls with lime wedge *or* 1 orange

DAY 12

	700	850
BREAKFAST	¾ cup *HOT OATMEAL* 2 tsp. raisins ½ cup nonfat milk, hot or cold ½ medium grapefruit	1 cup *HOT OATMEAL* 1 Tbsp. raisins ¾ cup nonfat milk, hot or cold ½ medium grapefruit
LUNCH	*CHEESE QUICHE* (⅛ recipe) *RAW VEGETABLE SALAD* No. 3 (¼ recipe) ¼ cup *SWEET–AND–SOUR VINEGAR DRESSING*	*CHEESE QUICHE* (⅛ recipe) *RAW VEGETABLE SALAD* No. 3 (¼ recipe) ¼ cup *SWEET–AND–SOUR VINEGAR DRESSING* 3 rye crackers (Ideal brand, ultrathin flatbread)

DINNER	1½ cups *CABBAGE SOUP*
	
	TUNA LOAF (¹/₆ recipe) with 3 Tbsp. *WHITE SAUCE* No. 1
	
	BAKED TOMATOES (¹/₆ recipe)
	
	VEGETABLE COMBINATION No. 2 (¼ recipe)
	
	Raw Vegetable Garnish:
	  2 leaves butter lettuce
	  ¼ medium cucumber, sliced
	  1 radish, sliced
	  1 lemon slice
	  1 sprig parsley
		1½ cups *CABBAGE SOUP*
		
		TUNA LOAF (¹/₆ recipe) with 3 Tbsp. *WHITE SAUCE* No. 1
		
		BAKED TOMATOES (⅓ recipe)
		
		VEGETABLE COMBINATION No. 2 (¼ recipe)
		
		Raw Vegetable Garnish:
		  2 leaves butter lettuce
		  ¼ medium cucumber, sliced
		  1 radish, sliced
		  1 lemon slice
		  1 sprig parsley

1000	1200
1 cup *HOT OATMEAL*	1 cup *HOT OATMEAL*
1 Tbsp. raisins	1 Tbsp. raisins
¾ cup nonfat milk, hot or cold	¾ cup nonfat milk, hot or cold
1 medium orange *or* ½ large grapefruit	1 medium orange *or* ½ large grapefruit
CHEESE QUICHE (¹/₆ recipe)	*CHEESE QUICHE* (¹/₅ recipe)
RAW VEGETABLE SALAD No. 3 (¼ recipe)	*RAW VEGETABLE SALAD* No. 3 (¼ recipe)
¼ cup *SWEET-AND-SOUR VINEGAR DRESSING*	¼ cup *SWEET-AND-SOUR VINEGAR DRESSING*
4 rye crackers (Ideal brand, ultrathin flatbread)	5 rye crackers (Ideal brand, ultrathin flatbread) *or* 1 slice whole-wheat bread
1½ cups *CABBAGE SOUP*	1½ cups *CABBAGE SOUP*
LONDON MEAT LOAF (¹/₆ recipe) with ½ cup *SPICY TOMATO SAUCE* *or* *TUNA LOAF* (¹/₆ recipe) with ½ cup *SPICY TOMATO SAUCE or* ¼ cup *WHITE SAUCE* No. 1	*LONDON MEAT LOAF* (¹/₅ recipe) with ¾ cup *SPICY TOMATO SAUCE* *or* *TUNA LOAF* (¹/₅ recipe) with ¾ cup *SPICY TOMATO SAUCE or* ⅓ cup *WHITE SAUCE* No. 1
VEGETABLE COMBINATION No. 2 (¼ recipe)	*VEGETABLE COMBINATION* No. 2 (¼ recipe)
GREEK SALAD (¹/₆ recipe)	*GREEK SALAD* (¹/₆ recipe)
BAKED STUFFED POTATOES (¹/₆ recipe)	*BAKED STUFFED POTATOES* (⅕ recipe)

DAY 13

	700	850
BREAKFAST	¾ cup *HOT CRACKED WHEAT* ¼ medium banana, sliced ¾ cup nonfat milk, hot or cold	1 cup *HOT CRACKED WHEAT* ½ medium banana, sliced ¾ cup nonfat milk, hot or cold

LUNCH	2 *VEGETABLE CUTLETS*
	  with 2 Tbsp. *TANGY SAUCE*
	RAW VEGETABLE SALAD No. 4
	(¼ recipe)
	¼ cup *THOUSAND ISLAND DRESSING*
		3 *VEGETABLE CUTLETS*
		  with ¼ cup *TANGY SAUCE*
		RAW VEGETABLE SALAD No. 4
		(¼ recipe)
		¼ cup *THOUSAND ISLAND DRESSING*

DINNER	⅔ cup tomato juice
	4 cups *STIR-FRIED CHINESE VEGETABLES WITH CHICKEN* garnished with 2 orange slices
		1 cup tomato juice
		4 cups *STIR-FRIED CHINESE VEGETABLES WITH CHICKEN*
		⌐ 1 medium tangerine
		   or
		  ½ medium grapefruit ⌐

1000	1200
1 cup *HOT CRACKED WHEAT*	1 cup *HOT CRACKED WHEAT*
½ medium banana, sliced	½ large banana, sliced
¾ cup nonfat milk, hot or cold	¾ cup nonfat milk, hot or cold
	½ slice whole-wheat bread, toasted
3 *VEGETABLE CUTLETS* with ¼ cup *TANGY SAUCE*	3 *VEGETABLE CUTLETS* with ¼ cup *TANGY SAUCE*
RAW VEGETABLE SALAD No. 4 (¼ recipe)	*RAW VEGETABLE SALAD* No. 4 (¼ recipe)
¼ cup *THOUSAND ISLAND DRESSING*	¼ cup *THOUSAND ISLAND DRESSING*
1 medium tangerine *or* ½ medium grapefruit	1 medium tangerine *or* ½ medium grapefruit
1 cup tomato juice	1 cup tomato juice
CHICKEN AND VEGETABLE TETRAZZINI (⅕ recipe) *ANTIPASTO SALAD* (¼ recipe) *VEGETABLE COMBINATION* No. 3 (⅕ recipe) *or* 4 cups *STIR-FRIED CHINESE VEGETABLES WITH CHICKEN* ⅓ cup *BROWN RICE*	*CHICKEN AND VEGETABLE TETRAZZINI* (¼ recipe) *ANTIPASTO SALAD* (⅓ recipe) *VEGETABLE COMBINATION* No. 3 (¼ recipe) *or* 4 cups *STIR-FRIED CHINESE VEGETABLES WITH CHICKEN* ⅔ cup *BROWN RICE*
⅔ cup sliced fresh pears *or* ½ cup *TAPIOCA PUDDING*	1⅓ cups sliced fresh pears *or* 1 cup *TAPIOCA PUDDING*

DAY 14

	700	**850**
BREAKFAST	¾ cup *HOT CRACKED WHEAT* ⅓ cup peeled, diced fresh peach *or* ¼ medium banana, sliced ¼ cup nonfat milk, hot or cold ½ medium grapefruit	1 cup *HOT CRACKED WHEAT* ⅔ cup peeled, diced fresh peach *or* ½ medium banana, sliced ½ cup nonfat milk, hot or cold ½ medium grapefruit
LUNCH	*CREOLE JAMBALAYA SALAD* (⅓ recipe) garnished with 6 tiny cooked shrimp ¼ cup *CREAMY CHEESE DRESSING* *HERBED GREENS* (mustard or turnip) (½ recipe)	*CREOLE JAMBALAYA SALAD* (⅓ recipe) garnished with 6 tiny cooked shrimp ¼ cup *CREAMY CHEESE DRESSING* *HERBED GREENS* (mustard or turnip) (½ recipe)
DINNER	*FISH BALLS WITH SAUCE* (¹/₆ recipe) *ZESTY BEET MOLD* (⅛ recipe) served on 2 lettuce leaves and garnished with 2 stalks celery, sliced *VEGETABLE COMBINATION* No. 1 (¼ recipe)	*FISH BALLS WITH SAUCE* (¹/₆ recipe) served over ½ cup hot whole-wheat noodles *ZESTY BEET MOLD* (⅛ recipe) served on 2 lettuce leaves and garnished with 2 stalks celery, sliced *VEGETABLE COMBINATION* No. 1 (¼ recipe)

1000	1200
1 cup *HOT CRACKED WHEAT*	1 cup *HOT CRACKED WHEAT*
1 cup peeled, diced fresh peach *or* 1 small banana, sliced	1 cup peeled, diced fresh peach *or* 1 small banana, sliced
½ cup nonfat milk, hot or cold	½ cup nonfat milk, hot or cold
	1 slice whole-wheat bread, toasted
CREOLE JAMBALAYA SALAD (⅓ recipe) garnished with 6 tiny cooked shrimp	*CREOLE JAMBALAYA SALAD* (½ recipe) garnished with 6 tiny cooked shrimp
¼ cup *CREAMY CHEESE DRESSING*	¼ cup *CREAMY CHEESE DRESSING*
HERBED GREENS (mustard or turnip) (½ recipe)	*HERBED GREENS* (mustard or turnip) (½ recipe)
	3 rye crackers (Ideal brand, ultrathin flatbread)
1 medium orange *or* ½ large grapefruit	1 medium orange *or* ½ large grapefruit
FISH BALLS WITH SAUCE (¹/₆ recipe) served over 1 cup hot whole-wheat noodles	*FISH BALLS WITH SAUCE* (¹/₆ recipe) served over 1 cup hot whole-wheat noodles
ZESTY BEET MOLD (¹/₆ recipe) served on 2 lettuce leaves and garnished with 2 stalks celery, sliced	*ZESTY BEET MOLD* (¹/₆ recipe) served on 2 lettuce leaves and garnished with 2 stalks celery, sliced
VEGETABLE COMBINATION No. 1 (¼ recipe)	*VEGETABLE COMBINATION* No. 1 (⅓ recipe)

"NO FUSS" MENU PLAN

	700	850
BREAKFAST	Shredded Wheat cereal (1½ oblong biscuits) ¼ medium banana, sliced ½ cup nonfat milk	Shredded Wheat cereal (1½ oblong biscuits) ¼ medium banana, sliced ½ cup nonfat milk
LUNCH	½ can tuna (3¼-oz. can, water-packed, chunk style) Salad: 1 cup shredded romaine lettuce 1 cup shredded butterhead lettuce ½ medium tomato 1 lemon wedge 3 triple rye crackers (Ry-Krisp brand)	½ can tuna (3¼-oz. can, water-packed, chunk style) Salad: 1 cup shredded romaine lettuce 1 cup shredded butterhead lettuce 1 small tomato 1 lemon wedge 3 triple rye crackers (Ry-Krisp brand) 1 medium apple
DINNER	2 oz. skinned and boned chicken breast, steamed, or ½ can tuna (3¼-oz. can, water-packed, chunk style) 3 stalks broccoli, raw or steamed Salad: 1 cup shredded romaine lettuce 1 cup shredded butterhead lettuce ½ medium tomato 1 lemon wedge 1 slice whole-wheat bread ½ medium grapefruit	2 oz. skinned and boned chicken breast, steamed, or ½ can tuna (3¼-oz. can, water-packed, chunk style) 3 stalks broccoli, raw or steamed Salad: 1 cup shredded romaine lettuce 1 cup shredded butterhead lettuce 1 small tomato 1 lemon wedge 1 slice whole-wheat bread ½ medium grapefruit ———— 2 cups air-popped popcorn

1000	1200
Shredded Wheat cereal (2 oblong biscuits)	Shredded Wheat cereal (2 oblong biscuits)
¼ medium banana, sliced	¼ medium banana, sliced
1 cup nonfat milk	1 cup nonfat milk
1 slice whole-wheat bread, toasted	1 slice whole-wheat bread, toasted

½ can tuna (3¼-oz. can, water-packed, chunk style)
 	
Salad:
  1 cup shredded romaine lettuce
  1 cup shredded butterhead lettuce
  1 small tomato
  1 lemon wedge
 	
3 triple rye crackers (Ry-Krisp brand)
 	
1 medium apple
	½ can tuna (3¼-oz. can, water-packed, chunk style)
	
	Salad:
	  1 cup shredded romaine lettuce
	  1 cup shredded butterhead lettuce
	  1 small tomato
	  1 lemon wedge
	
	3 triple rye crackers (Ry-Krisp brand)
	
	1 medium apple

2 oz. skinned and boned chicken breast, steamed, or ½ can tuna (3¼-oz. can, water-packed, chunk style)
 	
3 stalks broccoli, raw or steamed
 	
Salad:
  1 cup shredded romaine lettuce
  1 cup shredded butterhead lettuce
  1 small tomato
  1 lemon wedge
 	
1 slice whole-wheat bread
 	
½ medium grapefruit
 	
———
 	
2 cups air-popped popcorn
	2 oz. skinned and boned chicken breast, steamed, or ½ can tuna (3¼-oz. can, water-packed, chunk style)
	
	3 stalks broccoli, raw or steamed
	Salad:
	  1 cup shredded romaine lettuce
	  1 cup shredded butterhead lettuce
	  1 small tomato
	  1 lemon wedge
	
	1 slice whole-wheat bread
	
	½ medium grapefruit
	
	1 baked potato or ⅔ cup cooked long-grain brown rice
	
	———
	
	2 cups air-popped popcorn
	
	2 raw carrots

8

Practical Pointers for the Pritikin Dieter

The Pritikin Diet works, there's no doubt about it. It works not just on paper, not just in the laboratory, not just in the supportive environments of the Pritikin Centers. It works for individual people, following individual lifestyles. There are ways to make it work for you, too.

Your greatest concern may be those times when cooking a meal from the plan is exactly what you *don't* feel like doing, and occasions when you'll be eating out. There's the lunch date with an old college chum later this week, the dinner party you're going to on Saturday, the occasional restaurant meal that's a holiday from cooking. You're not about to give up these pleasures, and there's no reason you should. Taking the plunge into the Pritikin Diet is a commitment but it needn't make you a social hermit, and later in this chapter I'm going to give you tips for managing happily and successfully when you're eating away from home. But first, what about those times in your own kitchen when the menu plans, even with their built-in flexibility, are not flexible enough for *you*? The answer is free-form dieting.

FREE-FORM DIETING

Following the 14 menu plans produces weight loss at a fairly predictable rate. But if you wanted to, you could do as well or almost as well in your rate of weight loss by what I call free-form dieting, that is, eating meals based on your own food combinations and recipe creations. The essential requirements are that the foods composing your diet are mainly those low in caloric density, that high caloric density foods are never eaten and that a few simple nutritional guidelines are followed.

Applying the principles of free-form dieting is simple. If you're at home, pull from the fridge, freezer, or pantry shelf nutritious foods of low to moderately low caloric density and cook them the Pritikin way; if you're dining out, select dishes made from acceptable ingredients to provide a low-calorie meal.

Formal menu plans, set serving sizes, and calorie-counting are all bypassed by the free-form dieter, but close attention must be paid to the Caloric Density Table as the basic guideline in choosing foods to eat. The foods that should be emphasized in free-form dieting are those in the Use Freely and Use in Moderation groups. Foods from the Avoid group should be spurned completely, as they should by all weight-loss Pritikin Dieters. Foods from the Restricted group should be consumed only in small quantities, or caloric intake may be excessive and weight loss may not occur at all. (A few foods in the Restricted group are marked with [†]. These foods are not recommended for anyone following either the regular Pritikin Diet or its low-calorie weight-loss version because of their excessively high fat or cholesterol content. They are included in the listing only to show their caloric density relative to other foods.)

In cooking the free-form way, you can use recipes or not as you wish. Experienced free-form dieters sometimes use no recipe at all, just imagination and the principles of free-form dieting—the time-honored technique of "a little bit of this" and "a little bit of that," guided by their knowledge of Pritikin weight-loss cooking.

Most of the recipes in this book can be used as rough guides in free-form dieting. If, for example, a recipe calls for 1½ cups of bell pepper, you can just cut up as much as you like without bothering to measure—or you can leave it out. If you think the dish would be enhanced by tomatoes, go ahead and toss some in.

If you are following the menu plans but occasionally free-form dining at home or away from home for a day or two, you needn't worry about getting all the essential nutrients if you are eating a variety of vegetables, fruits, some grains, and moderate amounts of concentrated protein foods such as skimmed milk or other nonfat dairy products and lean fish, poultry, or meat. But the longer-term free-form dieter should follow the guidelines below to ensure adequate intake of all nutrients, especially when caloric intake is severely restricted (approximately 850 calories per day or less). The guidelines are designed to help the dieter comply with Pritikin Diet concepts and the RDAs (Recommended Daily Allowances). The particular foods in the quantities suggested will provide adequate nutrition on a calorie-restricted diet.

Guidelines for Free-Form Dieters

- Eat one to three pieces of fruit a day. If you eat only one, make it a citrus fruit.

- Several times a week eat some yellow or orange vegetables, raw or cooked.

- Eat plenty of raw and cooked green vegetables. Especially valuable are some lettuces (romaine and butterhead varieties such as Boston and Bibb), watercress, and cooked greens (turnip, mustard, and collard greens). If you are severely restricting your caloric intake (approximately 850 calories per day or less), several generous servings of one or more of these very low-calorie vegetables should be eaten daily.

- Include two small servings of whole grains or whole-grain products in your daily diet in the form of bread, crackers, cereal, rice or other grain, or pasta.

- Eat three daily servings of protein-concentrated foods. One of these should be a 3½-ounce serving of animal food. Preferred choices are white meat of chicken or turkey (skin removed), and halibut, swordfish, and tuna (fresh or water-packed). Also have a 3½-ounce serving of nonfat cottage cheese and an 8-ounce serving of nonfat milk or the equivalent in nonfat dairy foods (buttermilk—8 ounces; yogurt—6 ounces; dry milk—5 tablespoons; or cottage cheese—2 ounces).

On the regular Pritikin Diet, protein-concentrated foods are restricted to prevent the excessive intake of cholesterol. These restrictions are somewhat relaxed on the weight-loss diet. This is because of the need to limit the more caloric carbohydrate foods such as grains and legumes that normally contribute significant amounts of protein.

However, animal foods that are especially high in cholesterol should be avoided even though they may be low in calories. The body can get rid of only tiny amounts of cholesterol at a time, and any extra is stored in the tissues and arteries, causing blockage and eventually damage. The foods highest in cholesterol are egg yolks, organ meats, and some shellfish. Egg yolks (including caviar) and organ meats are never eaten on the Pritikin Diet. Lobster can be used as a substitute in equal amounts for white meat of poultry or other acceptable animal protein, but crab, oysters, clams, scallops, and shrimp, which are higher in cholesterol or other atherogenic (artery-blocking) sterols, are permitted only when used in half the amount. The free-form dieter who is not relying upon carefully constructed menu plans that ensure adequate nutrition should choose animal protein that is richest in certain nutrients, and should favor the kinds of animal protein listed in the guidelines over lobster and other shellfish, other kinds of fish, or beef and other kinds of meat.

Free-form dieting has obvious utility and appeal. How much of it you do is a matter that depends largely upon differences in personal style and individual circumstances. If you need the discipline of regular menu plans for every meal and every day, if you can prepare all or most of your meals or have them prepared for you, if you like to cook from recipes, it would be a mistake to choose free-form dieting except in special situations. But if you prefer a set of guidelines to a structured menu plan and if you eat out and travel a great deal, the choice of free-form dieting as your main approach is probably best for you.

ORGANIZING YOUR KITCHEN

Whether you are going to be following the menu plans almost all the time and rarely dieting free-form, or cooking free-form almost exclusively, you'll help ensure success if your kitchen is properly organized for your new way of eating.

If other members of the household will not be eating the same diet, a good first step is to create a space just for your personal food storage, preferably in distinctive containers, in the refrigerator, freezer, and in one or more cupboards. It prevents the upset of having other people get into your food, and you'll be less apt to get into theirs through confusion or temptation. A good investment would be a set of plastic containers in different sizes with well-fitting lids, and heavy aluminum foil disposable baking dishes in which you can store, freeze, and reheat. Zip-lock plastic bags are great space-savers in the refrigerator or freezer, since they conform to the shape of the food stored in them. Many of the recipes you'll be preparing lend themselves well to quantity preparation; by doubling or tripling a recipe, you'll save time and money. Most of the recipes will keep in the refrigerator for at least a week; for longer storage, many of them are suitable for freezing. On some mornings it will be a great comfort to be able, before you leave for work, to pull from the freezer a foil-wrapped packet containing your already home-cooked dinner entrée, and to know that salad dressing and soup are ready in the refrigerator. Some people find it helpful to plan their entire week's cooking and do most of it on one day, perhaps a Saturday. This has been the secret of their success in adhering to the diet; it may be yours, too.

Put up a bulletin board or, better, use your refrigerator door for Pritikin Diet notes and schedules. Post your shopping needs, a Xerox copy of the day's menu plan or Guidelines for Free-Form Dieters, and other relevant reminders. By posting the menu plans you'll have them handy for reference. Putting them up in plain view will also serve as a general proclamation to you and to others in your household (who will no doubt be eager to help you in your efforts) that today you'll be eating those foods *and no others*.

PRITIKIN WEIGHT-LOSS DIET SHOPPING LIST

Get organized from the start by putting in a small stock of the items on this list required for recipes in the fourteen-day menu plan. Bread, bread specialties, poultry, fish and meat may be frozen. In day-to-day shopping, you can buy fresh fruits and vegetables as needed. Add the beverages of your choice, and you'll have everything you need for your weight-loss program.

GRAIN STAPLES

Cracked wheat cereal
Rolled oats, regular (not quick-cooking)
Brown rice, long grain
Bran flakes, unprocessed miller's
Cornmeal, yellow, whole ground or bolted
Whole wheat pastry flour
Whole wheat flour, regular
Unbleached pastry flour

Rice flour
Spaghetti, whole wheat
Noodles, whole wheat (without egg yolk or soy flour)
Whole grain crackers:
  Kavli Norwegian Flatbread, thin
  Ideal Ultra-thin Flatbread
Ry-Krisp, unseasoned
Hol-Grain, wheat and rice crackers, unsalted

MISCELLANEOUS STAPLES

Nonfat dry milk
Cornstarch
Arrowroot
Unflavored gelatin
Active dry yeast
Baking powder (Rumford or other brand free of aluminum compounds)
Baking soda
Unsweetened carob powder
Pearl tapioca, quick-cooking
Matzo meal
Whey powder and agar (two health-food store items)

DAIRY REFRIGERATOR FOODS

Nonfat (or skim) milk
Buttermilk, up to 1% fat by weight
Yogurt, nonfat, or up to 1% fat by weight
Skimmed milk cheeses, up to 1% fat by weight (look for these possibilities: Knudsen's Hoop Cheese, Breakstone's Pot Cheese (½%), Borden's Dry Curd, Friendship Skimmed Milk Cottage Cheese, Safeway's Dry Curd Cottage Cheese, Lite 'n Lively Cottage Cheese, or other cheeses up to 1% fat by weight)
Sapsago cheese
Whole eggs (for whites)

CANNED GOODS

Artichoke hearts, water-packed
Bamboo shoots
Beets, sliced, whole, and shoestring
Chilies, whole green, and diced green
Chili salsa, green
Green beans, French-style
Pimientos, whole and sliced
Pumpkin
Water chestnuts
Pink salmon
Tuna, water-packed
Evaporated skimmed milk
Juices, regular unsweetened: apple, and pineapple
Pineapple, unsweetened, crushed, and slices in pineapple juice
Tomato juice and V-8 juice
Tomato sauce
Tomato paste
Whole-packed tomatoes
Italian plum tomatoes
Diced tomatoes in purée
Crushed tomatoes in purée

CONDIMENTS AND FLAVORINGS

Vinegars: white, cider, rice, red wine, malt
Wines: sherry, Sauternes, white, red burgundy, dry vermouth
Mustards: prepared, Dijon, stoneground (Inglehoffer's)
Green taco sauce
Tabasco sauce
Picanto sauce (Pace)
Soy sauce or tamari
Pickles, dill
Capers
Pepperoncini (peppers in wine vinegar)
Pure flavor extracts: vanilla and lemon

DRIED VEGETABLES, HERBS, AND SPICES

Bell pepper flakes, red and green
Red peppers, dried, and red pepper flakes
Chilies, large dried
Cilantro, dried
Parsley, dried
Mint flakes
Chives, freeze-dried
Onions, dried minced
Allspice, ground and whole
Anise
Basil leaves
Bay leaves
Caraway seeds
Cayenne pepper
Celery seed
Chili powder, mild and regular
Cinnamon, ground
Cloves, ground and whole
Coriander
Cumin, ground
Curry powder
Dill seed
Dill weed
Fennel seeds
Fines herbes
Garlic powder
Ginger, powdered
Gumbo filé
Horseradish, powdered
Italian seasoning
Mace
Marjoram
Mustard, dry
Mustard seeds, black
Nutmeg, ground
Onion powder
Oregano leaves
Paprika
Pepper, white, black, and red
Peppercorns and whole white peppercorns
Poppy seeds
Poultry seasoning
Rosemary leaves and ground rosemary
Saffron
Sage
Sesame seeds
Salad herbs
Tarragon leaves
Thyme leaves and ground thyme
Turmeric

LEGUMES

Small red beans (1200 cal./day diet only)

FREEZER FOODS

Broccoli, chopped
Corn niblets
Greens, mustard, turnip and collard
Okra, cut
Peas
Strawberries, whole, unsweetened
Blueberries, unsweetened
Fruit juice concentrates: apple, orange, and grapefruit
Whole-wheat bread (Pritikin or other acceptable type)
Sourdough bread
Corn tortillas
Whole-wheat tortillas (chapatis)
Turkey breast
Chicken breasts with bone in
Chicken breasts, skinned and boned
Chicken bones from boned breasts, for making chicken stock

Concentrated cooking stocks (Saucier brand)	Fish fillets: cod, halibut, and red snapper
Flank steak, lean	Cooked crabmeat
Beef, very lean, ground	Tiny shrimp (small quantity)

COOKING PRITIKIN-STYLE

As you look through the recipes you'll probably notice some unfamiliar cooking techniques. In Pritikin cooking you don't sauté vegetables in the usual way in butter or oil, but use instead water or another fat-free liquid. Merely bring a little of the liquid to a boil in the bottom of a skillet, add the chopped vegetables, and cook over moderate heat (stirring all the while) until the vegetables have cooked sufficiently and browned a bit and most of the liquid has evaporated. You'll really prefer the greaseless taste of vegetables sautéed this way.

One of the delights of Pritikin cooking is the adaptability of many traditional dishes to this approach. You can make marvelous sauces completely without butter or other fat! The liquid to be thickened is heated to a boil and a paste of cornstarch or arrowroot is stirred in. Continue cooking and stirring for a few minutes until the sauce is as thick as you want it to be. Wonderful white sauces and vegetable sauces can be made this way. All peculiarly Pritikin techniques are described clearly in the recipe directions.

The appliance you'll find most useful in Pritikin cooking is a good electric blender. Many people are equally enthusiastic about their food processors, but others seem just as happy chopping their vegetables by hand. For sautéing vegetables in fat-free liquids, an electric fry-pan or wok is also handy, especially if you like Oriental-style vegetables a lot. For steaming vegetables, the collapsible stainless steel steaming baskets are efficient and handy. You'll find that a good nonstick skillet and some nonstick baking pans in a variety of sizes will also be helpful.

Sodium should be restricted on any diet, weight-loss or not, to avoid unhealthful water retention. The Pritikin Diet restricts salt intake to a prudent level of about 3 or 4 grams per day. The relatively small amount of sodium you'll ingest using our recipes will come from the natural sodium in foods; from added salt in canned or frozen vegetables; and from some condiments, such as the small amounts of soy sauce, or tamari, a more authentic Japanese version of soy sauce, used in some recipes.

Many people have grown to depend upon salt and pepper as primary seasonings for their food. In our recipes, we have utilized many spices and dried herbs to provide flavor, minimizing the need for both salt and pepper. Some studies have suggested that black pepper especially may be harmful. When pepper seems important to a recipe, it has been included in the ingredients. Omit it if you wish, or use white pepper (an apparently less harmful form of black pepper) or, when appropriate, red pepper in smaller quantities.

SHOPPING PRITIKIN-STYLE

Now that you've organized your kitchen and have a place to put your food supply, check the shopping list on pages 112–115 for items you may wish to stock immediately: these include canned goods and other relatively nonperishable foods like spices, grains and grain products, and frozen items. If you have the freezer space, you can store poultry, fish, meat, and various types of breads, as well as frozen items. On your first shopping expeditions, buy as many of the items you expect to use as possible; on subsequent shopping trips your load will be considerably lighter. The list is complete for the 14-day menu plan at all 4 diet levels.

Once you've laid in a good supply of nonperishables, most of your regular shopping should be done in the supermarket in your area that boasts the best produce section. You'll be seeking out vegetables that are first-class quality, among them some you will emphasize to provide your nutritional needs while on a low calorie diet, like the dark green lettuces and other greens. It may still take a little hunting to find some of the foods you'll need, but once you've made your connections you should have the problem under control. In shopping, always check fat content. The Pritikin Diet recommendation for the *upper limit* of fat content for most foods is 15 percent of total calories. If the label does not give this percentage, you can figure it out yourself if the number of grams of fat and the total calories are stated. Multiply the number of grams of fat by 9 (the calories in one gram of fat) and divide by the number of calories. If the answer is .15 or less, the product meets Pritikin standards for fat content.

For some whole-grain products such as cracked wheat and ground whole-grain or bolted cornmeal, you may need to seek out a health-foods store if your supermarket does not have a well-stocked health-foods section. Incidentally, you need to use just as much care in selecting things from "health" counters as you do in supermarket shopping. On the supermarket shelves you'll find Quaker "Old-Fashioned" oats, which is satisfactory, beside Quaker instant oats, which is far less nutritious and is not recommended. Likewise, at the health store you'll find cracked wheat and other wholesome whole-grain cereals next to brands with undesirable ingredients such as added wheat germ. Wheat germ is oil-rich and adds calories. In cracked wheat, which is just the natural wheat berry that has been cracked for faster cooking, you'll get only the amount of wheat germ natural to the grain—sufficient but not excessive. If you can't find cracked wheat or if you prefer another whole-grain cereal, select one that is equally wholesome.

You'll have to do some careful label-reading before determining the best whole-grain bread available in your vicinity. Your bread intake will be quite limited for calorie considerations, but you do need some grain foods and you want to be sure that any bread you eat is the right kind. I must confess that my bread, marketed as Pritikin Bread, is just that. I decided to get a bread on the market because it was appalling to me that the country didn't have a nationally distributed bread that met high nutritional standards.

If you can't find my bread or another whole grain bread without added oil or fat in your area, settle on the next best thing: a whole-grain bread in which oil or fat appears last or nearly last in the list of ingredients. To be absolutely sure that fat content is not excessive, calculate the fat calorie contribution if grams of fat and calories are listed. Make sure, too, that any bread you buy contains no egg yolks and minimal sweeteners.

I hope you'll be able to find acceptable whole wheat pita bread, chapatis, corn tortillas, and/or whole-grain rye breads, which, in appropriately small quantities, will add interest to your diet.

The dairy foods you'll be eating will be nonfat or skimmed milk products. The terms are more or less synonymous, but skimmed milk products may be slightly higher in fat content, up to 1 percent by weight.

Buttermilk made from skimmed milk is not available in some communities, but it's worth checking around to see what the different dairies have available: you may be pleasantly surprised. You can reduce the fat content of commercial buttermilk somewhat by straining out the tiny globs of fat you'll see floating around. Most of the fat, however, will have been homogenized and so can't be removed by straining.

Don't let the labeling of fat content in dairy products (including cheeses) fool you. Because of the high water content, when fat content is given as a percentage of weight the result is a deceptively low figure. Lowfat milk and many brands of buttermilk are about 2 percent fat by weight, which means that the fat content contributes about 30 percent of total calories. As you know, that's too high for a weight-loss diet—and certainly too high for your health.

Many recipes call for uncreamed cottage cheese. Both regular and low-fat cottage cheese have had creaming mixtures added to them that make them unacceptably high in fat content, but in a pinch you can put them in a colander and run some cold water over the curds to rinse off as much cream as possible. Uncreamed cottage cheese can be used in many different ways—as is, as a recipe ingredient, or blended with nonfat buttermilk to make a sour cream substitute. The recipe for this excellent fat-free Mock Sour Cream is on page 355. You'll find uncreamed cottage cheese in many forms, including a dry curd type. Another variety, called hoop cheese, is made by pressing the crumbly white cheese into a brick form. But be warned: in some parts of the country the name "hoop cheese" refers to quite another kind of cheese which is unsuitable for the diet. In buying cheese, look for a milkfat content of 1·percent or less. Don't be fooled by *part*-skim milk cheeses, which are much too high in fat for your diet. In general, if a cheese melts and runs when it bakes its fat content is too high. Because the water content of different skimmed milk cheeses may vary, the consistency of certain recipes may be affected a trifle. After experimentation, you may want to make slight adjustments in the amount of liquid ingredients to compensate.

Hard cheeses, with the notable exception of Sapsago cheese, are much too high in fat content to be used on the diet. Sapsago, or green cheese, is reminiscent of Parmesan, and we use it in many recipes as a flavoring. But while Parmesan has almost 60 percent of its calories in fat, Sapsago has under 10 percent. Too few people are familiar with Sapsago, but many supermarkets carry it. If yours doesn't, ask the store manager if a distributor can supply it. Sapsago comes from Switzerland, where it is manufactured by Geska (they spell it as two words: Sap Sago).

Nonfat yogurt is called for in many recipes, and I regret to say that you may have some trouble finding it in stores. Don't use regular or low-fat yogurt; both are too high in fat content. One yogurt manufacturer in the Los Angeles area is developing a nonfat yogurt for wide distribution, but until that's available, unless you're very lucky you may have to make your own. A simple recipe appears on page 356.

A stock—vegetable, chicken, or beef—is frequently listed in many recipes in preference to water as the liquid ingredient. Water can certainly be used in most cases, but a flavored stock improves many recipes very considerably. Commercial chicken stock or bouillon cubes ordinarily contain much fat and other undesirable ingredients, but we can recommend one brand of flavored bases that has recently made its appearance, distributed by Saucier Cuisine Inc. (185 Madison Avenue, New York, N.Y. 10016; you can mail-order their products through Omaha Steaks International, 800 228-9055). The line includes concentrated chicken, beef, fish, and lobster stocks and can be found in the frozen-food sections of better food stores. If you prefer, you can make your own. There are recipes in the Recipe Section for chicken, beef, and vegetable stocks. You can also save the cooking liquid from your vegetables for future use in recipes, freezing it in zip-lock plastic bags or in ice-cube trays.

When you shop, watch out for hidden sodium compounds that are often present in bouillon cubes and other commercial products under names you may not recognize as sources of salt: monosodium glutamate, hydrolyzed yeast, sea salt, soy sauce, or garlic and onion salt.

It may take you a little while to get used to less salt, the absence of fat, and new ingredients and cooking techniques, but Pritikin Dieters tell me all the time that once they get into the swing of it, they begin to love their new eating style. You will, too.

EATING OUT PRITIKIN-STYLE

Can you take your lunch to work? Are you going to be doing some traveling and want to take some of your food along? In both situations you'll benefit from a little advance planning.

Carrying a Pritikin lunch to work should be no problem once you've dealt with the hurdles you think exist—like how do I get it there? Get yourself a good lunchbox with a wide-mouthed Thermos and a variety of containers. Soups and hot vegetable combinations can go into the Thermos. Salads can go into a plastic container with a well-fitting lid and your salad dressing in a small jar with a screw top. Crackers or raw veggies and the like for your morning or afternoon snacks can go into plastic bags. If you like a hot drink during the day or with your lunch, pack some herb tea bags or keep a small jar of Postum in your desk. (If giving up coffee at the office is more than you can bear while getting used to a new style of eating, you're forgiven. But remember, coffee does stimulate the appetite, so you'd be working at cross-purposes with yourself.)

You'll survive very nicely traveling if you combine free-form dieting with carrying along a little food of your own. Pat Walters, Director of the Alumni Program of the Pritikin Center in Santa Monica, who travels frequently to visit groups of alumni, does just that. This vibrant, slim lady, who swears by the Pritikin Diet, never leaves home without a six-pack of low-sodium vegetable or tomato juice in her suitcase, which together with a few crackers gets her through tight spots on a busy schedule when she's hungry and can't get to a restaurant or supermarket. (Getting hungry is something she simply doesn't permit herself to do; she claims it makes her irritable, nonproductive, and tired.)

Pat and others have discovered that in strange cities a trip to the supermarket can provide the makings for a fine impromptu diet meal. She recommends stocking up on vegetable juices, the best bread or crackers you can find, fruit, and a few veggies such as tomatoes, cucumbers, and even cabbage. On a recent trip I kept a head of cabbage in my hotel room, cutting off chunks now and then for a quick and easy salad. In normal weather, cabbages do fine without refrigeration for a few days.

When traveling by car, some people like to pack edibles in a Styrofoam picnic basket or icebox to keep foods cold. When I travel by air, I take along a loaf of bread, several boxes of whole grain rice crackers, and some fruit. On long trips when I will have access to kitchen facilities, I take along some whole grains and cereals, supplementing them with produce purchased locally.

You can even diet on the Grand Tour. Barbara Harris and her husband, both following the Pritikin Diet, recently traveled in France for a month. Mrs. Harris, a writer, reported on their experience in a *New York Times* piece called "France Along the Diet Route." She told of wonderful times shopping in open-air markets for fresh fruits and vegetables. Sometimes their meals were picnics, but they also fared very well at elegant restaurants, simply by making their needs known. Mrs. Harris wrote, "Our trip convinced us that dietary restrictions can be dealt with with surprising ease. We both returned home slimmer, healthier, and more energetic than we were when we left; though poorer in pocket, we feel enriched in every other way."

What assures success in eating in restaurants? Knowing what to order and where to find food that best meets your requirements, and *communication with your waiter or waitress*. Communication is vital: you may think that your waiter or waitress fully understands your order only to discover after a long wait that the fish you asked to have broiled dry is glistening with butter and your baked potato has been doused with sour cream. State your needs pleasantly and clearly, and ask to have them repeated back to you. It sometimes helps to explain that you are on a special diet and are not permitted to eat certain foods (many Pritikin Dieters have found that this approach focuses the waiter's attention on their order by arousing sympathy or interest). If the food that arrives is not as ordered, gently but firmly refuse it. It's your diet, your health, and your money—don't permit yourself to be intimidated.

As to the other half of the battle—knowing what to order and where to find food that meets your requirements—you'll have varying degrees of success depending upon where you live. In large cities or communities where there is more awareness of nutrition, you may do better, but it's hard to generalize. It's usually possible to come up with something suitable in any restaurant situation, but don't sally forth expecting miracles. If you are going to be eating in an unfamiliar restaurant, it may be wise to have something to eat before you leave home so you don't arrive famished and susceptible to temptation if the menu offers you a meager selection.

Restaurants featuring salad bars are lifesavers if the bar is a good one, but watch out for salad ingredients already in oil marinades or creamy dressings. You'll have to pass up the separate dressings, which are all very high calorically, but there are various things you can do to add flavor to your salad. There is usually a cruet of vinegar at salad bars. Or, you can flavor your salad by squeezing some lemon on it, or pouring over it some tomato juice you've ordered. Some people go a step further and concoct their own salad dressings right at the table, while others bring their own with them in a tight-capped container. Using tomato juice, prepared mustard and Tabasco, or vinegar mixed with one part water and one part prepared mustard, you too can make instant salad dressings at your table. The ingenuity of Pritikin Dieters is indeed impressive!

Many people have had very good success in Chinese restaurants, where they order plain steamed (not stir-fried) vegetables with a little breast of chicken added. Some Chinese restaurants use considerable amounts of oil in the wok, so ask that the vegetables be steamed in water or chicken broth instead. If your waiter or chef insists that's not possible, ask that the barest minimum of oil be used in the wok. Ask also to have the dish seasoned only with garlic and ginger and to hold the usual sugar, salt, and MSG. Monosodium glutamate, a sodium compound, causes water to be retained in your tissues just as salt does; many people also have allergic responses to it. The vegetables with a bit of chicken, a little rice, and a pot of Chinese tea should keep you quite happy. Choose plain boiled or steamed rice in a Chinese restaurant; don't be fooled by the appearance of fried rice, which takes on a brown color when fried in oil with soy sauce. Chinese restaurants serve white rice, not whole-grain brown rice, no matter how it's prepared.

Most restaurants serving American food, from coffee shops to the most elegant dinner clubs, will offer what I call a core menu. In the evening you can generally get a plain salad, tomato juice, plain baked potato, and fish broiled dry or broiled chicken from which you can remove the skin. Many establishments will be able to provide unbuttered steamed vegetables and, for dessert, a half melon or grapefruit in season. During the day the baked potato may not be available, but sometimes you'll see a low-fat

HOW TO ORDER YOUR PRITIKIN-CHINESE MEAL
(Show this to your waiter)

No oil, no salt, no sugar. Especially no MSG! Assorted
steamed vegetables, please. Thank you.

If you like, photocopy and keep in your purse or wallet.
The Chinese instructions are for a fairly bland dish of
steamed vegetables; you could ask for chicken, ginger,
and garlic to be added.

soup such as a vegetable soup with a tomato base. Of course,
you may hit the jackpot: a few restaurants in larger cities in
several parts of the country are featuring Pritikin-Diet food, and
you may be in luck in your community.

If you are going to be eating in the same restaurant or hotel for
several days or are a regular patron, take the maitre d' or dining
room manager into your confidence. Pat Walters does this
regularly. When she checks into a hotel, she makes her breakfast
arrangements for the duration of her stay. Hot oatmeal is prepared for her every morning, and the loaf of Pritikin Bread she
brings with her is used for her morning toast. You'll be surprised
at the degree of cooperation you receive when you make your
needs known to people pleasantly and cheerfully. (Of course,
you may not be so lucky. If cooked cereal isn't available or the

only variety offered is the wretched instant kind, order some Shredded Wheat or Grape-Nuts, the next best choices. If there's no skimmed milk, try a small amount of apple juice on it. You can get through many tight spots with a bit of flexibility and imagination.)

At friends' homes you can expect to have a little more control over the situation than when eating in unfamiliar restaurants. You're not in hostile territory, but it is necessary for you to speak up and make your needs known in advance, as always, pleasantly and cheerfully. If your friends aren't willing to make *any* deviation in their menu plans, perhaps they are not really friends. While you can hardly expect a harried hostess to fix a whole special meal for you, it is usually not too much trouble to set aside some salad before tossing with oil and vinegar, to omit butter or sauces from a portion of the vegetables, or to reserve a plain baked potato while the others are stuffed with cheese and bacon bits. Your hostess will probably make suggestions as to what she can most easily do to accommodate your diet requirements. Just be open about your needs and ask amiably for her cooperation. If later at the dinner she urges you to have some of her German chocolate torte with whipped cream, just assume she's flustered by the pressures of hostessing and has forgotten you're on a diet—stand firm in passing it up.

At club and organization luncheons and banquets, it may be a little more difficult to arrange proper food. Sometimes you can talk to the person in charge a day or so in advance and arrange to have something served that you can eat. If the function is held regularly, every month or so, it's worth finding out if you can make special arrangements. When there is not much that you can do to assure yourself a suitable meal, have your meal at home before leaving for the event or pack yourself a picnic that you can enjoy in your car en route.

ENTERTAINING PRITIKIN-STYLE

Many of the recipes in this book work for gourmet entertaining. In fact, many of the menu-plan dinners themselves will do fine for company meals with the addition of generous servings of grain or potato dishes, a dip with vegetables and crackers to offer your guests before they come to the table, and a dessert to wind up the meal.

If you think about it, it's likely many of your friends know they would benefit from eating this kind of diet either for weight or health reasons and probably would welcome the opportunity to have a Pritikin-style meal. As your friends become aware of the wide range of delicious dishes that can be made even on the weight-loss version of the Pritikin Diet, they may even surprise you with a Pritikin dinner when you're invited to their homes. Your social life may even pick up as you and your friends share this new way of eating. One caution, though: people like to make up their own minds about whether or not to go on a new regimen, and may resent being told that they should. Let your example of loss of weight and gain in health and the delicious foods you've prepared speak for you.

STAYING ON THE DIET

Food diaries, contracts with yourself, all the devices that are often used to keep people on diets do not play much of a role in Pritikin-style dieting. While overeating and compulsive eating may have a psychological component, the problems of over-weight that result occur largely because of the high caloric density of the foods consumed. If low-caloric-density food is eaten, rarely do these behavioral tendencies cause obesity. In fact, frequent eating is more in tune with our biological needs than a few widely spaced meals, since blood-sugar levels are thus kept more constant. People trying to lose weight may especially benefit from dividing their caloric intake into frequent small meals, as research suggests that less weight is gained that way.

The incentive you need for adhering to a new dietary lifestyle both during the weight-loss period and afterward on maintenance will become stronger each day as you feel better and look better. You won't feel deprived because you'll be eating considerable bulk, which will keep you from being hungry. Still, it may take a while before you get used to some new tastes and stop missing the old ones. If you like butter, you'll find there is nothing on the Pritikin Diet that tastes quite like it, nor do we have the gustatory equivalents of prime rib of beef or Roquefort cheese. But you will begin to enjoy many new food tastes and textures that have been lost to you in the world of high-fat cholesterol-laden foods that ruin health as they add pounds. Palate is truly a matter of conditioning. In a short while you'll be surprised to find that you actually prefer the new tastes to the old.

Naturally, during the transition period it makes good sense not to expose yourself to temptation unnecessarily. If you can, it's best to keep the household as free as possible of foods you should not be eating—the cookies, cake, and other high-caloric-density foods for which you may have a weakness. At least keep them separate from your own stores. If you have to be around foods you should not be eating, keep the contact minimal. If you're cooking other foods for your family and have to taste now and then for seasoning, take the barest taste possible.

Be patient with yourself. Good habits, like bad ones, feed on themselves, and you must recognize that you won't acquire a shiny new set of fully formed habits overnight. It may take a little while for you to get into the new eating style completely, but you *will* get into it wholeheartedly as you begin to notice the many rewards that will come to you. You'll find that your weight loss, your greater energy, your generally improved health, and your attractive new appearance are gains that you value tremendously—so much so that you will soon become firmly attached to eating the Pritikin way.

9

Exercise the Pritikin Way

This chapter is for everybody—no cop-outs, please. You'll lose weight just by the diet, of course. But to lose weight faster, to firm and condition your muscles so you won't sag as the weight comes off, and to give yourself the look and feeling of well-being, you need to exercise. The same exercise program that will accomplish all this will also help to build your resistance to heart disease; for those who already have heart disease, these exercises when medically supervised can help restore normal function. In sum, if you're healthy when you embark on a regular exercise program, you'll get healthier; if you're not as healthy as you should be, your health will improve. And all the time you'll be losing weight faster than with the diet alone and conditioning your muscles for a firm body. Isn't that an irresistible proposal?

In the days before lawn mowers and automobiles, vacuum cleaners and elevators, physical activity was a normal part of daily human existence. Technology has changed that. In our society we need to make a conscious effort to keep our bodies active, our muscles working the way they were designed to.

Fortunately, regular exercise is growing more acceptable, and many people, especially young people, are beginning to make this conscious effort. We see them riding their bicycles or jogging on the streets at the end of the day. I was forty-two when I first made the decision to build exercise into my daily routine on a regular basis. At the time—1957—I was president of a firm that manufactured electronics specialties utilizing my patents. The routine I settled on for my exercise—riding from home to office and back on my ten-speed bicycle—raised a few eyebrows. Top executives were supposed to drive to their offices in fancy automobiles. Worse yet, I carried my lunch on my bike in a brown paper bag.

My fall from social grace was nearly completed a few years

later when I decided to jog instead of bike. Joggers about town were rare birds twenty years ago; the jaunty warmup suits and bright-colored running shorts that identify today's growing army of joggers hadn't yet been invented by the fashion industry, nor were special running shoes readily available to the amateur. So my reputation for oddball behavior picked up a point or two as I jogged about in business clothes and my most comfortable sneakers. My exercise was frequently interrupted by motorists stopping to ask whether my car had broken down—why else would I be running?

THE AUTHOR AS AN UNSTYLISH
PRE-JOGGING-ERA JOGGER
(lunch is in the briefcase)

Today you'll be in good company and have plenty of it when you begin to build exercise into your daily life.

EXERCISE AS AN AID TO WEIGHT LOSS

Weight gain over the years is generally an insidious process. Our calorie-dense diet and lack of sufficient physical activity cause most people to put on pounds over the years, and if you gain only one pound per year between the ages of twenty-five and fifty you'll be 25 pounds overweight by age fifty. Gain two pounds a year, and at fifty you'll be 50 pounds overweight!

There are no magic ways to halt and reverse this trend; the solutions lie exclusively in calorie relationships. You need to take in fewer calories or expend more calories, preferably both. Some calories are always being burned even when we are at rest as the body maintains its vital functions. Even without lowering your present calorie intake, you could tip the balance between calories consumed and calories expended just by exercise, because exercise is a concentrated form of energy expenditure. When at the same time you lower your calorie intake, your weight-loss progress can be pushed along quite rapidly.

If you think that exercising will only make you hungrier, you're wrong. You may actually notice a decrease in appetite with exercise: most studies with humans indicate either no change in food consumption with moderate exercise of extended duration, or even some suppression of intake with more vigorous exercise of shorter duration.

Of course, you need an efficient exercise. You see lots of fatties pedaling along on bicycles, hoping for miracles. They'd be surprised to learn they'd do better with a brisk walk.

AEROBIC EXERCISE

The most effective exercises you can do for weight loss are the so-called aerobic exercises, and one of the best of the aerobic exercises you can do is just plain walking (not strolling, not moseying, but purposeful *walking*).

Aerobic exercise is a term that's used a lot in popular parlance, often without a clear idea of its meaning. As the name might suggest, aerobic exercises are those that cause the need for additional oxygen to produce the extra energy you're using. Walking, swimming, and jogging are aerobic activities: in all these exercises, the large voluntary muscles of the arms and legs can be worked vigorously in a continuous repetitive pattern, creating a greater demand for oxygen. This results not only in improved functioning of the cardiovascular system, but also in a greater rate of weight loss because of the increased caloric expenditure and gradual growth in metabolically active lean body tissue.

To derive maximum benefits from aerobic exercising, you must work strenuously enough to make you breathe harder and your heart beat faster, but not so strenuously that you can't carry on a conversation. This simple "talk test" will tell you whether you are exercising sufficiently but not excessively. If you're exercising alone and don't want to be overheard talking to yourself, hum or sing a song. If you're out of condition, you will huff and puff from relatively slight exertion and you probably won't be able to exercise long enough at this level to do the maximum amount of good, but you'll still be deriving some benefit in promoting weight loss and improving body condition. As you continue your exercise program over a period of time, your endurance will increase and eventually you'll be able to exercise at this level for at least an hour.

Your choice of an exercise to help in your weight-loss program is important. Let's look at some of the most popular exercise activities and see how they rate. Various sporting activities, such as golf or volleyball, do not serve the weight-loss purpose as well as the aerobic exercises, either because the large muscles are not sufficiently involved or the pattern of use is not continuous and repetitive. I call these activities recreational exercises. There are still other forms of activity that may be aerobic in their effect if they are performed continuously for a long enough period of time at a sufficiently high level of exertion.

AEROBIC EXERCISES	RECREATIONAL EXERCISES	EXERCISES THAT MAY BE AEROBIC IN PERFORMANCE
Walking	Golf	Jumprope
Jogging	Bowling	Dancing
Swimming	Tennis doubles	Skating
Indoor machines	Horseback riding	Tennis singles
Motorized treadmill	Weight-lifting	Racquetball
Stationary bicycle	Sailing	Squash
Rowing and/or	Calisthenics	Cross-country skiing
cycling machine	Downhill skiing	
	Outdoor bicycling	
	Volleyball	

For most readers of this book the best choice of aerobic exercise would be a regular walking program. Slow jogging (at 5 to 7 miles per hour), or walking alternated with slow jogging, may also be a good choice for some, especially after their weight has dropped sufficiently and endurance has built up. Both walking and jogging are very beneficial because of the continuous expenditure of effort and the repetitive use of the large leg muscles. On the other hand, unless you are a near-professional, an exercise such as outdoor bicycling does not use the body the same way. You may work very hard climbing a hill on your cycle, but then you just sit while you coast downhill; you may even stop completely for traffic lights, pedestrians, and stray dogs.

Recreational exercises have important benefits, of course. They provide fun and enjoyment as well as definite physiological improvements. But they are far less effective than aerobic exercises in promoting weight loss and body conditioning. If you can find time for both forms of exercise in your life, that's great. But it it's a toss-up between an aerobic exercise and a recreational one, choose an aerobic exercise.

WALKING

Man has been walking for perhaps a million years or more, and human beings are the only true walkers among the creatures of the earth. The skill of our hands and the size of our brain also make us unique, and there is reason to believe both developments slowly evolved in relationship to our assuming the walking stance. Running is also natural to man, but since the beginning of our time on earth our primary form of locomotion has been walking.

Until today. Our primary form of locomotion is now the automobile. People who take long walks for pleasure are often regarded as eccentrics by their friends behind wheels. Fashion is an enemy, too, especially of women: even if they wanted to, most women would find distance walking an ordeal in the shoes that are considered stylish.

Nonetheless, enlightened souls in growing numbers are asserting their natural biological right to *walk*. They simply park their cars and wear good walking shoes. A walking program may be the best and easiest exercise for you, too, especially if you are just beginning to move your body after many years of inactivity.

Because walking is an exercise so readily available, because it requires no special equipment, because it doesn't necessitate

Build Exercise Into Your Daily Routine

In addition to your regular aerobic exercise program, begin to *think exercise!*

- Take the stairs at work instead of the elevator.

- Park your car at the far end of the lot and walk to your destination.

- Don't take the bus at the nearest stop; walk to a stop 20–30 minutes away.

- Ride your bicycle to work, to market, on errands.

- Take exercise breaks instead of coffee breaks.

Find an Exercise Buddy

It helps many people to stay on their exercise program when a friend exercises with them. Make a commitment to meet a friend for exercise at a specific time daily.

Be Prepared for Inclement Weather

Don't let a good start on your exercise program get away from you when the weather turns bad. Think ahead and make appropriate arrangements for yourself.

- Join an aerobic fitness or aerobic dance class at your local Y or community college.

- Buy a treadmill or stationary bicycle and use it while watching television or listening to radio.

- Join a health club or Y that has treadmills, stationary bicycles, a swimming pool, and/or a walking/jogging track.

- Walk inside a covered shopping mall. Shopping malls are heated in winter and air-conditioned in summer. (But do your shopping at another time!)

- Jump rope. Begin with a single-step jump and work up to a double jump.

joining a club, there's a tendency to overlook it. Walking is a vastly underrated exercise for weight loss. Did you know that without altering your food intake at all, you could have a weight loss of almost 20 pounds a year simply by walking four miles a day at a casual pace of two miles an hour? When in time you bring your pace up to about 3 to 4 miles an hour, you'll be even more efficient in burning calories and improving body conditioning.

When you begin your walking program, start at a pace that is just comfortable, then work up to a faster pace over days, weeks, even months, as your endurance grows. But remember, even at a slower pace, if you are walking at a rate appropriate to your present level of conditioning, you are deriving important health and weight-loss benefits.

On page 359 in the Appendix is a structured progression plan for your walking program. Use it as a guide to building your endurance—you'll be surprised at your rapid progress. Start your walking program right away. It will work beautifully together with the diet to take pounds off quickly and give you a wonderful sense of well-being.

WARMUP AND COOLDOWN

"Warmup" and "cooldown" sound like factory terminology. In truth, your body *is* very much like an industrial operation, and its equipment, which includes your heart and muscles, needs a warming-up period and a cooling-down period in order to run most efficiently and without mishap.

The warmup period is simply five minutes of slow exercise at the beginning of the session to allow your heart rate to increase gradually. Warmup also allows your blood vessels to dilate gradually until they have enlarged as much as possible to accommodate the increased blood flow that results from strenuous exercise. Most walkers naturally start walking at a slower pace, then gradually ease into brisker walking, but joggers and other aerobic exercisers should make a conscious point of always beginning with five minutes of slow and easy exercise.

Your serious exercising starts after the warmup, in the workout phase. During this time you will be burning the most calories and deriving the most benefits. When you have worked up to a maintenance-level fitness program, your workout phase must be at least 20 to 30 minutes long to be effective. Your goal is to work up to a regular walking pace of 3 to 4 miles per hour or a jogging pace of 5 to 7+ miles per hour.

The cooldown period is the reverse of the warmup phase: your heart rate gradually declines and the blood vessels return to their resting size. Stopping your workout too suddenly may cause blood to pool in the legs, making you feel dizzy or faint. After your workout, don't just flop down: walk slowly and continuously for a few minutes in order to provide a steady muscular pump that will keep the blood flowing back to the heart and brain and prevent the pooling effect from occurring.

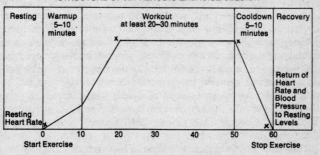

STRUCTURE OF AN AEROBIC EXERCISE SESSION

The phases of an aerobic exercise session—warmup, workout, and cooldown—are depicted in the diagram. If you're giving thought to serious jogging and have even mild cardiovascular disease, your doctor may advise you to monitor your pulse to make sure you do not exceed a safe pulse rate; the X's indicate points at which pulse rate should be checked. Checking pulse rate is not necessary for walkers unless you have special medical problems; for some strenuous exercisers, however, it may be good practice.

JOGGING

There's a great temptation to get into an activity when everyone else seems to be doing it. Fight the temptation, and make your jogging decision on cool, rational grounds. There are some people who should not even consider jogging. If you are more than 20 pounds overweight, jogging can put unwelcome stress on the ankles, knees, and hips.

If you have any orthopedic limitations, jogging may not be for you. Do you have one leg appreciably shorter than the other, or an ankle that swells easily from an old injury? Did you ever break a hip or have arthritis in the ankles, knees, or hips? If you have ever had any of these conditions, jogging may aggravate the situation.

For many individuals with a cardiac condition, high blood pressure, or any of the major cardiovascular risk factors including high cholesterol and triglycerides—and especially if they smoke—jogging is inadvisable. Fortunately, this diet will almost certainly reduce not only your weight but your cholesterol and triglyceride levels and also your blood pressure if it is high. Jogging may be possible for you after you've reduced your cardiovascular risk factors sufficiently; your doctor will advise you when you're ready for strenuous exercise. Before embarking on a strenuous exercise program, the American Heart Association and the American College of Sports Medicine recommend that everyone over the age of thirty-five take an EKG stress test. We concur. Coronary insufficiency sets in early on the American diet, and too many cases are reported of joggers who never should have been jogging who died in their tracks.

If you want to jog and are over thirty-five, tell your doctor you want a stress test, not just the resting EKG (which merely tests heart action at rest). The results of the stress test will enable your doctor to tell you the exercising heart rate that's safe and effective for you. With that information, you'll be able to monitor yourself during exercise by checking your pulse.

Some people simply don't find jogging enjoyable. It takes most joggers a while before they build up enough conditioning and endurance to find it pleasurable, and there are those who never find it an enjoyable acitvity. Jogging does provide exercise benefits faster than does walking (a half-hour of jogging is roughly equivalent to one hour of brisk walking), and this may prove an incentive for people who are able to jog and like it. But if walking is enjoyable for you and jogging isn't, by all means stick with walking.

If your own inclinations, your past history, and/or your doctor give you the go-ahead, start your jogging program slowly. If you have not been exercising for the past three months, it is advisable to begin with at least a month of walking before starting to jog. This preparation will give your muscles and other tissues a chance to adapt and will reduce the stress on your joints.

Beginning joggers should start at a very slow jogging speed of 5 to 6 miles per hour, gradually increasing that rate as their weight declines and their fitness level improves. Six and a half to 7½ miles per hour is a good rate for a maintenance-level fitness program: if you exceed that rate, you will be metabolizing carbohydrates more than fats and you may fatigue quickly. All joggers should begin and end their exercise session with the calf-stretching exercise below.

TO STRETCH CALVES

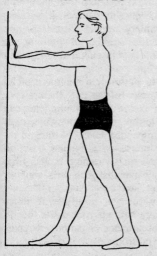

1. Stand with your arms straight ahead of you and place your hands flat against the wall.

2. Move one foot directly forward and the other back so that the distance between them is about 10-12 inches.

3. Keeping your body straight and heels on the floor, bend your forward knee and your arms. This will bring your head close to your hands and stretch your straight back leg. Hold for five seconds.

Stretch each leg five times.

The best way to work toward the goal of a full session of continuous jogging is through a combination walking/jogging program. As endurance builds, the jogging component is increased. The Walk/Jog Progression Plan on pages 360–362 in the Appendix provides the framework for a prudent rate of advance. After your aerobic exercise program has helped you to have reached your optimum weight, continuing it as a way of life will help you keep your weight where you want it as well as keep you fit.

SWIMMING

Do you like to swim? Do you have access to a large pool on a regular basis? If the answer to both questions is yes, swimming is a viable choice for you as a primary aerobic exercise or one you can alternate with another, such as walking. Swimming can be an excellent aerobic exercise and is very effective in improving muscle tone.

You should be able eventually to swim for a minimum of 30 minutes using the crawl or breaststroke (of the two, the crawl is the more effective as an aerobic exercise). Swimming lessons may help you to build your skills to this point. Meanwhile, until your endurance is up to the recommended level, be sure to do your walking or other aerobic exercise on a regular basis to supplement your swimming. Once your swimming is at a high skill and endurance level, you may interchange it with walking or another form of aerobic exercise, as you choose.

Swimming is still a possibility for you even if you don't possess an Olympic-size pool. Check with your local Y's, health clubs, community colleges, and department of parks and recreation for pools and endurance swim programs.

INDOOR MACHINES

People who live in parts of the country where the weather may put a damper on their activities often find that indoor machines help them to keep up their regular daily exercise program.

There are no special physical benefits to be derived from the use of an indoor machine, but having one can prove useful. For one thing, it's immediately available to you. Also, on a motor treadmill you will have to keep your pace constant at the speed you select, while in outdoor walking you may be unaware that your pace has slowed. Of course, outdoor walking is a lot more interesting, so if you do use a motor treadmill it's not a bad idea to set it up in front of the television set or near a radio so you can be entertained during your exercise time. Some people even like to read while on a treadmill.

You can also maintain your aerobic exercise program by stationary cycling. But be aware that cycling uses different leg muscles than does walking, and many people find the initial stages of an exercise program using the stationary bicycle can be somewhat painful. Walking uses the muscles in the back of the thigh, the hamstring muscles; the muscles used in cycling are the quadriceps muscles in the front of the thigh, which in most people tend to be untrained. As you cycle more and the muscles become more trained, you will be able to pedal against resistance for at least 30 minutes. But until you are able to do so, use walking as your primary exercise form. Once you have built your endurance, you may interchange walking and cycling as you choose.

If indoor cycling is your choice for an aerobic exercise program, be sure to use a good machine, preferably one that has numbered variable resistance and a heavy front flywheel. Start with a low resistance and keep your speed constant. As your leg strength increases, gradually increase the resistance on the bicycle. You should be aware that cycling is not a "total-body" exercise. It will burn calories, train your cardiovascular system and improve muscle tone in your legs. Cycling will not, however, develop muscle tone in the hips or upper body (although you can work your arm muscles by turning the bicycle upside down and operating the pedals by hand, increasing resistance as needed).

For people who cannot use their legs in aerobic exercising, rowing machines offer a good alternative. Those who want to use both arm and leg muscles in aerobic exercising can use machines that combine rowing and pedaling, permitting you to row or pedal or perform both actions simultaneously. As endurance grows, resistance can be increased for either motion.

Which machine is best for you, motorized treadmill, stationary cycle, or rowing machine? While motorized treadmills do have the advantage of not requiring the training of special muscle groups before they can be used effectively, *the best machine of all is the one you'll use*! Just don't get an electric cycle or rowing machine—the whole point is that *you* do the work!

How often should you be exercising? How hard should you exercise? How long should your exercise sessions last? You'll notice that these questions deal with Frequency, Intensity, and Time—or FIT—which you will soon be as you get going on your exercise program!

HOW OFTEN SHOULD I EXERCISE?

Try to exercise five or six times a week, usually once a day, until your body is conditioned and your excess weight has been lost. One day a week should be reserved for rest. Try not to miss exercising more than two days in a row because triglycerides, driven down by exercise, rise rapidly after that period. Excess triglycerides will soon be stored as excess fat.

You need to expend at least 2000 calories per week through exercise for physical activity to be a significant factor in your rate of weight loss. If you burn 400 calories in each exercise session (for example, by walking briskly about one hour for about four miles), you will need to have five such sessions during the week. If you were to burn even more calories through exercise (assuming the same caloric intake), your weight would of course drop more quickly.

Until you become proficient at your exercise, you may need to have several short exercise sessions daily. As your endurance builds and your exercise capacity increases, you'll be able to merge these into a single continuous session. Walkers may use the Walking Progression Plan as a guide. Begin the plan at any level that is comfortable. In a number of months, even if you haven't done much exercise for years, your proficiency should be built up enough so that one good walking session a day will be all that you'll require. That schedule is not only more convenient for most of us, it also happens to be the best for weight loss. The body burns fat more effectively in one long exercise session than in several short ones.

If you can keep up your five-or-six-times-a-week exercise schedule *after* you've reached your optimum weight, this is ideal. In any case, don't go below a three-times-a-week schedule.

HOW STRENUOUSLY SHOULD I EXERCISE?

A sustained walking pace of 3 to 4 miles an hour or slow jogging at 5 to 7 miles an hour will result in a significant increase in your rate of weight loss and in your cardiovascular fitness. Once you have built up your endurance, you should be able to exercise at that level for about an hour with no problem. You'll naturally want to increase the intensity of your exercise as rapidly as possible, but you don't want to exceed a prudent level of exertion at any time. Use the "talk test" to make sure you're not overdoing it.

To calculate your actual pace, you'll need to use a watch in combination with a street map or pedometer (remember the old formula: Distance divided by Time equals Rate). If you have access to a high school or college walking track, time yourself as you do laps (these tracks are almost always a quarter of a mile). If it takes you 15 minutes to walk 4 laps—a fast walking pace—you're doing 4 miles per hour.

HOW LONG SHOULD EACH EXERCISE SESSION BE?

In time, just as soon as your endurance permits, you should be exercising continuously in each session for 60 minutes. If your schedule makes it difficult for you to spend an hour in continuous exercise, try to arrange two daily sessions of 30 to 40 minutes each. Until you reach your optimum weight, you should also exercise one day on the weekend, when, if you wish, you can set a slower pace but exercise for a longer period of time. Your weekend exercise could be a leisurely 1½-to-2-hour walk.

The above is a suggested *minimum* exercise schedule for people on my weight-loss diet who want to accelerate their rate of weight loss. If you want to lose weight even faster, double the amount of time, or at least add another shorter exercise session to your daily schedule. The more aerobic exercise you do, the faster you will lose weight.

Set aside at least one hour out of each day during the week in which exercise will be your top priority. For some people, it's an hour in the morning before the day's activities begin; others may prefer an hour in the early evening immediately after work. On the weekend, the couple of hours you spend in casual walking will help to promote your weight loss.

No matter what schedule you choose, *be regular!* Changing schedules undermines your efforts to build an effective exercise program. To build up your endurance you'll need to work out regularly on a daily basis—that's what will give you maximum returns in burning calories to accelerate your weight loss, plus the body conditioning that will make you look and feel terrific.

EATING AND EXERCISE

You will happily observe that on the Pritikin Diet you will have improved endurance. Endurance studies comparing a high-fat diet and a high-carbohydrate diet (the design of the Pritikin regimen) show that the subjects' endurance in exercising on the high-carbohydrate diet was more than three times greater, measured in the length of time they were able to exercise, than when they were on the high-fat diet.

Should you eat before exercising and, if so, how much? Since the long muscles and the stomach may be in competition for blood supply if you exercise following a large meal, eating before exercise can be a problem for some people. Those with heart disease ought to eat only lightly before exercising. Almost everyone is able to eat a snack, such as fruit, before exercising with no ill consequences. Some people, myself included, have no problem whatsoever with strenuous exercise even after a large meal, but many others do. You'll need to experiment to find out what's best for you.

HOW TO DRESS FOR EXERCISE

Many people who get into exercise programs to lose weight overdress in the mistaken notion that if they make themselves sweat they will lose more weight. Any additional loss, of course, is water, which the body gains back when you drink your next glassful. Overdressing when exercising strenuously can also lead to dangerous heat exhaustion.

Dress in comfortable clothes and avoid becoming overheated. If you are chilly when you start out, wear layers of clothing that can be shed as you warm up. More calories are burned when your skin is cool.

A backpack can be convenient for the discarded layers of clothing shed as you get warmer during your exercise period. Carrying a backpack, or any weight for that matter, will also increase the number of calories you burn during exercise, and substantially improve your aerobic physical fitness.

Proper shoes are of the utmost importance. Tennis shoes or sneakers are not good for either walking or jogging (as I sadly discovered in my pre-jogging-era running days) because they do not cushion your weight adequately or give proper support. Good jogging shoes are the best shoes for walkers, too. Look for these qualities: excellent fit and comfort, good arch support, rounded heel for shock absorption, light weight, flexibility, and cushioned sole. Pinch the sole to check cushioning. Wearing suitable socks, try on several brands until you find the one that's right for you. Make sure there is plenty of room for the toes, because your feet will swell slightly when you exercise.

All the while you're burning calories and losing weight faster thanks to your regular exercising, you're deriving a host of other benefits that will make you healthier and happier. Your new way of eating is one cornerstone of your new lease on life, exercising is another.

In addition to longterm benefits, such as building your resistance to heart disease and other cardiovascular and degenerative diseases, exercise gives you important bonuses that will make everyday living *right now* much more enjoyable. Decrease in stress is one such bonus. Many people depend on drug therapy to relax; regular aerobic exercise provides a natural tranquilizer that reduces stress and anxiety. It appears that exercise metabolizes chemicals produced by stress—adrenaline, for example—

REGULAR AEROBIC EXERCISE

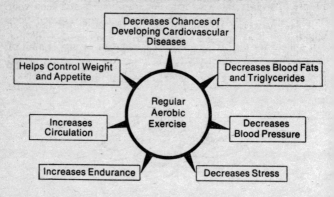

that cause tension and increased heart rate and may contribute to cardiovascular disease and hypertension.

People who exercise regularly tend to sleep better and deal more effectively with the conflicts of daily life. Exercisers tend to have fewer psychological problems and a more positive self-image than those who do not exercise. While the physical benefits of the Pritikin Program may not solve all your problems, reducing the stress in your life will certainly help.

Another bonus you'll discover is lessened fatigue. You might have expected just the reverse as a result of trying to crowd an hour of exercise into each day's already crowded schedule, particularly because in that hour you'll be working so hard at your exercise! But exercise trains your heart muscle. As the heart muscle becomes capable of pumping out more blood with each beat, its increased efficiency is accompanied by an increase in the oxygen content of the blood. The muscles respond to aerobic exercise training by developing a stronger ability to extract oxygen from the blood for energy production. Exercise will also result in increased delivery of oxygen-rich blood to the muscles by causing the development of more blood vessels surrounding the muscles. Your brain cells will also have a greater supply of oxygen, which will keep you more alert. All these changes will mean increased endurance, less fatigue, a slower resting-heart rate, and improved recovery time (the time it takes for your heart rate and blood pressure to return to resting levels after exertion).

There's really nothing like regular aerobic exercising to give you a sense of well-being—*and* help you lose pounds and keep your weight where you want it to be after you have reached your weight goal.

It's there for the taking. All that is required of you is a bit of determination and consistency. Using the Pritikin Diet supplemented by a good exercise program, results will begin to show surprisingly fast. You, your family, and your friends will rejoice and be happy with the *new you*.

10

How to Slow and Stop Weight Loss: Your Maintenance Diet

Yes—what a dream come true!—there actually comes a time when the Pritikin Dieter may have to be concerned about stopping weight loss.

Many who have attended our rehabilitation program at the Pritikin Centers were primarily interested in combating the life-threatening diseases which afflicted them, and loss of excess poundage was a welcome bonus to their main achievement in alleviating the debilitating symptoms of artery closure, diabetes, and other illnesses. About one out of every six of these formerly overweight people actually found that as they acquired a taste for some of our lower-calorie recipes for soups, vegetables, and other dishes, they were losing more weight than they wanted.

Once you have reached your optimum weight according to the height-weight tables, you may find that you are still a little heavier than you would like to be. If that's your situation, stay on the low-calorie diet until you reach your desired weight. But if you find that you lose weight exceptionally rapidly, it may be necessary for you to start eating foods of higher caloric density while you are still 5 pounds or so above what you want to weigh.

Changing images of ideal body configuration inevitably color our views of what optimum weight should be. Some women become so enamored of the supersvelte fashion-model look that they try to bring their weight down too far. This is not desirable, because an excessive drop in weight is accompanied by loss of muscle mass that once lost is difficult to replace. Sometimes so much weight is lost that these women stop menstruating. Over-weight is certainly detrimental to your health—and being too thin doesn't do much for it either.

On the other hand, we aren't used to seeing lean people in great numbers in our country, and some people (men especially) may worry that they're "too thin" when they're just fine. These

men—who usually say they feel better than they ever remember feeling—may be concerned about looking "masculine." Their paunchiest peers may admonish them for "overdoing a good thing," and their mothers may concur. Some women believe that to be plump is to be healthy, and they enjoy having portly sons and chubby grandchildren. Still, slowly but surely, beefcake, like cheesecake, is on its way out. The physique of the weight lifter is being supplanted as an ideal by that of the marathon runner, and plumpness in a woman is no longer automatically equated with femininity. Don't be pressured into accepting an image for yourself that isn't what you *know* looks and feels best for you. Use the Pritikin Diet to maintain your weight at the level you think is right for you.

Popular belief would have it that you have more "reserve" when you have more fat on your bones. Although in fact most people have more energy when they're thin, the placebo effect of putting on a few pounds if you think you look too thin may have emotional benefits that are not to be underestimated in the maintenance of a feeling of well-being, and in some cases this may outweigh other considerations.

To gain or maintain weight, you'll be moving up the Pritikin Diet from its low-calorie end to the opposite higher-calorie end. Of course, *don't* bump up calories by eating more fats. Fats do contain more than twice as many calories as do starches, but don't succumb to the temptation to eat foods with high fat content now that you can afford to consume more calories. You'd be running not only the risk of returning to your former undesirable weight condition by permitting yourself to get hooked on fatty foods again, but also of developing certain degenerative diseases. The principle for increasing caloric intake the Pritikin way is much safer and healthier: minimize your consumption of high-water-content, high-fiber foods (which were so helpful on the weight-loss program because they were filling *and* low calorie), and eat complex-carbohydrate foods of higher caloric density in liberal amounts. In practice, this means decreasing the amount of high-water-content vegetables in the diet and replacing them with starchy foods that contain less water—bread, potatoes, corn. On the 700- and 850-calorie diets especially, certain green vegetables were emphasized. Now, if you wish, vegetables such as mustard, turnip, or collard greens may be eliminated, but the dark green lettuces or butterhead lettuces that were specified for all four diets should always be chosen in preference to the nutritionally inferior iceberg type. Skimmed milk dairy products, too, may be decreased or eliminated once normal caloric intake is resumed, because protein and other nutrients they provide will be present in ample amounts on the regular Pritikin Diet. Snack time, too, is an opportunity for taking in more calories from healthful foods. Perhaps during the time you were trying to lose weight you occasionally nibbled on hot air-popped popcorn while watching TV or reading. The high-fiber (and thus calorie-diluting) content of popcorn made it an ideal snack food then, but now it should be replaced by a goodie of higher caloric density. A good substitute might be roasted garbanzo beans, which taste much like roasted nuts (a recipe for them is on page 348).

The chart on page 149 summarizes the foods to emphasize or limit in your diet if you wish to gain weight. Grains and legumes contain the highest number of calories, with starchy vegetables and fruit next in line (fruit, however, should not be overly emphasized because of its high sugar content).

As you can see, I want you to fill up on good food of higher caloric density. Because salads and soups contain so much water, we often suggest to people who are having trouble maintaining their weight that they restrict themselves to one small raw vegetable salad daily and completely eliminate soups. Some

FOR MAXIMUM WEIGHT GAIN	
LIMIT	EMPHASIZE
Vegetables with high water content: Cucumbers, celery, cabbage, asparagus, cauliflower, etc. Raw vegetable salads	*Grains and grain products:* Wheat, oats, barley, cornmeal, millet, bulgur, kasha Bread, crackers, cereal, pasta
Soups: Clear soups and broths, soups with a lot of broth, and especially vegetable soups	*Legumes:* Lentils Beans (navy, garbanzo, kidney, black-eyed peas, split peas, etc.)
Water and other noncaloric beverages	*Starchy vegetables:* White and sweet potatoes, corn, parsnips, winter squash (acorn, butternut, Hubbard, etc.)

people can continue to eat soups if they're very thick or made as stews, using split peas, lentils, beans, and pasta and a minimum of vegetables; other people must discontinue them completely to avoid further weight loss because of the water present even in the thicker high-calorie soups.

Water and other noncaloric beverages need to be restricted because of their filling effect. When you eat foods in their natural state, you need only drink when you are thirsty, as thirst is the way the body lets us know of its need for fluid replenishment. If you do take fluids, drink them only after eating; if you drink right before or during your meals or snacks, you'll be too full to eat as much as you should.

Refrigerators and their seductive contents are usually considered the bane of the overweight. Now you can turn your former enemy into your ally by the use of a few simple tricks. Keeping a pot of cooked rice in the refrigerator can provide a healthful way to keep your weight from dropping. Rice is relatively caloric and very versatile. You can heat cold rice quickly in a small amount of liquid and use it as a base for leftovers, or eat it plain. With leftover beans, we like rice heated in a little tomato juice. If the leftovers to go with the rice have a curry or sweet-sour flavor, try heating the rice in a little pineapple juice. A sprinkling of onion and garlic powders over the rice as it heats adds flavor interest to either preparation. To heat, use a covered nonstick skillet so that the liquid will steam through the rice, and stir occasionally over low heat to break up the rice and keep it from sticking.

Cold rice can serve as a caloric ingredient in a fast fruit cup. Slice up some bananas, strawberries, or other fruit, mix in some rice, and sprinkle a little cinnamon over it if you like.

Another trick for adding calories to your food intake is to save leftover baked potatoes in the refrigerator, where they will keep well for days. Add some thinly sliced peeled baked potato to a green salad, mixing it with the other ingredients. Leftover cooked beans can also be refrigerated and used in the same way to add interest to a green salad. For more calories, use lots of potato and beans and small amounts of the low-calorie greens.

Now, more than ever, bread should be your staff of life. If you make your own bread and always have some on hand, you'll find you're eating a lot more. Nothing could be healthier, and breadmaking can be more enjoyable than any other kind of cooking. You have to get the knack of it because you're working with something live—the yeast are microscopic plants and you have to cater to them—but it's fun once you learn how. You can make bread more interesting by adding fresh or dried onions and caraway seeds, or apples, raisins, and cinnamon. Having raisin bread and a bread knife on a cutting board on your kitchen counter is a sure way of putting on a few pounds: you'll find you're snacking on it all day. Tuck some in your briefcase, glove compartment, wherever it will be readily available so you can nibble throughout the day. Snack on bread the way you snacked on vegetables when you were on the weight-loss diet.

From the point of view of overweight people, I am one of the lucky ones who have to work at keeping my weight up. My special trick to keep my weight from dropping is having a sandwich as a bedtime snack. Sometimes I slice a banana, sprinkle a bit of cinnamon over it, and put it between two slices of bread. It's a simple snack, I enjoy it, and it works for me. Recipes for two of my favorite breads are on pages 325 and 326 of the Recipe Section. If you don't have time to bake, always have a variety of good quality store-bought bread on hand.

Although you still should avoid breads made with oils or fats, now you can eat some that are made with refined grains. At this point you will be consuming enough calories from natural foods that you will be getting sufficient fiber, vitamins, and minerals in your diet. Make sure, though, that *most* of the grain in your diet is in the form of whole grains, which contain valuable nutrients that are removed in the refining process. They also contain more of the type of fiber that is many times more efficient in increasing the bulk of the intestinal contents than the kinds of fiber that predominate in other types of foods. This is important in maintaining the health of the intestinal tract.

While you're losing weight the amount of fruit in the diet is restricted because it contains a lot of sugar. Of course, the sugar limitation is important for reasons other than calories, but you now can increase the amount of fruit you eat to six to eight pieces a day. Snacks shouldn't consist only of fruit, however, because they are not as fattening as other foods; in spite of their sugar content, many of them—especially summer fruits, like peaches—contain a good deal of water. One of the best fruit choices for you is the banana—keep lots on hand. If they start to ripen too quickly, put them in the refrigerator. The skins will blacken, but the ripening process will be stopped. Or, you can cut them into bite-sized pieces and freeze them. You'll be surprised to find they taste like ice cream! (Don't let them thaw out, though, or they'll be mushy.)

Four ounces of juice can be used in place of one or two pieces of your fruit allotment, as you no longer need to be so concerned about removing some of the calorie-diluting fiber content of foods. The rest of your fruit intake, however, should be eaten whole, since whole fruit contains valuable kinds of fiber, including pectins, not found in large amounts in other foods. Pectin lowers cholesterol levels much more effectively than do other constituents of the fiber complex.

If you use fruit juices as sweeteners in desserts and other recipes, and if you drink fruit juice, be sure to consider that part of your total fruit allotment. Eating too much fruit can cause elevated triglycerides (fats) in the blood. Some people find their triglycerides rise too high when they eat eight pieces of fruit a day, and they must limit themselves to three to five. A laboratory test ordered by your physician will tell you if you're one of these people. If you are, you should also avoid juices and frozen fruit (juicing and freezing don't increase sugar content, but they remove the fiber or break it down and so the sugar is more accessible).

For dessert, try to have pudding, cake, or cookies fairly often, using recipes in the Recipe Section. Now is the time *not* to pass up healthy desserts—this kind of treat will encourage you to eat a little more even after you're "full." You should emphasize starchier desserts and eat your fruit if you like *after* you've filled yourself with these more caloric foods.

Although exercise is extremely important, it can be overdone when you are trying to reverse weight loss. While you are trying to gain weight, exercise only 15 minutes to half an hour a day. Since exercise is a concentrated form of energy expenditure, you will be burning off too many calories with extended exercise sessions. Once you have attained your desired weight, you can resume your regular exercise program. Keeping warm while exercising (and at all other times) will prevent you from burning an excessive number of calories; but don't get too hot when exercising, as this could lead to heat exhaustion.

Perhaps during your weight-loss period you had consciously tried to concentrate on aspects of your daily life other than food to help you achieve your weight-loss goals. Hang on to your new interests and other beneficial changes you've made in your lifestyle, by all means. But now you do need to make food as enticing to you as possible through suitable recipes and the creative uses of spices, seasonings, and other flavor enhancements that will make you want to have second and third helpings of the calorie-denser healthful foods you should be eating to stop or reverse your weight loss. Just make sure you stay within the guidelines of the Pritikin Diet so you don't undermine your health in your weight-gain efforts.

Remember that if the pounds start to creep up, the sweeter foods should be the first to go. Grain foods need also to be restricted. When you need to cut down your calories, your intake of nutrients is more critical, so choose whole-grain foods only, avoiding those that are refined. Experimentation will lead you to your maintenance diet. You'll learn from trial and error the amount of grains, legumes, vegetables, etc. you can eat. These amounts will be different for everybody, and will vary for you if you significantly increase or decrease your level of physical activity.

After you have been on the Pritikin Diet for a while, you will be in touch with your body and its needs. You will automatically know which foods you should emphasize in your diet. In time, as you get the hang of it, the amount of food you eat will be fairly constant: if you want to lose, you simply include a little more food of low caloric density in your diet; if you want to gain, you avoid these foods and eat more foods of high caloric density. You don't need to starve to lose weight, and you don't have to stuff to maintain it.

You have a new way of eating, and a new slim and healthy you.* My last word on the subject is—Congratulations!

---

*If you are interested for yourself or others in learning more about the Pritikin Program or aids to following it, read my book *The Pritikin Program for Diet and Exercise* (New York: Grosset & Dunlap, 1979), and write for information on classes, live-in Centers, and our line of food products in development to Pritikin Programs, P.O. Box 5335, Santa Barbara, California 93108.

11

For the Health Professional

Medical Aspects of the High-Carbohydrate Diet in the Treatment of Obesity

This chapter has been prepared in conjunction with physicians familiar with the Pritikin program.

Obesity is regarded by many authorities as one of the leading public-health problems in the United States. The relationship between obesity and hypertension, diabetes mellitus, heart disease, mental distress and orthopedic disorders is well accepted by those acquainted with the available data. Dieting has become an intermittent way of life for millions of American adults, and many battle overweight continuously. Using popular current diet and drug therapies, physicians experience great difficulty in treating their overweight patients. Yet at the Pritikin Centers in a four-week residential program with over 7,000 participants, two-thirds of whom were overweight and one-third obese, remarkable success in controlling obesity has been achieved using a diet that has been eaten for millennia in many parts of the world and adapted for American tastes.

Since January 1976, experience with a high-carbohydrate diet consisting of vegetables, tubers and legumes, grains, and fruits, with very small amounts of animal products, has shown that this can be a very natural, healthy, and enjoyable diet for most people. Once accustomed to the new regimen, the dieter usually finds the typical American high-fat, high-salt, high-sugar diet distasteful. Patients feel and function better, and most of them adopt the diet as a basic feature of a permanent lifestyle. Because the high-carbohydrate diet is made up mainly of foods as grown, it has fewer calories than the typical American diet of predominately high-fat animal foods and refined foods, and therefore it can easily be adapted to a permanent program for controlling obesity. The reasons a high-carbohydrate diet should be the general treatment of choice for obesity are developed in this chapter. When combined with a simple exercise program, such as walking, the results can be dramatic.

BACKGROUND OF THE PROBLEM OF OBESITY

Prevalence of Obesity in America

There is abundant evidence that there have been marked alterations in the American diet as well as an increase in the prevalence of obesity in the last hundred years.[6,23] A person whose weight for a given body size exceeds the average by 20 percent or more is judged to be obese. A recent report from the Society of Actuaries indicates that mortality rates are increased by about 50 percent in moderately obese persons (approximately 35 percent overweight) and by nearly 100 percent in persons with severe obesity (approximately 50 percent or more overweight). Even with a weight excess of only 10 percent above normal, life expectancy is significantly reduced. The Health and Nutrition Examination Survey (HANES) measured the nutritional status of the U.S. population from a nationwide random sample of 28,000 persons.[1] The incidence of severe obesity among men aged 20–74 was 4.9 percent, whereas in the same age group among women it was 7.2 percent. The incidence of severe obesity was considerably higher in the middle age groups, roughly 45–54 years, than in older or younger age groups.

Complications of Obesity

Major morbid effects of obesity include hypertension, cardiovascular disease, diabetes mellitus, gallstones, arthritis, gout, and menstrual abnormalities.[51,56,57] There is also an association of obesity with several kinds of cancer that needs further study. Obesity is associated with higher blood levels of glucose, cholesterol, and triglycerides, and with lower levels of serum high-density lipoproteins than in people whose weights are normal. Of all the potentially preventable etiologic factors, obesity ranks second only to smoking as a contributing factor to cardiovascular diseases. It should be recognized, however, that the health hazard of obesity is intimately related to the high consumption of salt, fats, and cholesterol.

Besides the obvious physiologic problems of obesity, there is a special burden that patients suffer that can be called the psychological consequences of obesity affecting self-image and social relationships. The psycho-social problems from which severely obese people suffer go far beyond such problems characteristic of those who are relatively unattractive physically according to contemporary standards. The tendency to prejudge obese persons appears to begin in early childhood and is not much diminished even in adult life. The obese are often the butt of rude humor and have attributed to them traits and characteristics that are quite irrelevant to obesity. Moreover, most obese people tend to be repeatedly unsuccessful in their endeavors to lose weight and thus blame themselves and are blamed by others for their failures. For some people the stigma of obesity is an unbearable burden, and for others the lifelong struggle against it may rob them of much creative energy and vitality. Most people seriously underestimate the difficulties that obese people have in becoming and remaining thin, and the negative impact of undeserved criticism from others is exacerbated by the failure of most obese people to find a feasible solution for their predicament.

Aging, Nutrition, and Health Care

Physicians and other health professionals are often insufficiently aware of the interrelationships among aging, nutrition, and health.[53] Since the incidence and adverse impact of obesity on human health increases with advancing age, it is a morbid condition that can and should be controlled utilizing every resource available in our society. A variety of studies has shown that obesity is strongly influenced by the social environment.[48,25] For example, in the United States there is a striking inverse correlation between socio-economic status and prevalence of obesity, whereas in less affluent societies the reverse is the case. Studies of this kind suggest that whatever the genetic or biochemical determinants for obesity may be, their importance is relatively trivial compared with factors that can be modified by physicians, nutritionists, and other health-care professionals.

Within a short period of time, the physical and economic health of the country could be jeopardized by the disastrous consequences of mal- and overnutrition. In its bicentennial year, the United States already had a population of 32 million people age 60 or above, over half of whom suffered from one to six degenerative diseases that began either in childhood or young adulthood. Making inroads to reverse this trend is difficult. One obstacle is the veritable avalanche of food fads, useless gimmicks, and quackery that distracts the public. Another is the lack of understanding, even among health professionals, of the concept that nutrition and other features of lifestyle from infancy through early maturity have a tremendous impact on the incidence of the degenerative diseases and disabilities of late maturity and old age, and on longevity.

Definitions of Obesity

Among both medical and lay people obesity is usually defined in terms of weight for a given height and frame size. For most purposes this is accurate enough, particularly when we are dealing with those persons who are severely obese. Except in certain deviant groups, such as highly trained muscular athletes, the measurement of weight for a given height usually bears a very close correlation with more direct indices of percentage of fatty tissue such as skin-fold thickness or underwater weight.

Some patients who do not greatly exceed ideal weight are nevertheless moderately obese because of a small muscle mass, a relatively small and light frame, and a relative excess of adipose tissue. This body type tends to be associated for obvious reasons with a rather sedentary lifestyle. Adoption of a healthier diet and incorporation of a regular exercise program may lead to a remarkable change in body configuration due to loss of adipose tissue, increase in muscle mass and bone density, but a surprisingly small decrease in overall body weight. An important contributing factor to the problem of excess weight in patients has to do with water retention. Most persons ingest large excesses of sodium and therefore retain large amounts of water. The habitual intake of excess sodium can be shown to be associated with a 5 percent or even greater increase in body weight above that to be expected in persons on a low sodium intake. In women, particularly at certain times during the menstrual cycle, sodium and water retention can increase above the base line and produce a rise of body weight as well as a wide variety of symptoms giving the patient a sense of discomfort. Too often this condition is treated with diuretics, which tend to compound the problem. Indeed, it is now felt that the inappropriate use of diuretics may actually cause such edema.[35]

Causes of Obesity

A variety of animal and human studies have been performed to investigate the causes of obesity and have shown that, in general, there are two types: primary obesity and primary hyperphagia, or excessive food intake, with secondary obesity.

Primary obesity is uncommon. The mechanisms may involve genetic, endocrine, anatomic, or biochemical abnormalities, which may lead to inappropriate and excessive formation of adipose tissues, with a secondary increase in food intake.[50] One mechanism postulated to explain the increase in caloric intake involves the formation of increased amounts of insulin, a lipogenic factor, which by stimulating formation of adipose tissue and precipitating a fall in blood sugar could stimulate hunger and lead to progressive weight gain. The increased insulin-induced fat synthesis may account for the fact that overeating in early childhood sometimes leads to an increased number of adipocytes. This can perpetuate obesity in later life.[8,10]

Genetic obesity in animals has been studied in a variety of models. For example, there is a genetically obese strain of mice that spontaneously eat excessive amounts on an ad lib diet. These mice have an increased percentage of body fat even when weight gain is prevented by food restriction. The possibility that such phenomena exist in human subjects remains to be proved.[19]

In the vast majority of cases, obesity is related to primary hyperphagia. This can be due to a variety of environmental and psychological factors. In affluent societies, there is an overabundance of easily accessible, highly palatable and attractive, but calorically concentrated foods, i.e., foods high in fat and sugar and low in fiber and bulk.[22] The promotion of these foods as a source of pleasure, recreation, social interaction, and stress reduction has been incredibly successful. The socio-economic control of the prevalence of obesity tends to be related to cultural factors within families or larger social groupings. In some societies and in some populations within societies, there is literally an epidemic of obesity. There are emotional factors that are very important also. For example, it has been postulated that some men and women use obesity as a way of avoiding sexual relationships or dealing with their sexual conflicts.

Physiology of Weight Loss

One pound of weight loss from the body requires an accumulated deficit of approximately 3500 calories. This is accomplished mainly by the loss of fat but, depending upon the diet, there may be varying amounts lost as water, protein and carbohydrates (from glycogen stores).[52] Glycogen and protein exist in the body as part of a complex of hydrated material with a ratio of water to carbohydrate (or protein) of approximately 3 or 4 to 1. Thus when protein or carbohydrate is lost from the body, there is an obligatory water loss as well. This does not seem to be true for fat stores.

It is rarely possible to achieve combustion of fat as the only fuel, although the composition of the fuel mixture can vary. In patients who are on a calorie-restricted intake for several weeks or months, the percent of fat in the fuel mixture gradually rises and can reach nearly 80 percent. After a long duration of calorie restriction, weight loss can decrease as much as 20 to 40 percent, the consequence of a fall in the basal metabolic rate.[52] In one study of weight loss in nonobese subjects studied for up to 24 weeks, the average energy level of weight loss initially was about one pound per 1910 calorie deficit and subsequently was one pound for a deficit of 2460 calories. The decrease in the rate of weight loss was due to diminished water loss. In obese subjects the weight loss was more exclusively from body fat and often the caloric deficit resulting in the loss of a pound of body weight exceeded 3000 calories.[52]

One factor in the slowed rate of weight loss is that during dieting people tend to reduce their voluntary physical activity, sometimes by as much as 50 percent or more, especially on high-protein diets that induce fatigue as toxic breakdown products accumulate.[43,23] The fall in physical activity can be modified by a program designed to maintain or increase physical activity.

The therapy of obesity is one of the most difficult, challenging, and often frustrating endeavors that a physician may encounter in the practice of medicine. Initial weight loss is relatively easy to achieve, almost regardless of the type of program prescribed. However, maintaining ideal or near ideal body weight has proved so difficult with the methods currently employed as to discourage all but a few hardy souls from the practice of bariatrics.

NONDIETARY APPROACHES TO THE PROBLEM OF OBESITY

Failure to achieve results in producing weight loss by dietary means in obese and overweight individuals has given impetus to countless nondietary regimens, devices, and therapeutic agents that have no scientific basis. An example of such an ineffectual remedy for excess weight is the use of plastic covers and wraps that impair heat loss from some particular portion of the body. Testimonials to the effectiveness of such products may fail to mention other measures employed simultaneously that may have been responsible for weight loss.

For the severely obese patients (sometimes called morbidly obese) who are nearly 300 pounds or more in weight, there are various radical measures that have been proposed in recent years.[55] Their implementation is testimony to the desperation of the patient's plight. Jaw-wiring has been shown to produce weight loss in the short term, although in time compulsive eaters may get around even this impediment quite readily by ingesting very large amounts of high-calorie liquid or semiliquid foods. The ever present danger of asphyxiation from aspiration of vomitus makes one question the wisdom of such a radical procedure. Moreover, when the wires are removed the patients usually return to their previous feeding habits and regain their lost weight.

A variety of surgical procedures has been attempted for weight control, including stomach stapling, partial gastric resection, and intestinal bypass. These clearly are not the panaceas originally envisioned.[5,56] They are associated with a wide range of side effects, some of which can be serious or even life-threatening. Intestinal bypass produces a form of malabsorption that accounts for a maximum daily deficit of only 450 kcal and in some circumstances considerably less.[56] After the procedure most patients lose weight for a period of time and then stabilize. Stabilization at a weight considerably higher than ideal is quite easy in patients who habitually have large intakes of food. While some degree of weight loss may be guaranteed by surgery, it is purchased at an extremely high cost. Before considering surgery, the causes of medical failure should be carefully analyzed. This is not to say that surgical procedures are never indicated; however, their use constitutes an extreme measure to be undertaken only after all medical measures have failed and with a clear understanding of their limitations and the great risks involved. The effects associated with these surgeries are disturbing, and it is still not known what additional adverse effects may appear 15, 20, or more years postoperatively.[42,16]

Drug Therapy for Obesity

The drugs used in the treatment of obesity fall into several categories: those that suppress appetite; those that increase metabolic rate; and a group that includes a variety of pharmacologic agents some of whose mechanisms of action are not clearly understood.

Anorectic drugs possess many of the pharmacologic properties of the naturally occurring hormones adrenaline and noradrenaline. The one in most common use is amphetamine. The side effects associated with this drug include decreased fatigue, insomnia, increased alertness, euphoria, and increased energy. The drug causes a decrease in food intake because of a central suppression of appetite. A large number of other drugs, many of them amphetamine derivatives, has been developed in an effort to reduce the central stimulation that occurs with amphetamine and amphetamine-like drugs. Although weight loss is greater with these drugs than with placebos, they are associated with a host of side effects and it has not been possible to show that they contribute anything to sustained weight control once the drug is stopped. In addition, many obese people eat compulsively without paying attention to their hunger or lack of it.[5]

Calorigenic agents such as thyroid and similar drugs increase oxygen consumption and basal metabolic rate and have been used in the treatment of obesity for almost a century. Most obese patients do not have abnormally low basal metabolic rates, nor do they have abnormally low concentrations of thyroid hormone. In fact, some studies have actually shown slightly increased levels of thyroid, which may indicate a mild resistance in obese subjects to this hormone.[5] A variety of studies has shown that the use of thyroid hormones usually effected a greater degree of weight loss than did placebos. However, this weight may have been enhanced by the use of diuretics, often employed in conjunction with thyroid therapy. As with the amphetamine-like drugs, there is no evidence that calorigenic drugs have any persistent effect after therapy is discontinued; the only possible effect is to accelerate initial weight loss.

There are inherent dangers in the practice of using excessive quantities of thyroid hormones. In studies using d-thyroxine to lower serum cholesterol in patients with atherosclerosis, it was found that the small effect on cholesterol was accompanied by an increased mortality. Besides increasing oxygen consumption, thyroxine increases protein catabolism and nitrogen loss in the urine so that patients often go into negative nitrogen balance. Indeed, in the short term the majority of weight loss caused by thyroid hormone is due to protein loss rather than fat loss. Since for every pound of protein loss there are three pounds of water loss, the overall weight loss may be encouraging to the patient but in fact is very harmful.[5] A potentially more dangerous side effect of thyroid hormone is its modification of the strength and rhythmicity of cardiac contraction. Since in the obese there is increased stress on the heart due to excess weight and to hypertension often associated with obesity, the use of thyroid hormone in these patients could have deleterious effects. In fact, it was this sort of side effect that led the Coronary Drug Project of the National Institutes of Health to discontinue the study of the lipid-lowering effects of thyroxine.

Diuretics have also been extensively used in the treatment of idiopathic edema, a common condition in young women. Women seem to be unusually sensitive to the mild edema that occurs extensively among Americans and people of other developed nations, who ingest excessive amounts of sodium. This is aggravated in most women by the sodium-retaining properties of contraceptive hormone preparations as well as endogenous hormones involved in the menstrual cycle. Women who see a physician and complain of generalized puffiness, a bloated feeling, heaviness in the extremities, swollen eyes in the morning, inability to put on or remove rings, or excessive tightness of shoes at the end of the day are usually given diuretics rather than an explanation for their condition. De Wardner[35] has suggested that primary idiopathic edema of women is often caused by the diuretics given to them for the water retention resulting from a high dietary intake of sodium. In almost all these women, dietary sodium restriction is the treatment of choice; the use of diuretics merely compounds and perpetuates the problem.

Diuretics tend to induce increased serum levels of renin, angiotensin, aldosterone, and antidiuretic hormone (ADH), and often may increase levels of catecholamines. This tends to aggravate the water- and sodium-retaining state, making it very difficult to discontinue the drug therapy. In addition, patients given diuretics commonly lose potassium as well and may need supplementation. Use of diuretics raises serum uric acid, and in an occasional patient may precipitate an attack of gout.

In obesity control, diuretics induce some degree of dehydration that may be welcomed by women who suffer from fluid retention. The resultant weight loss may be dramatic and very encouraging. But salt and water loss are only temporary. Since they have no effect on fat stores in the body, diuretics are not indicated in weight control. Because of the hormonal changes they induce, they may convert a minor problem of fluid retention into a serious one.*

Human chorionic gonadotropin is a hormone that has been used to treat obesity both because of its purported appetite-suppressing effect and its effect in changing body configuration. It was initially proposed that injections of HCG, in conjunction with a 500-calorie diet, would help mobilize fat that in the ordinary course of events would not be easily mobilized. It was thought that the hormone would facilitate weight loss as well as the development of a more ideal body configuration. Extensive testing of these hypotheses has failed to substantiate the original claims or to show that HCG contributes in any substantial way to the weight loss achieved by obese people eating a 500-calorie diet.[5]

A variety of other hormones has been examined for their possible effect on weight loss and body configuration. At present, the endocrine approach to obesity has little to offer. Other drugs used have been those that impair intestinal absorption or bulking agents that fill the intestine and stomach in an attempt to diminish appetite. There is no evidence that any of these approaches has anything to offer beyond what would be expected from their placebo effect alone.

The pharmacologic approach to the treatment of obesity has been very disappointing. In many instances it is relatively inef-

*A case history providing such an example appears on pages 16–17.

fective, particularly in producing any sort of sustained weight loss, and in some cases the toxic side effects of drugs are serious.

Behavior-Modification Approaches in the Treatment of Obesity

Behavioral approaches have been used in an attempt to influence caloric intake by making changes in self-awareness and manipulating circumstances so that food intake is inhibited. Keeping calorie-counting ledgers and becoming more aware of the amount of food and the frequency of eating are approaches that have met with only small success. Such simple tricks as using smaller plates and dishes so that the amount of food appears relatively large, making agreements to eat only when seated, not to eat in certain rooms or at certain times of the day, have all been used in an attempt to control excessive caloric intake. Chewing the food more carefully and for a longer period of time, ceasing to eat the instant that hunger is diminished, purposely leaving half the food on the plate, keeping food diaries, and meeting with other obese persons to discuss the results of such programs are also very popular techniques, although generally not very effective. For some people, however, excessive food intake is a problem comparable to alcoholism and other destructive addictions, and as such it may be more effectively managed by peer groups than by physicians or other medical or paramedical authority figures.

LOW-CARBOHYDRATE DIETS

High-protein, high-fat diets require rigid restriction of carbohydrate. These low-carbohydrate diets have been very popular with the lay public. Few of them are high only in protein, since if meat and dairy foods are the principal sources of protein the intake of fat is high as well. Ketosis, suppression of appetite, osmotic diuresis, and, in many people, rapid weight loss do result, but the toxic effects of such diets have led many physicians to abandon their use and responsible medical authorities and institutions to condemn them.[11,17]

Adherence to the high-protein (high-fat/low-carbohydrate) diet involves limiting the amount of food ingested. The most widely promoted and popular form of this diet is that described in R. C. Atkins's *Dr. Atkins' Diet Revolution* and, more recently, *Dr. Atkins' Super Energy Diet*. Atkins claims that on a diet in which there is little or no carbohydrate, a substance he calls the fat-mobilizing hormone is produced, which causes fat from tissue stores to be oxidized. While it is true that on a low-calorie, low-carbohydrate diet body fat is burned, there is no evidence that this involves a specific hormone.[11] The fat is mobilized because of the hypocaloric nature of the diet, and any isocaloric regimen would have the same effect.

The essential mechanism by which a low-carbohydrate diet reduces weight is by the catabolizing of fat in the absence of carbohydrate, resulting in ketosis, which suppresses appetite. Ketosis also affects the central nervous system and can cause headaches and gastrointestinal upset. Low-carbohydrate diets have been around for many years, and there is nothing innovative about these highly promoted programs.[11] Indeed, more than a century ago Dr. William Harvey used a low-carbohydrate diet in the control of obesity. In 1974, the Council on Foods and Nutrition of the American Medical Association considered the low-calorie, low-carbohydrate diets as outlined by Atkins, Stillman, and others. In their strong condemnation of such dietary practices, they specifically commented on the false claims and metabolic concepts, relative lack of efficacy, and untoward side effects associated with these diets.[11]

High-protein, low-carbohydrate diets produce weight loss in part by markedly restricting the caloric intake of one entire food category—carbohydrates—automatically assuring reduction in total caloric intake. Such reduction is further assured by ketosis-induced anorexia. Decreased caloric intake is the principal mechanism for consistent weight loss on these dietary programs. However (and this is especially important initially), a low-carbohydrate diet induces very significant water and saline loss and tissue dehydration. In part, this is due to the fact that on a low-carbohydrate diet the carbohydrate stores are significantly depleted and as carbohydrate stores shrink, water is lost as well. Of even more importance are the other mechanisms by which high-protein, high-fat diets induce water and electrolyte loss. With the exception of the initial loss of fluids on the low-carbohydrate diet, they cause no more weight loss than does any other isocaloric regimen. Some of the advertisements for the low-carbohydrate diets suggest that calories don't count, because "metabolic changes" are induced enabling relatively sedentary patients to lose weight in spite of a high caloric intake. In careful scientific observations, none of these claims has been substantiated. There is no evidence to suggest that the low-carbohydrate, ketogenic diet has any advantage over other diets for the purpose of rapid or permanent weight reduction.[11,27]

Since low-carbohydrate diets ordinarily contain a high proportion of animal protein, particularly animal protein with a high fat content, there is a real danger of inducing or exacerbating hyperlipidemia.[38,47] Many "refugees" from Dr. Atkins's diet who developed serious symptoms of atherosclerosis and cardiovascular disease have been treated at the Pritikin Centers.

There is by now an enormous literature linking high dietary intake of meat, dairy products, and eggs with elevated serum levels of cholesterol and the subsequent development of atherosclerosis and coronary heart disease.[38,47] Prominent health organizations are advocating major alterations in the American diet to reduce fat and cholesterol and increase the intake of complex carbohydrates.

Although carbohydrates have often been indicted in causing weight gain, weight can readily be lost or maintained at or near ideal levels on high-carbohydrate diets when the carbohydrates are in their natural form.[20] Data from the Pritikin Centers' four-week residential program demonstrate the effectiveness of a high-complex-carbohydrate diet for weight loss. A further discussion of the results obtained on this program, including a chart summarizing these data, may be found on pages 172–176.

The literature relating high carbohydrate intake and physical performance and endurance is extensive.[4,20,55,15] The association is so convincing that many athletes interested in endurance routinely use a high-carbohydrate diet in training and prior to competitive events. On the other hand, physical performance is adversely affected by low carbohydrate intake, since liver and muscle glycogen stores are depleted by this type of diet. Troops in the Canadian Army during World War II were shown to have markedly deteriorated performance after just a few days on a low-carbohydrate intake.[11] Patients on a low-carbohydrate diet with depleted glycogen stores can have problems if they engage in any strenuous physical activity. Diminished liver glycogen stores will adversely affect blood sugar levels and brain function. Nausea, dizziness, and even blackouts are possible if blood sugar falls low enough. Although muscle glycogen is somewhat better preserved than liver glycogen, muscle fatigue occurs much earlier during exercise on a low-carbohydrate intake than on one including adequate carbohydrates. It has been demonstrated that there is nearly a sixfold increase in muscle glycogen stores when one is on a high-carbohydrate rather than a low-carbohydrate diet, and this is associated with a significant increase in physical endurance.

A high-protein, high-fat diet has often been touted as the ideal treatment for hypoglycemia. Many "refugees" from this therapy have also been treated at the Pritikin Centers. These patients, erroneously diagnosed as hypoglycemic, developed serious side effects on such diets.

Hypoglycemia is an overdiagnosed disease entity. On a high simple-sugar or refined-carbohydrate intake, blood-sugar levels do undergo drastic and rapid elevations and depressions that produce central nervous system symptoms in some persons. However, in a careful study of many hundred "hypoglycemic" episodes in such patients there seemed to be no consistent relationship between symptoms and blood-sugar levels.[28] Whether or not patients are truly hypoglycemic, proper nutrition seems to have a favorable impact on their symptoms. The actual explanation for the presence of the symptoms becomes less important since they can be controlled by diet. The treatment of choice involves frequent small feedings of unrefined complex carbohydrates. This provides the same stabilization of blood sugar without the multitude of disadvantages of high protein/high fat intake.

A problem with diagnostic testing for both hypo- and hyperglycemia is the questionable validity of the glucose tolerance test, which involves the rapid ingestion of a large simple-carbohydrate load followed by measurement of blood sugar over a period of several hours. The body's response to such an abnormal challenge is of relatively little interest. The fasting blood sugar and the sugar level after a standard meal are much more significant. For this reason, postprandial testing is preferable to the GTT. However, the adverse effects of the high-fat diet and the beneficial effects of the high-carbohydrate diet will be evident with both types of testing.

The relationship between fat in the diet and blood sugar is complex. It appears that a high-fat, low-carbohydrate intake induces a state of relative insulin resistance. Normal men have been shown to develop abnormal glucose tolerance after several days on this type of diet. On high-carbohydrate diets, glucose tolerance normalizes.

A high-carbohydrate diet has a stabilizing effect on the blood sugar even in patients with mild diabetes. At Harvard University's Joslin Clinic, which advocates very strict control of blood sugar in order to prevent diabetic complications, a trial high-carbohydrate diet showed no increase in insulin and no destabilization of blood-sugar control. For several hours after the ingestion of large amounts of fat, however, there was a variety of postprandial phenomena, presumably related to the high levels of fat in the blood for several hours after their ingestion. Interestingly, after ingestion of polyunsaturated fats, blood levels of fat remain elevated longer than after ingestion of animal fat. High fat levels seem to impair the normal function of the cellular elements in the blood, and this may be associated with their impaired passage through the microcirculation.

Since the intake of vitamins may be dangerously low on the Atkins Diet, it is recommended that the diet be supplemented with large amounts of vitamins and minerals. In some cases, the recommendations are for intake of these substances in grossly unphysiologic amounts. In many patients on this diet, an elevated level of uric acid may occur. If there is any susceptibility to development of gouty arthritis, this diet is contraindicated for that reason alone, since adherence to the diet would necessitate the taking of uricosuric agents. Finally, there are the deleterious effects of excessive protein intake. These diets may double or triple the customary protein intake calculated as percent of total caloric intake. On the Atkins maintenance diet, in which caloric intake is adjusted upward to maintain weight, the protein intake may be even more excessive.

High protein intake is associated with the development of skeletal demineralization. If the protein intake is high enough it is not possible to ingest sufficient calcium to stay in calcium balance. High-protein diets have a very high phosphate-to-calcium ratio (3 or 4 to 1). This excessive intake of phosphorus is associated with increased levels of calcium in the urine and skeletal demineralization.[29] It appears that a more ideal dietary ratio of phosphates to calcium is approximately 1 to 1,* which is not achievable on a high-protein, high-fat diet. Some investiga-

*Analysis of the Pritikin weight-loss diets (700–1200 kcal/day) indicates a P/C of 1.0 to 1.5.

tors believe that a high phosphorus-to-calcium ratio is the most important contributing factor to the development of osteoporosis in the later years.[29]

In order to be used as a source of fuel, protein is deaminated and the released ammonia converted in the liver to urea. In patients with impairment of liver function, it is usually necessary to reduce protein intake to prevent serious central nervous system toxicity due to the accumulation of ammonia. Headache is one of the symptoms due to the buildup of ammonia. The concomitant accumulation of urea is related not only to its greater production but also to its diminished excretion due to dehydration and impaired renal function.

There is a propensity for renal calculi to develop on high-protein diets.[9,41] There appears to be a direct relationship between the average amount of protein ingested (i.e., per capita meat consumption) and the prevalence of renal calculi. In a study of nations whose protein intakes varied widely, the United States had both the highest per capita protein intake and the highest prevalence of renal calculi.

The gastrointestinal tract is also affected adversely by a diet excessively high in protein. Higher than normal levels of blood urea may be associated with an unpleasant taste and odor in the mouth. High-protein, high-fat, low-carbohydrate diets are also associated with increased amounts of ammonia formed in the gastrointestinal tract. The ammonia and fat profoundly affect the number and type of intestinal bacteria. It is presently believed there is a strong relationship between the type of intestinal flora predominating in the bowel and the subsequent development of colon cancer.[57]

Liquid Protein Diets

Liquid protein diets, for example those promoted in Robert Lynn and Sandra L. Stuart's *The Last Chance Diet,* have been universally condemned by medical authorities everywhere.[3,11,18,32,33,36] Many liquid protein diet drinks sold in drugstores and health food outlets have been taken with absolutely no medical supervision. Little attention was paid to their nutritional value and in many instances patients who received most or all of their caloric intake from such drinks developed serious mineral and vitamin deficiencies. More alarmingly, there have been some 60 reported fatalities associated with the use of liquid protein drinks.[18,36] Many of these deaths have occurred with no warning in relatively young women. The exact mechanisms for these deaths remain an enigma. It is very likely, however, that they are the most severe manifestation of widespread cardiotoxicity associated with these diets.[7] Since liquid protein diets commonly consist of very low-quality protein (predigested collagen or connective tissue), serious negative nitrogen balance may have ensued.

Numerous products of the *Last Chance* type of liquid protein have been marketed under a variety of tradenames; the diet has also been called the predigested protein diet. This type of diet is usually associated with low levels of blood calcium and potassium, but serious cardiac arrhythmias can result even when these levels are normal.[33]

Protein-Sparing Modified Fast

In an attempt to make liquid protein diets more acceptable to the medical community, the quality of the protein has been upgraded considerably (for example, by the use of egg-white protein instead of gelatin), and descriptions of a variety of regimens that involve careful medical supervision have been published. The generic term for such programs is "protein-sparing modified fast," and the purported advantages are:

1. The development of ketosis with anorexia.
2. Relative sparing of body protein and maintenance of nitrogen balance despite very severe caloric restriction and negative calorie balance. (Actually, body protein is spared to a much greater extent on an isocaloric high-carbohydrate regimen.)
3. Little need for food choices at the grocery store, restaurants, or at home.
4. Impressive early weight loss that is encouraging to the patient (this early weight loss primarily involves loss of sodium and water).

Medical supervision may involve a visit to the physician or nurse at least weekly, careful monitoring of blood electrolyte levels, and frequent EKG monitoring. Such medically supervised programs have been instituted by private physicians and also in university medical centers. Because of their popularity, they have stimulated the growth of a considerable line of related commercial products. Protein powders may be used to make drinks or soup, and some manufacturers have even developed low-carbohydrate, high-protein desserts.

The problems of the protein-sparing modified fast (PSMF) are similar to those encountered with high-protein diets in general, whether liquid or solid. Although caloric intake can be rigorously controlled while the patient is on the program because no food choices have to be made during this period, no skills are learned to maintain or further weight loss once the PSMF program is discontinued.[27] The most damaging information to date regarding PSMF is reported in a recent study in *The New England Journal of Medicine* by cardiologists from the University of Rochester, New York (Strong Memorial Hospital).[33] These investigators studied a group of relatively healthy obese volunteers who went on a PSMF program for a period of several weeks. Careful monitoring of blood electrolytes, resting electrocardiograms, and 12- and 24-hour Holter-monitored electrocardiograms were performed at frequent intervals. The physicians were surprised repeatedly that they found potentially life-threatening cardiac arrhythmias in the Holter-monitored electrocardiograms of some of the patients during their fasting periods. Blood electrolyte measurements and resting electrocardiograms alone would not have suggested these serious abnormalities. The investigators strongly condemn the use of PSMF and recommend that its use be terminated pending extensive investigation of these ominous phenomena, for which there was no obvious physiologic or biochemical explanation.

In summary, there are numerous and serious disadvantages to all variants of high-protein diets. The use of high-protein, high-fat, solid-food diets offers the dubious benefit of transitory weight loss due principally to fluid loss and dehydration, but this approach is condemned by a broad spectrum of the medical community. Such diets tend to be associated with elevated levels of cholesterol and serum lipids; diminished body stores of glycogen and reduction in endurance for physical activity; increased incidence of renal calculi; and elevated levels of uric acid that must be treated pharmacologically to eliminate the risk of attacks of gouty arthritis. The chronic ketosis found in patients on low-carbohydrate diets may suppress appetite but also may lead to untoward central nervous system symptoms. The apparent suppression of the sympathetic nervous system in these patients may aggravate the tendency to orthostatic hypotension, frequently present because of dehydration.[14]

The dangers of low-carbohydrate liquid protein diets are even more dramatic.[24] Despite the rash of deaths associated with this type of diet, in recent years there has been a growing literature from the medical community suggesting that liquid protein diets can be administered safely if there is adequate medical supervision. This supervision would provide for replacement of minerals and vitamins, monitoring of serum electrolytes, and administration of routine electrocardiograms at frequent intervals. However, the University of Rochester study suggests that this intermittent monitoring creates a false sense of security. Holter monitoring of patients on liquid protein diets reveals potentially life-threatening arrhythmias in many individuals that otherwise would not have been detected. This study also suggests that the whole story has not been told regarding the cardiac complications of the high-protein, low-carbohydrate diets.

HIGH-CARBOHYDRATE DIETS

In order to circumvent the problems with the high-protein/high-fat diets discussed above, there is a growing interest in the medical community in high-carbohydrate diets. More than thirty years ago Dr. Walter Kempner utilized a high-carbohydrate diet consisting of white rice and fruit in the treatment of renal insufficiency and severe hypertensive cardiovascular disease. The diet was later adapted for the treatment of diabetes mellitus. Since then, it has been shown repeatedly that high-carbohydrate diets such as the rice/fruit diet are associated with improved glucose tolerance, even in normal subjects. Both improvements in glucose tolerance and a fall in serum triglycerides are often very rapid on this kind of diet.

In recent years use of the Kempner rice diet[31] for the treatment of severe or massive obesity has received considerable attention from lay and medical communities. In a group of 106 massively obese patients reported on in 1976, the average weight loss was 64 kgrams over a period of 8 to 11 months, or about half a pound per day. Due to extreme sodium restriction, sodium retention was usually not a problem in these patients.

Weight-Loss Results at the Pritikin Centers

Experience at the Pritikin Centers with a high-carbohydrate diet suggests that this is the ideal regimen for both weight loss and long-term weight maintenance. The diet for overweight participants has the same basic format as that served to everyone at a Center, i.e., six to eight daily feedings of unrefined natural complex-carbohydrate foods with small amounts of low-fat or nonfat animal and dairy food. However, participants who need to lose weight are expected to restrict their caloric intake to approximately 700–1200 kcal/day.

The Center diet is designed primarily to promote reduction of blood lipid levels and control of blood glucose, and the foods served vary in caloric content from very low to moderately high. Patients needing to lose weight are provided with caloric guidelines and counseling in an effort to encourage them to avoid higher-calorie foods at the self-service buffets and when placing food orders. However, they are not monitored. Since the main concern of the patients is usually their symptoms of degenerative disease, adherence to the low-calorie regimen in some of these individuals is less than optimal. In addition, many of the overweight participants are on medications that slow their rate of weight loss. Despite these negative factors, significant weight losses in the groups above normal weight are achieved as shown in the chart on the following page.

Exercise as an Adjunct to the Dietary Regimen

Although the average weight loss in four weeks at the Pritikin Centers is in the vicinity of ½ pound per day, subjects (usually male) with large muscle mass can lose as much as 1 to 1½ pounds per day, providing they are very active physically. Many of the patients rapidly increase their level of physical activity, walking at their training heart rate up to 10 or 15 miles a day. Frequent small feedings of high-carbohydrate foods are ideally suited to maintaining adequate glycogen stores for such vigorous activity. However, with this level of exercise, the principal source of fuel after a few days is the fat stores of the body.

A regular exercise regimen is an important adjunct to the dietary calorie restriction and is an integral part of the program at the Centers. Since liver or muscle glycogen depletion does not occur on a high-carbohydrate diet, the level of activity and endurance remains intact or is increased. Also, because adequate amounts of protein are ingested, nitrogen balance can be maintained and, with proper exercise, muscle mass may increase. As it does, the metabolic rate will increase as well, making it possible

Weight Changes in 21-Day Period* During Pritikin Center Inpatient Program (Paired T-tests)

Analysis of a cohort of 893 Pritikin Center participants by Loma Linda University, Department of Epidemiology and Biostatistics

Females

Initial Percent of Ideal Weight	Mean Weight in Pounds			t	df	P	Projected Weight Loss in Pounds for 30-Day Period
	Initial	After	Change				
110–119	143.57	135.55	−8.02	14.67	52	<0.001	11.47
120–129	156.36	148.23	−8.13	16.48	43	<0.001	11.63
130–139	167.54	157.08	−10.46	20.08	25	<0.001	14.96
≥140	201.67	188.15	−13.52	19.20	38	<0.001	19.33

Males

Initial Percent of Ideal Weight	Mean Weight in Pounds			t	df	P	Projected Weight Loss in Pounds for 30-Day Period
	Initial	After	Change				
110–119	177.56	166.74	−10.82	30.71	158	<0.001	15.47
120–129	195.29	181.67	−13.62	29.83	78	<0.001	19.48
130–139	206.65	191.30	−15.35	27.00	42	<0.001	21.95
≥140	242.04	222.86	−19.18	16.05	27	<0.001	27.43

*Day 2 to Day 23.

to burn calories at an increased rate, especially during exercise. A proper aerobic exercise program in conjunction with calorie restriction tends both to enhance weight loss (specifically loss of fat) and to normalize body configuration.[54] In exercising, it is most important to sustain the level of exertion for 30 minutes or longer at the training heart rate that has been determined to be safe and effective for the individual patient.

Compliance with the High-Carbohydrate Regimen by Center Patients

Because of the increased amount of bulk in the diet and the multiple feedings, a feeling of satiety is produced several times a day, and the needs of compulsive eaters may be substantially satisfied. This is in contrast to the ravenous hunger that usually accompanies hypocaloric diets. Also, the low-calorie food served, because of the absence of fat, sugar, and salt, is relatively less conducive to overconsumption by those persons who eat excessively when confronted with rich, sweet, or highly salted foods. These factors work together to enhance compliance while at the Centers.

Recidivism is lower in patients leaving the Pritikin Centers than in many other programs, possibly due to additional motivation associated with the high incidence among them of cardiovascular and endocrine disorders such as hypertension, coronary heart disease, and diabetes. Continuing weight loss appears to be achieved at home on three feedings a day with some snacks between meals. Surveys of patients who attended one of the Pritikin Centers showed that 75 to 80 percent of them stay on the dietary program about 75 to 80 percent of the time.

A plateau can occur in any weight-loss regimen. It happens to some patients on the high-carbohydrate diet and can be explained by the physiological adjustments that occur during weight loss, changes in the intestinal flora, and an increase in intestinal contents. In addition, in some patients, particularly women, there may be a certain degree of fluid retention. These factors may slow weight loss (but not the loss of body fat) in the first few weeks and discourage patients. Fluid retention can be handled quite easily by restricting sodium to about 2 grams or less and suggesting that fluid intake be reduced and governed by thirst. Also, while exercise has the beneficial effect of increasing bone density and muscle mass, this causes a slight increase in the weight of these tissues. If a plateau occurs, it is necessary to provide the patient with encouragement so that he or she persists on the diet through the periods of minimal or zero weight loss. Fortunately, this is not a common problem. Even when it does occur, in the long run weight loss on the high-carbohydrate diet is the same or greater than that on any other isocaloric diet if one takes into account the dehydration that usually occurs on low-carbohydrate diets. Even total fasting offers no advantage over a 600–800 calorie diet, since at most it would provide only about 1 to 1½ more pounds of fat loss per week.

Nutritional Adequacy of a High-Carbohydrate Regimen

A major problem with most weight-loss diets is their nutritional inadequacy. Vitamin supplementation is especially necessary on low-carbohydrate hypocaloric diets. One example of the problems that can arise as a result of these diets is the bilateral optic neuropathy with decreased visual acuity and particularly decreased night vision that was recently reported in two patients adhering to this type of diet.[24] It was determined from a decrease in the serum level of transketolase, an enzyme requiring thiamin as a co-enzyme, that a thiamin deficiency state was present in these patients. On a high-protein/high-fat diet, if the protein is principally from animal sources, the intake of thiamin may be deficient.

Vitamin supplementation is not necessary, however, on a hypocaloric diet (even as low as 700 kcal/day), if it is composed predominately of a variety of unrefined complex-carbohydrate foods since adequate amounts of vitamins and minerals are contained in these vegetable foods. The diet plans in this book provide for adequate quantities of all nutritive factors. Nutritional analyses of the 700–1200 calorie diets (for protein, fat, carbohydrate, calcium, phosphorus, iron, sodium, potassium, vitamins A and C, and thiamin, riboflavin, and niacin) are based on data in *Nutritional Value of American Foods,* published by the U.S. Department of Agriculture. The values for the other vitamins, minerals, linoleic acid, and the P/S ratio have been determined by chemical analysis. Based on these analyses, we do not recommend supplements, even for those who have a hundred pounds or more to lose.

The nutritional analysis charts on pages 363–371 in the Appendix, based on a typical day's menu, enable comparison of the nutrient intake at the four levels of hypocaloric diet with the most recent RDA guidelines and with average American nutrient intake as shown in a 1977–78 U.S. Department of Agriculture national food consumption survey.[40,49] Because of the caloric deficiency of these four levels, especially the 700-calories-per-day level, one might expect the amounts of the various nutrients to fall considerably below both the RDA and intake levels on the average high caloric American diet. However, whereas the intake of nutrients on the weight-loss Pritikin Diet meets the RDA guidelines, calcium and iron intakes on the average American diet are less than the RDAs. The food consumption survey showed levels of both below the RDAs for both men and women aged 23 and over, and of iron in women aged 23 to 50.

The typical day's menu on which these charts are based is comparable nutritionally to the other menu plans in this book, though slight variations in the amounts of some of the nutrients may exist from day to day.

Although the RDA guidelines are met on our four hypocaloric diet levels, it should be noted that minor deviations from the RDAs usually do not represent a health risk. In addition, on our diet the requirement for many nutrients is lower than it would be if a person were eating a typical American diet because the large proportion of protein and fat in the diet of most Americans increases the need for many vitamins and minerals.

The RDA standard tables are based upon nonrestricted caloric intakes. In order to determine the RDA for calorie-restricted diets, it is necessary to refer to the text of the ninth edition of *Recommended Dietary Allowances*, National Research Council, 1980.

On page 13: "For many members of the adult population, total energy consumption should be reduced in order to restrict or maintain body weight. Consequently, those who, for one reason or another, reduce their calorie consumption below the average energy allowance for their age or sex would need to select foods having a higher nutrient concentration than the RDA/1000 kcal. For example, a 1000-calorie weight-reduction diet, in order to be nutritionally adequate, would have to supply most nutrients in at least double the allowance per thousand calories...."

All of the Pritikin hypocaloric diets supply most nutrients in at least double the allowance per thousand calories. The following discussion includes a comparison of amounts present and recommendations in the RDA text for various nutrient levels for hypocaloric diets.

Thiamin. On page 84: "... a thiamin allowance for adults of 0.5 mg/1000 kcal is recommended. Because there is some evidence that older persons use thiamin less efficiently (Horwitt *et al.*, 1948; Oldham, 1962) it is recommended that they maintain an intake of 1 mg/day, even if they consume less than 2000 kcal daily." The four levels of the Pritikin hypocaloric diets have a minimum of 1 mg/day.

Riboflavin. On page 89: ". . . the riboflavin allowances in this report have been computed as 0.6 mg/1000 kcal for people of all ages. However, for elderly people and others whose caloric intake may be less than 2000 kcal, a minimum intake of 1.2 mg/day is recommended." All levels of the Pritikin hypocaloric diets have a minimum of 1.2 mg/day.

Niacin. On page 93: "The allowance recommended for adults, expressed as niacin equivalents, is 6.6 niacin equivalents per 1000 kcal (1.6 NE/MJ) and not less than 13 niacin equivalents at caloric intakes of less than 2000 kcal (8.4 MJ)." All levels of the Pritikin hypocaloric diets have a minimum of 13 mg (niacin equivalents)/day.

Vitamin A. All calorie levels of the diet contain at least twice the RDA, mostly from plant foods.

Vitamin C. The diets all contain at least five times the RDA, mostly from noncitrus foods.

Vitamin E. On page 66: "The minimum adult requirement for vitamin E when the diet contains the minimum of essential fatty acids (3 percent of calories) is not known but is probably not more than 3–4 mg δ-α-tocopherol equivalent (4.5–6 IU) per day."

This recommendation is for daily intakes up to 3000 kcal. Analyses of all diets indicate that this requirement is met.

Vitamin B_6. On page 98: "A ratio of 0.02 mg of vitamin B_6 per gram of protein eaten has been suggested as a basis for calculating the vitamin B_6 allowance. . . ." Based on this, 56 grams of protein would require 1.12 mg of B_6. Analyses of all diets indicate that this requirement is met.

Vitamin B_{12}. Analyses of all diets indicate that the requirement for vitamin B_{12} is met. The RDA is 3 mcg/1200–3000 kcal/day. And since the body stores at least a two-to-five-year supply of B_{12}, even 1 mcg would be adequate for a year or two, over which time up to 150–200 pounds of weight can be lost.

Both high-protein and high-fat diets cause increased requirements for B_{12}.[46,45,39] The ketosis produced on high-protein, high-fat weight-loss diets causes an enormous depletion of thiamin, and deficiency of these vitamins can result in B_{12} deficiency. (Ketosis also depletes body stores of niacin and vitamin C.) The

Pritikin Diet, because it is low in both protein and fat, conserves B_{12}.

Folacin. Plant foods, especially leafy greens, are highest in folic acid, and analyses of all diets indicate that this requirement is met.

Calcium. Calcium requirements are substantially greater when the intake of protein is high. On the diet served at the Pritikin Centers and proposed in this book, calcium retention is greater and is utilized more efficiently than on the average American diet. Although all of the diets meet the 800 mg RDA, 500 mg of calcium would probably be quite adequate. On page 129: "It is recognized that persons consuming less than the customary United States intake of protein and phosphorus [abundant in protein foods and cola drinks] will remain in calcium balance with intakes considerably below the allowance recommended."

Phosphorus. Although all the diets meet the 800-mg RDA, 500 mg of phosphorus would probably be quite adequate. In Western societies, the intake of phosphorus to calcium is too great. This excessive phosphorus consumption contributes to bone demineralization resulting in the extremely high incidence of osteoporosis in these societies. Too much phosphorus (or calcium) can also diminish the ability to absorb dietary iron.

Magnesium. Although all of the diets meet the RDA, on page 135 it is stated: "Magnesium deficiency is usually seen only in pathological conditions, such as malabsorption syndromes and gastrointestinal-tract diseases requiring prolonged total parenteral nutrition." This indicates that even on substantially lower intakes of magnesium, deficiency is not likely.

Iron. Iron nutriture is adequate on the Pritikin Diet although it is lower in meat, fish, and poultry (sources of heme iron) than the average American diet. Heme iron is more readily absorbed than nonheme iron if the diet does not contain adequate ascorbic acid. Layrisse[34] has studied absorption of vegetable food iron and finds that only 66 mg of ascorbic acid increases iron absorption fivefold, resulting in absorption of dietary iron equal to that when the diet is high in heme-iron-containing foods. The average vitamin C content of the Pritikin weight-loss diets is more than 300 mg per day. In addition, tests on humans using radioactive iron (Fe-59) demonstrated that for normal subjects iron in liver is absorbed at twice the rate of iron in lettuce and greens. For iron-deficient patients, however, there is no difference. Lettuce and liver iron both were absorbed at the 25–30 percent level.[37]

Too much calcium or phosphorus can diminish the ability to absorb dietary iron. Cola drinks, which are high in phosphoric acid, contribute significantly to the excessive dietary intake of phosphorus. Iron absorption may also be adversely affected by the widespread use of the preservative EDTA, a chelating agent, which is added to many prepared foods and to carbonated soft drinks, beer, and liquor to prevent oxidative damage by free minerals. The iron intake of a large segment of our population, especially menstruating women, may fall below the RDA. Possibly the RDAs for iron are set so high because the American diet is so high in fat; fat interferes with oxygen release from hemoglobin iron to the tissues, increasing the body's need for iron. The Pritikin diets are so low in fat and processed additive-containing foods that they probably contain a good deal more than adequate amounts of iron.

All levels of the Pritikin weight-loss menu plans are designed to provide a minimum of 10 mg of iron per day. Iron content ranges from 10 to 18 mg per day and averages 14 mg per day, which is midway between the RDA for men (10 mg per day) and for menstruating women (18 mg per day). For menstruating women who wish to achieve the RDA level, the 18 mg daily plans should be emphasized. (Eighteen mg or more of iron are provided at all calorie levels by menu plans 6, 11, and 13; at calorie levels of 1000 and up by menus 4, 5, 6, 11, 13, and 14; and at the 1200-calorie level by menus 1, 3, 4, 5, 6, 7, 8, 9, 12, 13, and 14.)

In my view, 14 mg per day is adequate for both sexes, including menstruating women, especially for those adhering to the Pritikin Diet, which is low in protein and high in vitamin C.

William Crosby, M.D., of the editorial board of the *Journal of the American Medical Association*, has written, "The standards of adequacy of dietary iron have been systematically inflated. Ten years ago, the recommended daily allowance (RDA) of iron was 12 mg for women. In 1964, it was increased to 15 mg. In 1968, it was increased again to 18 mg. Nothing has changed in the U.S. diet. There has been no increase of women with anemia. Furthermore, none of these levels of RDA was established as a consequence of careful examinations of actual requirement. The changes were made after 'deliberation' by the Food and Nutrition Board, National Academy of Sciences–

National Research Council. By setting artificial standards, it is possible to claim that any diet is deficient, but it does not follow that the people who eat the diet are iron-deficient. Today, after this manipulation of the RDA, it is claimed that in the United States 95% of women 18 to 44 years of age have iron-deficient diets. Yet, with low serum iron values as the index of deficiency, less than 2% are found to be iron deficient. Thus, epidemics can be created in Washington by the shuffling of papers.''[12]

Because many women's diets are deficient in iron according to the inflated level at which the RDA is set, there has been talk of the iron-fortification of American foods. However, since iron is excreted inefficiently, there is concern that such a measure would cause the intake for our male population to be too high. Crosby and others are concerned because of the Swedish iron-fortification data[13] indicating a significant percent of males have hemochromatosis that apparently developed after fortification of food with iron. This is a condition common among the Bantus of South Africa, who cook exclusively in iron pots, and an estimated 80 percent of the population have siderosis.

According to the RDA manual (page 137), the average amount of iron lost by healthy males is about 1 mg/day, and the average amount lost by healthy menstruating women is 1.5 mg per day. In about 94 percent of normal women, the loss is less than 2.4 mg. On page 141: "The evaluation of absorbable iron, although subject to future refinement, *expresses more appropriately than the calculation of total iron* [italics ours] the present state of knowledge by taking into account the nearly tenfold variability of iron absorption, depending on source and dietary composition." Both the amount of iron in the diet and the rate at which it is absorbed are far greater on the Pritikin Diet than on the normal American diet.

Zinc. Zinc varies from approximately 10 mg on the 700-calorie diet, to 15 mg per day on the 1200-calorie diet. The RDA, which includes a substantial safety factor, is 15 mg/day. The RDA manual states on page 146: "The average zinc content of mixed diets consumed by the American adult has been reported as between 10 and 15 mg (Sandstead, 1973). However, a recent study measuring the zinc content in duplicate samples of self-chosen food of 20 free-living adults over a period of 6 days detected an average intake of only 8.6 mg/day, ranging from 6 to 12.4 mg (Holden *et al.,* 1979)." Zinc deficiency is essentially unknown in this country, and yet the high protein diet normally eaten increases the requirements for zinc. Based on the population studies, a 10–15 mg zinc intake per day is more than adequate.

Iodine. On page 148, the RDA manual states: "The daily iodine requirement for prevention of goiter in adults is 50–75 mcg, or approximately 1 mcg/kg of body weight (FBN, 1970)." The RDA of 150 micrograms has a substantial safety factor. According to analyses, the Pritikin Diets (prepared from foods purchased in California) meet the RDA for iodine. It is not certain that this is the case when the diets are prepared from foods obtained in other parts of the country. However, since iodine deficiency in this country is rare, this should not be of concern.

Fiber. A diet of predominantly unrefined carbohydrate foods is higher in fiber than the ordinary diet consumed by Americans. Some preliminary studies suggested that diets high in fiber might have the effect of inhibiting the absorption of minerals from the intestinal tract. Subsequent studies have attempted to answer this question. The consensus is that a varied diet containing large amounts of unrefined carbohydrate foods, although high in fiber, would not have this effect. One of the most recent studies in this area was conducted by Dr. James Anderson, Chief of Endocrinology at the University of Kentucky Medical Center, who sought to determine whether a diet relatively high in fiber content would deplete mineral nutriture. He observed no evidence of mineral deficiency in patients on high-fiber diets for up to 51 months. In addition, although diabetics are commonly deficient in magnesium, there was no deficiency in this mineral in the diabetic patients studied.[2] There is an apparent tendency when there is a sudden change from a diet quite low in fiber to one that contains larger amounts for the blood levels of certain minerals to drop a little temporarily; however, this phenomenon is transient and the levels of minerals rapidly normalize.

The high fiber content of the diet usually prevents the constipation that occurs with most hypocaloric diets. To insure spontaneous frequent bowel movements, however, supplementary bran is advocated, using one to six heaping tablespoons of unprocessed miller's bran a day. The calories of the bran are balanced by the more rapid transit time which reduces caloric absorption. Bran absorbs several times its weight in water, significantly increasing the bulk of the stool. This not only prevents constipation but also tends to reduce fluid retention. If constipation continues to be a problem, the daily amount of bran ingested should be increased or other bulk-forming laxative provided. If the constipated patient is advised to increase bran intake, it is best to direct that it be taken sprinkled over food at three different times during the day and followed by a glass of fluid within the hour. The use of any drugs or chemical agents which produce bowel spasms should be strictly avoided, since this perpetuates bowel hypotonia and induces dependency on such agents.

Fatty acids. Although the Pritikin Diet contains substantially less fat than does the average American diet, all caloric levels of the Pritikin regimen amply meet requirements for fat. The Pritikin Diet has a P/S ratio of 1.8 and intake of linoleic and linolenic acids, the essential fatty acids, is more than adequate.

In summary, all diets, from 700 to 1200 calories, not only meet the RDA guidelines for nutrients, but supply more nutrients than are available on the full-calorie average American diet.[49]

There is some overanxiety among dietitians about meeting the RDAs. It is not critical to meet these allowances for the various nutrients at all times, because there is a large safety factor built into them. The intake of some nutrients could be 20 to 50 percent lower and in the case of vitamin B_{12}, the intake could be 80 percent lower for the period during which the weight-loss diets are used. Even for longer durations on a Pritikin-type diet, we could ingest much lower levels than the RDAs for most nutrients and still receive sufficient amounts to maintain optimum health.

The benefits of a high-carbohydrate diet for weight loss over other approaches, dietary or nondietary, are numerous. Diets high in unrefined, complex carbohydrates associated with intact fiber tend to lower blood insulin levels and normalize carbohydrate and lipid metabolism. The water and high fiber content of the foods permitted provide sufficient bulk in the diet to appease the hunger of the average dieter. Because these foods are low in caloric density, the high-carbohydrate diet is of great help even to compulsive eaters in controlling their weight. While success for such individuals in the use of this type of diet is naturally enhanced in the partially controlled environment at the Pritikin Centers, intelligent and motivated individuals may be able to achieve excellent results under the care of their own physicians despite poor eating habits and a history of failure in previous efforts to lose weight. It is to be hoped that the extensive experience at the Pritikin Centers* in effectively using a high-carbohydrate diet for weight loss may encourage physicians to employ this approach with suitable patients.

*Data reporting results at the Pritikin Centers with obese patients, many with hypertension, adult-onset diabetes and cardiac disease, may be obtained by physicians by writing to me at P.O. Box 5335, Santa Barbara, California 93108. Physicians may also wish to ask for the medical packet, which gives information about the live-in Centers and community classes teaching the Pritikin Program. Further information about the Pritikin Program may be found in my book, *The Pritikin Program for Diet and Exercise* (New York: Grosset & Dunlap, 1979).

Comments from a Behavioral Scientist on Problems of Dieting

by
Steven M. Zifferblatt, Ph.D.
Associate Director
Pritikin Center, Santa Monica, California

As a researcher in the area of health and behavior change, I have spent a great deal of time studying eating habits and have witnessed the comings and goings of a plethora of theories, therapies, and diets. Their endless proliferation reflects, of course, the obvious fact that none of them up to now has proved successful.

Over the years I have devoted many hours to consoling patients who were frustrated at not being able to maintain the weight loss they struggled so hard to achieve. Most had optimistically tried numerous diet fads that promised quick and dramatic weight loss through minimum effort and deprivation only to return to their original eating patterns and regain the weight they had so much wanted to lose.

One of the unfortunate consequences of this cycle of losing and regaining weight is a progressive diminution of self-esteem. Unfortunately, people who follow diet fads assume their weight loss will be permanent. When the inevitable backslide starts, their conclusion is that they and not the diets are at fault.

Seeds of inadequacy are firmly embedded in us all—slim, fat, tall, short, rich or poor. It merely requires certain circumstances to allow them to germinate and thrive. People who go on most popular diets recognized a problem and selected a solution assuring quick and easy weight loss. When the diet is carefully followed but the weight is regained, a sense of failure is inevitable. Repeating this cycle several times, as most dieters do, results not only in a lifelong weight problem but also in the feeling the dieter is a loser.

Too many overweight people are under the illusion that weight loss can be easily and quickly achieved and maintained if only the right short-term diet could be found. Permanent weight loss can be a reality only if permanent changes of eating habits are achieved. The dieter with unrealistic expectations is the dieter forever doomed to cyclic weight loss and gain. The dieter with realistic perceptions of the time, effort, and skills required to maintain weight loss is guaranteed success.

Most popular fad diets do not change eating patterns permanently. It takes more than a brief and bizarre flight from reality to change lifelong eating patterns. The popular high-protein, high-fat, and liquid diets require eating foods of abnormal types or amounts. The water loss they produce often results in abnormally rapid weight loss during the first few days, but the combinations and amounts of required foods constitute a dramatic departure from the type of diet that can be followed on a lasting basis. Therefore the dieter returns to old eating habits and regains weight.

Permanent weight control needs to be achieved not by using such artificial diets but by following a natural diet that uses the same type of foods both to lose and to maintain weight once weight-loss goals are achieved. A natural diet lends itself to the maintenance of desired weight because as weight is lost the eating patterns are acquired that will be continued on a permanent basis. With the natural diet, the only skill to be learned once weight loss is attained is that of making some adjustments in the amount of certain foods that have been eaten all along, i.e., increased intake of some of the more caloric foods.

Achieving permanent weight loss requires the dieter to rebel against historically strong and firmly learned patterns of eating. It is always easier to resist change and persist with familiar, comfortable eating habits. It is also easier to change eating habits for a short period of time as one does on typical fad diets. For most people, dieting is not perceived as true change but as an intense but brief departure from everyday eating rituals. It is possible to eat foods you don't like, eat excessive amounts of certain types of foods, or even to fast for a few weeks. Some may even enjoy the radical change from the everyday tedium of fighting a losing battle to the dramatic excitement of a new and fashionable diet. However, people who embark on such an artificial diet know they will return to their old familiar eating habits. We tend to persist in what we know well and in what is comfortable and predictable, whether or not we think it is good or healthy for us. However, permanent weight change is ensured not by brief or periodic dieting but only by long-term commitment.

Changing eating patterns that have been honed and shaped over thirty or forty years may not come about at the first proclamation of intent without occasional lapses. It always surprises me to hear mature men and women proclaim their despair when they backslide in their attempts to develop new eating patterns. Success is assured by taking setbacks in stride, learning from them, and getting back to work. Failure is assured by believing that an occasional dietary indiscretion signals the futility of one's efforts.

Most people are concerned with losing as much weight as they can in as short a time as possible. To be solely concerned with losing as much weight as possible as fast as possible is self-defeating. It is much better to set both immediate and long-range goals. The approach in use at the Pritikin Centers and recommended in this book is based on an approach that enables the dieter to pursue both goals. Fat stores are depleted as rapidly as on any other weight-loss regimen containing the same number of calories, and in a healthful way. At the same time, the dieter is growing accustomed to a new and enjoyable way of eating which can be adhered to throughout life—a way of eating that will guarantee normal weight and improved health prospects. By concentrating on a new way of eating rather than only on initial weight loss, weight loss will be achieved and maintained.

Source Notes

CHAPTER 1

Atkins, R. C. 1972. *Dr. Atkins' Diet Revolution*, p. 289. New York: Bantam Books.

Bendezu, R., *et al.* 1976. Certain metabolic consequences of jejunoileal bypass. *Am. J. Clin. Nutr.* 29: 366–370.

Bistrian, B. R. 1978. Clinical use of a protein-sparing modified fast. *JAMA* 240: 2299–2302.

Community Nutrition Institute. 1980. Diet aids boom. *CNI Weekly Report* 10 (14): 4.

Council on Foods and Nutrition, American Medical Association. 1974. A critique of low-carbohydrate ketogenic weight reduction regimens: a review of Dr. Atkins' Diet Revolution. *JAMA* 224: 15–22.

Elliott, J. 1978. More help for the morbidly obese: gastric stapling. *JAMA* 240: 1941.

FDA Drug Bulletin. 1978. Liquid protein and sudden cardiac deaths—an update. May–July.

Kuldau, J. M., *et al.* 1980. Jejuno-ileal bypass: general and psychiatric outcome after one year. *Psychosomatics* 21 (7): 534–539.

Jowsey, J. 1976. Prevention and treatment of osteoporosis. In *Nutrition and Aging,* ed. M. Winick, pp. 131–144. New York: John Wiley.

Lantigua, R. A., *et al.* 1980. Cardiac arrhythmias associated with a liquid protein diet for the treatment of obesity. *N. Engl. J. Med.* 303: 735–738.

Lawlor, T., *et al.* 1969. Metabolic hazards of fasting. *Am. J. Clin. Nutr.* 22: 1142–1149.

Med. Trib. 1979. Stomach-stapling corrects obesity and preserves digestive tissue. 20 (Oct. 10).

d. *World News*. 1978. Stapling creates mini-stomach for obese patients. 19 (Oct. 16): 17–18.

tr. *Rev.* 1974. Current status of jejuno-ileal bypass for obesity. 32 (11): 333–338.

tr. *Rev.* 1975. Obesity, jejuno-ileal bypass and death. 33 (2): 38–40.

tr. *Rev.* 1978. The nature of weight loss during short term dieting. 36 (3): 72–74.

Sunyer, F. X. 1976. Jujunal bypass surgery for obesity. *Am. J. Clin. Nutr.* 29: 409–416.

ckman, F., *et al.* 1974. Changes in serum cholesterol during the Stillman diet. *JAMA* 228: 54–58.

dgers, S. 1977. Jaw wiring in the treatment of obesity. *Lancet* II: 1221–1222.

ss, M. 1979. Cardiovascular complications during prolonged starvation. *West. J. Med.* 130 (2): 170–177.

agrin, J. W., *et al.* 1971. Polyarthritis in obese patients with intestinal bypass. *Ann. Intern. Med.* 75: 377–380.

err, H. P., *et al.* 1974. Bile acid metabolism and hepatic disease following small bowel surgery for obesity. *Am. J. Clin. Nutr.* 27:1369–1379.

ein, J. R., *et al.* 1976. Ineffectiveness of human chorionic gonadotropin in weight reduction: a double-blind study. *Am. J. Clin. Nutr.* 19: 940–948.

pping, D. C., *et al.* 1977. Synthesis of macromolecules by intestinal cells incubated with ammonia. *Am. J. Physiol.* 233 (4): E341–E347.

S. Dept. of Health, Education, and Welfare. 1977. *HEW News.* Nov. 9.

ung, J. B., *et al.* 1977. Suppression of sympathetic nervous system during fasting. *Science* 196: 1473–1475.

CHAPTER 2

ams, C. F. 1975. *Nutritive Value of Foods in Common Units.* U.S. Dept. of Agriculture. Agriculture Handbook No. 456.

nsumer Reports. 1978. Too much sugar? March.

eenberg, J. 1978. The fat American. *Science News* 113 (12): 188–189.

ber, G. B., *et al.* 1977. Depletion and disruption of dietary

fiber: effects on satiety, plasma glucose and serum insu
Lancet II: 679–682.

Hartz, A., *et al.* 1977. Relative importance of the effect
family environment and heredity on obesity. *Ann. Hu*
Genet. 41: 185–193.

Higgins, I. T. 1976. Fatness similarities in adopted pairs (let
Am. J. Clin. Nutr. 29: 1067–1068.

JAMA. 1977. Obesity in children: environment or genes? 2
2009.

Karam, J. H. 1979. Obesity: fat cells—not fat people. *West*
Med. 130 (2): 128–132.

Kolata, G. B. 1977. Obesity: a growing problem. *Resea*
News (December): 905–906.

Pediatric Ann. 1978. Obesity in childhood. June.

Pi-Sunyer, F. X. 1976. Jejunal bypass surgery for obesity. *Am*
Clin. Nutr. 29: 409–416.

Rodin, J. 1978. The puzzle of obesity. *Human Nature* (Fel
ary): 38–47.

CHAPTER 3

Anderson, J. W., *et al.* 1980. Mineral and vitamin status
high-fiber diets: long-term studies of diabetic patients. *Dia*
tes Care 3 (1): 38–40.

Connor, W. E., *et al.* 1978. The plasma lipids, lipoproteins,
the diet of the Tarahumara Indians of Mexico. *Am. J. C*
Nutr. 31: 1131.

Kempner, W., *et al.* 1975. Treatment of massive obesity v
rice/reduction diet program. *Arch. Intern. Med.* 135: 1575–15

Lantigua, R. A., *et al.* 1980. Cardiac arrhythmias associa
with a liquid protein diet for the treatment of obesity. *N. E*
J. Med. 303: 735–738.

Lee, C., *et al.* 1971. Nitrogen retention of young men fed
with or without supplementing chicken. *Am. J. Clin. Nutr.*
318–323.

Patillo, D., *et al.* 1981. Body weight and composition
laboratory rats: effects of diets with high or low prot
concentrations. *Science* 211: 185–186.

U.S. Dept. of Agriculture. 1980. *Nationwide Food Consump*
Survey 1977–78. Preliminary Report No. 2.

West, K. M., *et al.* 1966. Glucose tolerance, nutrition,

diabetes in Uruguay, Venezuela, Malaya, and East Pakistan. *Diabetes* 15:9–18.

CHAPTER 4

Burkitt, D. P., ed. 1975. *Refined Carbohydrate Foods and Disease: Some Implications of Dietary Fibre.* New York: Academic Press.

Friedman, M., *et al.* 1965. Effect of unsaturated fats upon lipemia and conjunctival circulation. *JAMA* 193: 110–114.

Grace, C. S., *et al.* 1970. Blood fibrinolysis and coagulation in New Guineans and Australians. *Aust. Ann. Med.* 4: 328–333.

Hartroft, W. S. 1960. The pathology of obesity. In *The Prevention of Obesity,* ed. R. L. Craid, pp. 32–41. Dallas: American Heart Association.

Iacano, J. M., *et al.* 1975. Reduction in blood pressure associated with high polyunsaturated fat diets that reduce blood cholesterol in man. *Preventive Med.* 4: 426–433.

Jowsey, J. 1976. Prevention and treatment of osteoporosis. In *Nutrition and Aging,* ed. M. Winick, pp. 131–144. New York: John Wiley.

Moore, C. V. 1973. Iron. In *Modern Nutrition in Health and Disease,* ed. R. S. Goodhart and M. W. Shils, pp. 301–304. Philadelphia: Lea & Febiger.

Weisinger, J. R., *et al.* 1974. The nephrotic syndrome: a complication of massive obesity. *Ann. Intern. Med.* 81: 440–447.

CHAPTER 8

Harris, Barbara. 1980. France along the diet route. *The New York Times,* September 28, Section C, p. 1.

Metzner, H. L., *et al.* 1977. The relationship between frequency of eating and adiposity in adult men and women in the Tecumseh Community Health Study. *Am. J. Clin. Nutr.* 30: 712–715.

CHAPTER 9

Åstrand, P.-O., *et al.* 1977. *Textbook of Work Physiology,* 2d ed. New York: McGraw-Hill.

Franklin, B. A., *et al*. 1980. Losing weight through exercise. *JAMA* 244: 377.

CHAPTER 11

1. Abraham, S., *et al*. 1980. Prevalence of severe obesity in adults in the United States. *Am. J. Clin. Nutr.* 33: 364–369.

2. Anderson, J. W., *et al*. 1980. Mineral and vitamin status on high-fiber diets: long-term status of diabetic patients. *Diabetes Care* 3: 38–40.

3. Apfelbaum, M. 1976. The effects of very restrictive high protein diets. *Clin. Endocrinol. Metab.* 5: 417–430.

4. Åstrand, P.-O., *et al*. 1977. *Textbook of Work Physiology*, 2d ed., pp. 483–521. New York: McGraw-Hill.

5. Bray, G. A. 1976. *The Obese Patient*. Major Problems in Internal Medicine, vol. IX. Philadelphia: W. B. Saunders.

6. Bray, G. A., ed. 1979. *Obesity in America*. Bethesda: National Institutes of Health. Available from Publications Unit, Fogarty International Center, Bldg 16A, Rm 205, National Institutes of Health, Bethesda, MD 20205 (NIH Publication No. 79-359).

7. Brown, J. M., *et al*. 1978. Cardiac complications of protein-sparing modified fasting. *JAMA* 240: 120–122.

8. Charney, E., *et al*. 1976. Childhood antecedents of adult obesity: do chubby infants become obese adults? *N. Eng. J. Med.* 295: 6–9.

9. *Clin. Nutr.* 1980. Diet and urinary calculi. 38: 75–76.

10. Committee on Nutrition of Mother and Preschool Child. 1978. Fetal and infant nutrition and susceptibility to obesity. *Am. J. Clin. Nutr.* 31: 2026–2030.

11. Council on Foods and Nutrition, American Medical Association. 1974. A critique of low-carbohydrate ketogenic weight reduction regimens: a review of *Dr. Atkins' Diet Revolution*. *JAMA* 224: 15–22.

12. Crosby, W. 1974. The iron-enrichment-now-brouhaha. *JAMA* 228: 1651.

13. Crosby, W. 1978. The safety of iron-fortified foods. *JAMA* 239: 2026.

14. DeHaven, J., *et al*. 1980. Nitrogen and sodium balance and sympathetic-nervous-system activity in obese subjects

treated with a low calorie protein or mixed diet. *N. Eng. J. Med.* 302: 477–482.

15. DeVries, H. 1974. *Physiology of Exercise for Physical Education and Athletics*, pp. 26–34. Dubuque: William C. Brown.

16. Drenick, E. J., *et al.* 1978. Renal damage with intestinal bypass. *Ann. Intern. Med.* 5: 594.

17. Felig, P. 1978. Four questions about protein diets. *N. Eng. J. Med.* 298: 1025–1026.

18. Frattali, V. P. 1979. Deaths associated with the liquid protein diet. FDA, By-lines No. 4.

19. Garn, S., *et al.* 1975. Does obesity have a genetic basis in man? *Ecol. Food Nutr.* 4: 57.

20. Genuth, S. M. 1976. Effect of high fat vs. high carbohydrate feeding on the development of obesity in weanling ob/ob mice. *Diabetologia* 12: 155–159.

21. Greenberg, I., *et al.* 1979. Obesity: facts, fads, and fantasies. *Compr. Ther.* 5: 68–76.

22. Grinker, J. 1978. Obesity and sweet taste. *Am. J. Clin. Nutr.* 31: 1078–1087.

23. Hegsted, M. 1974. Energy needs and utilization. *Nutr. Rev.* 32: 33–36.

24. Hoyt, C. S., *et al.* 1977. Low-carbohydrate diet and optic neuropathy. *Med. J. Austr.* 1: 65–66.

25. Huenemann, R. L., *et. al.* 1980. Cultural factors in the development, maintenance, and control of obesity. *Cardiovascular Reviews & Reports.* 1: 21–26.

26. Hultman, E. 1967. Adverse effects of high fat, low CHO diet on performance. American Heart Association Monograph. 15: 106.

27. Johnson, D., *et al.* 1977. Therapeutic fasting in morbid obesity: long-term follow-up. *Arch. Intern. Med.* 137: 1381–1382.

28. Johnson, D. D., *et al.* 1980. Reactive hypoglycemia. *JAMA* 243: 1151–1155.

29. Jowsey, J. 1976. Osteoporosis: its nature and the role of diet. *Postgrad. Med.* 60: 75–79.

30. Kannel, W., *et al.* 1967. Relation of adiposity to blood pressure and development of hypertension. Framingham study. *Ann. Intern. Med.* 67: 48–59.

31. Kempner, W., *et al.* 1975. Treatment of massive obesity

with rice/reduction diet program. *Arch. Intern. Med.* 135: 1575–1584.

32. Kennedy, D., *et al.* 1978. Protein diets. *FDA Drug Bulletin* January-February.

33. Lantigua, R. A., *et al.* 1980. Cardiac arrhythmias associated with a liquid protein diet for the treatment of obesity. *N. Eng. J. Med.* 303: 735–738.

34. Layrisse, M., *et al.* 1974. Measurement of the total daily dietary iron absorption by the extrinsic tag model. *Am. J. Clin. Nutr.* 27: 152–162.

35. MacGregor, G. A., *et al.* 1979. Is idiopathic edema idiopathic? *Lancet* I: 397–400.

36. Michiel, R. R., *et al.* 1978. Sudden death in a patient on a liquid protein diet. *N. Eng. J. Med.* 298: 1005–1007.

37. Moore, C. V. 1973. Iron. In *Modern Nutrition in Health and Disease*, ed. R. S. Goodhart and M. E. Shils, pp. 301–304. Philadelphia: Lea and Febiger.

38. Nash, D. T., *et al.* 1979. Progression of coronary atherosclerosis and dietary hyperlipidemia. *Circulation* 56: 363–365.

39. Nath, N., *et al.* 1967. Effect of aceto acetate and b-hydropybutyrate on vitamin B_{12} in rats. *Proc. Biol. & Med.* 124: 210–213.

40. National Research Council. 1980. *Recommended Dietary Allowances*, 9th ed.

41. *Nutr. Rev.* 1980. Urinary calculi and dietary protein. 38: 9–10.

42. Parfitt, M. D., *et al.* 1978. Metabolic bone disease after intestinal bypass for treatment of obesity. *Ann. Intern. Med.* 2: 193.

43. Rabinowitz, D. 1970. Some endocrine and metabolic aspects of obesity. *Ann. Rev. Med.* 21: 241–258.

44. Schwartz, R. S., *et al.* 1978. Increased adipose-tissue lipoprotein-lipase activity in moderately obese men after weight reduction. *Lancet* I: 1230–1231.

45. Siddons, R. C. 1974. The experimental production of vitamin B_{12} deficiency in the baboon (Papio Cynocephalus): a two-year study. *Brit. J. Nutr.* 32: 219–225.

46. Sikvakumar, B., *et al.* 1969. Effect of various high protein diets on vitamin B status in rats. *J. of Vitaminology* 15: 141–142.

47. Stamler, J. 1978. Lifestyles, major risk factors, proof and public policy. *Circulation* 58: 3–19.

48. Stunkard, A. J. 1977. Obesity and the social environment: current status, future prospects. New York Academy of Science. *Food and Nutrition in Health and Disease* 300: 298–320.

49. U.S. Dept. of Agriculture. 1980. *Nationwide Food Consumption Survey 1977–78.* Preliminary Report No. 2.

50. Van Itallie, T. B. 1980. "Morbid" obesity; a hazardous disorder that resists conservative treatment. *Am. J. Clin. Nutr.* 33: 358–363.

51. Van Itallie, T. B., *et al.* 1979. Appraisal of excess calories as a factor in the causation of disease. *Am. J. Clin. Nutr.* 32: 2648–2653.

52. Van Itallie, T. B., *et al.* 1977. Current concepts in nutrition. *N. Eng. J. Med.* 297: 1158–1161.

53. Watkin, D. M. 1977. Aging, nutrition and the continuum of health care. New York Academy of Science. *Food and Nutrition in Health and Disease* 300: 290–297.

54. Weltman, A., *et al.* 1980. Caloric restriction and/or mild exercise: effects on serum lipids and body composition. *Am. J. Clin. Nutr.* 33: 1002–1009.

55. Williams, M. H. 1976. *Nutritional Aspects of Human Physical and Athletic Performance,* pp. 44–75. Springfield: Charles C. Thomas.

56. Wooley, S. C., *et al.* 1980. The case against radical interventions. *Am. J. Clin. Nutr.* 33: 465–471.

57. Wynder, E. L. 1977. Nutritional Carcinogenesis. New York Academy of Science. *Food and Nutrition in Health and Disease* 300: 360–378.

Part II
Recipes

About the Recipes...

A caloric value is given for each recipe. That information plus the information in the Caloric Density Tables should provide most of the figures you'll want to refer to as you proceed on your diet. In addition, the values given below for a few common

Fruit	*Calories*
½ medium apple	44
½ small banana	40
½ cup grapes	35
½ eating orange	32
1 small peach	38
½ small pear	43
½ cup fresh pineapple	40
5 Damson plums	33
1½ Tbsp. raisins	39
1 medium tangerine	39
¼ of 5" canteloupe	41
1 cup pieces watermelon (¹/₁₆ of 16"x10" melon)	111
2"-wide wedge of 7"-long honeydew melon	49

Bread and Crackers

	Calories
1 slice whole-wheat bread	65
1 slice sourdough bread	74
1 triple Ry-Krisp cracker	25
1 Kavli Norwegian thin cracker	15
1 Ideal ultrathin flatbread	12
1 Hol-Grain rice cracker	12
1 Hol-Grain wheat cracker	7

Raw Vegetables	*Calories*
1 medium carrot	30
1 large celery stalk	7
1 medium cucumber	35
1 cup lettuce	9
5 medium radishes	4
1 medium tomato	27
1 cherry tomato	4

Cooked Vegetables

	Calories
1 cup broccoli	40
1 cup cauliflower	28
1 cup summer squash	29
1 cup baked winter squash	129
1 cup boiled winter squash	93
1 cup peas	109
1 cup corn	135
1 large baked potato (long-type)	173
1 medium boiled potato (round-type)	104

foods will help you make substitutions for foods on the menu plans when desired.

A FEW IMPORTANT POINTS

- Occasionally an ingredient is called for that is itself a preparation for which a recipe is given in our book and listed in the recipe index. These ingredients appear in the recipe in capital letters (e.g., *MOCK SOUR CREAM*).

- When the size of a fruit or vegetable is not indicated in the ingredient list, assume it to be medium size. One tomato, for instance, means one average-sized tomato.

- Although it is not specified in the recipes, all vegetables and fruits should be washed thoroughly before they are used. If they have been waxed, peel before using whenever possible. (Cucumbers and apples, for example, are often waxed.) Oranges are often colored with artificial coloring. When grated orange or lemon rind is called for, peel the fruit and grate the inside of the rind to avoid any wax or coloring on the outside.

- Stock (the liquid in which vegetables, chicken, or meat has been cooked) is called for in many soup and entrée recipes. Usually, water is given as an alternate, but stock is preferable because of the flavor it contributes. A group of stock recipes appears on pages 240–244. You may often substitute liquid left over from cooking vegetables with satisfactory results.

- Nonfat yogurt is another ingredient frequently listed. A recipe for preparing nonfat yogurt appears on page 356, if you are unable to find commercially prepared yogurt low enough in fat content (up to 1 percent fat by weight).

- A few recipes call for chili peppers to add zest to sauces or other preparations. Chili peppers range from mild to fiery hot. Choose peppers according to your tastes, then use them as desired—mincing finely for maximum spicing, or using them whole, then discarding them after the cooking period is over for a subtler taste. The seeds of chili peppers need to be removed before the peppers are chopped or minced, as they can be *very* hot. When you remove them, be sure to wash your hands afterwards. You can cause irritation to the skin of your face or your eyes by contact after touching the seeds.

- There are scattered reports in the literature that suggest possible problems associated with the use of black pepper. We have therefore tried to minimize its use in the recipes. When pepper is listed as an ingredient you may wish to omit it, or to use white pepper, which is apparently less irritating.

- Some higher-calorie recipes are included in this section for use after you have attained your optimum weight, or, if desired, in suitably small quantities before then. These recipes—mostly grain recipes or dessert recipes using grains—are readily identifiable by their higher caloric value per serving.

Salads

The first four salad recipes, designed especially for the menu plans, are good ways to vary your daily mixed green salad, whether or not you are following the plans.

RAW VEGETABLE SALAD No. 1

> 8 cups torn romaine lettuce leaves
> 1 cup bean sprouts
> 1 tomato, diced
> ½ cucumber, sliced
> ½ cup grated carrots
> ½ cup sliced cauliflower
> ½ cup chopped celery
> ½ cup chopped green pepper

Chill ingredients and combine, tossing gently.
Makes 4 servings
Calories per serving: 58

RAW VEGETABLE SALAD No. 2

> 4 cups torn butter lettuce leaves
> 4 cups torn romaine lettuce leaves
> 1 cup shredded red cabbage
> 1 cup bean sprouts
> 1 small cucumber, sliced
> 2 green onions, chopped
> 4 radishes, sliced
> ½ small carrot, thinly sliced
> 2 small tomatoes, quartered

Chill ingredients. Combine all the ingredients except the tomatoes, tossing gently. Arrange the quartered tomatoes over the salad.
Makes 4 servings
Calories per serving: 59

RAW VEGETABLE SALAD No. 3

4 cups torn butter lettuce leaves
4 cups torn romaine lettuce leaves
2 cups torn watercress
1 cup diced celery
½ cup sliced mushrooms
½ cup grated carrots
½ basket cherry tomatoes
¼ red onion, thinly sliced
1 green or red bell pepper, sliced in rings

Chill all ingredients and combine all except the bell pepper, tossing gently. Arrange pepper rings on top of salad.
Makes 4 servings
Calories per serving: 54

RAW VEGETABLE SALAD No. 4

6 cups torn romaine lettuce leaves
2 cups torn or sliced iceberg lettuce leaves
2 cups bean or alfalfa sprouts
½ small cucumber, sliced
3 stalks celery, sliced diagonally
4 radishes, sliced
1 cup water-packed artichoke hearts, drained and quartered
1 cup sliced cooked beets
Garnish: chopped chives or green onions

Chill all ingredients and combine all except the beets and chives, tossing gently. Transfer the salad to individual serving bowls. Garnish each salad with the beets and chives.

VARIATION: Add 4 hard-boiled egg whites, sliced, for additional garnish.
Makes 4 servings
Calories per serving: 66

CUCUMBER SUNOMONO SALAD

2 large cucumbers
1/3 cup white vinegar
4 teaspoons frozen apple juice concentrate
1 teaspoon soy sauce or tamari
2 slices fresh ginger, finely chopped or slivered

Cut cucumbers in half lengthwise and remove any large seeds.
Slice crosswise into very thin slices. Marinate in refrigerator in
mixture of vinegar, apple juice concentrate, soy sauce or tamari,
and ginger for one hour or longer. Serve chilled.
Makes 6 servings
Calories per serving: 22

CARROT DELIGHT

6 carrots, thinly sliced
2 apples, peeled and cut into chunks
1 tablespoon frozen apple juice concentrate
Juice of 1 lemon
1/2 teaspoon cinnamon

Mix all the ingredients and chill before serving.
Makes 6 servings
Calories per serving: 67

CAULIFLOWER SALAD

1 cauliflower, cut into flowerets
1 carrot, thinly sliced
1 green pepper, diced
½ cup lemon juice or juice of 1 lemon or ½ cup vin
2 cloves garlic, minced
½ bunch parsley, minced
3 green onions, thinly sliced

Place the cauliflower, carrot and green pepper in a stea
basket or a pot with a little water and steam covered f
minutes. Drain and cool, then transfer to a salad bowl.

Combine the lemon juice or vinegar, garlic, parsley, and g
onions and pour over the vegetables, tossing gently to distri
dressing. Chill and serve.

Makes 4 servings
Calories per serving: 90

CUCUMBER AND TOMATO SALAD

1 small cucumber
1 firm, ripe tomato
¼ cup red onion slices
4 canned artichoke hearts, water-packed (optional
½ cup water
½ cup rice vinegar or other mild vinegar
1 tablespoon frozen apple juice concentrate
1 tablespoon parsley
1½ teaspoons oregano
2 cloves garlic, minced

Peel the cucumber, slice in half lengthwise, and scoop out
seeds; slice in ¼-inch pieces. Cut the tomato in wedges and
the artichoke hearts. Prepare the marinade by mixing the o
ingredients. Pour over the vegetables and allow to sit at least
hour.

VARIATION: Add ½ cup water-packed tuna. Instead of tomato wedges, use as many scooped out large tomatoes as needed and stuff the salad inside.

Makes 2–3 servings
Calories per serving (⅓ recipe): 47

GREEN BEAN SALAD

> 2 pounds fresh green beans, cut into 1-inch or 2-inch
>   pieces
> Juice of 1 lemon
> 2 cloves garlic, finely minced
> ¼ bunch parsley, minced
> Pinch basil

Cook the green beans in a skillet in a small amount of water until just tender. Drain and cool. Combine the beans with remaining ingredients. Chill and serve.

Makes 4 servings
Calories per serving: 80

ORIENTAL SALAD BOWL

Dressing:
> 1 teaspoon unflavored gelatin
> 1 tablespoon cold water
> ⅓ cup boiling water
> ¼ cup lemon juice
> 2 tablespoons soy sauce or tamari
> 1 teaspoon frozen apple juice concentrate
> 1 teaspoon grated lemon rind
> ½ teaspoon garlic powder
> Powdered ginger to taste

Salad:

> 2 cups bean sprouts
> 2 tomatoes, diced
> 1 cucumber, thinly sliced
> 1 green pepper, minced
> ½ cup diced celery
> ¼ cup minced green onions
> ¼ cup chopped red radishes
> ¼ cup sliced canned water chestnuts

To prepare the dressing, sprinkle the gelatin over the cold water in a small bowl to soften. Add the boiling water and stir until the gelatin is dissolved. Place the gelatin mixture with the remaining dressing ingredients in a blender and blend to mix thoroughly. Use at room temperature.

Combine all the salad vegetables in a bowl. Pour dressing over the vegetables and toss gently until thoroughly mixed.

Makes 3–6 servings
Calories per serving (¼ recipe): 73

ORANGE, ONION, AND BUTTER LETTUCE SALAD

> 2 large heads butter lettuce
> 3 large oranges
> 1 small red onion
> ¾ cup finely chopped parsley
> 1 cup ORANGE VINAIGRETTE DRESSING
> ½ teaspoon celery seed

Chill all the ingredients. Tear the lettuce into bite-sized pieces in a suitable bowl. Carefully section the oranges, removing membranes. Halve each section of orange, removing any seeds. Slice onion in paper-thin rings. Toss all with *ORANGE VINAI-GRETTE DRESSING*, sprinkle on celery seed, and toss again.

Makes 6 servings
Calories per serving (including dressing): 72

SPINACH AND BUTTER LETTUCE SALAD

1 bunch spinach, stems removed
1 head butter lettuce, torn in bite-sized pieces
½ cup loosely crumbled hoop cheese or other uncreamed
  cottage cheese
½ cup chopped parsley
⅔ cup "CAESAR" DRESSING

Combine all the ingredients in a large salad bowl and toss with *"CAESAR" DRESSING* until salad is well coated.
Makes 6 servings
Calories per serving (including dressing): 38

GREEK SALAD

2 large, firm tomtoes
2 cucumbers
1 red bell pepper, cut in strips
1 small red onion, thinly sliced
2 cloves garlic, minced
½ cup rice vinegar or other mild vinegar
¼ cup red wine vinegar
2 teaspoons frozen apple juice concentrate
1 tablespoon minced fresh oregano or ½ tablespoon
  dried oregano
1 tablespoon minced fresh mint or ½ tablespoon dried
  mint
⅓ cup loosely crumbled hoop cheese or other uncreamed
  cottage cheese

Cut each tomato into 8 wedges. Peel the cucumbers, halve them lengthwise, scoop out seeds, and cut in ¼-inch slices. Place the tomatoes, cucumbers, red pepper, and onion in a large bowl.

Combine the garlic, vinegars, and apple juice concentrate in a saucepan. Heat just until steam appears; cool. Pour over the vegetables, add the minced herbs, and toss to coat well. Marinate the salad in the refrigerator until fully chilled. Just before serving, add the cheese and toss lightly.
Makes 4–6 servings
Calories per serving (⅙ recipe): 49

CONFETTI STRIP COLESLAW

¼ head each of red cabbage and green cabbage, core
1 red bell pepper, halved lengthwise
1 green bell pepper, halved lengthwise
2 stalks celery, halved crosswise
4 green onions, halved crosswise
2 carrots, halved crosswise
1 turnip or parsnip, peeled

Dressing:
 ½ cup rice vinegar or other mild vinegar
 ¼ cup frozen apple juice concentrate
 ¼ cup lemon juice
 1 teaspoon powdered ginger
 1 teaspoon dry mustard
 ¼ teaspoon garlic powder
 ½ teaspoon celery seed

Shred the red cabbage in long fine strips and place in a bowl
Shred all the other vegetables in long fine strips and place them
in a separate bowl. Add ice water to both bowls. (The red
cabbage is iced separately to avoid discoloring the other vegeta
bles.)

Mix in a blender all the dressing ingredients except the celery
seed. When the vegetables are well chilled, drain them thorough
ly and pat dry with a towel or spin dry in a lettuce spinner
Combine all vegetables in a large serving bowl. Just before
serving, stir the celery seed into the dressing and pour the
dressing over the shredded vegetables. Toss gently to distribute
dressing evenly.

Makes 10–12 servings
Calories per serving (¹⁄₁₀ recipe): 58

CREOLE JAMBALAYA SALAD

Marinade:

> ¾ cup rice vinegar or other mild vinegar
> ⅓ cup water
> 2 tablespoons frozen apple juice concentrate
> 1 tablespoon powdered horseradish
> 1 tablespoon onion powder
> 1 teaspoon garlic powder
> 1 teaspoon caraway seeds
> ⅛ teaspoon pepper

Salad:

> 1 cup thickly sliced mushrooms
> 2 cups canned water-packed artichoke hearts, drained
> 1 8-ounce can bamboo shoots, drained
> 1 cup diagonally cut celery
> 4 tomatoes, quartered
> 1 green pepper, cut in chunks
> ½ white onion, thinly sliced
> ½ cup diced green onions
> 4 cups torn romaine lettuce leaves
> 4 cups torn butter lettuce leaves
> Garnish: a few tiny cooked shrimp for each serving
>   (optional)
> *CREAMY CHEESE DRESSING* (optional)

Heat the marinade ingredients and mushrooms together; do not boil. Add the artichokes and bamboo shoots. Refrigerate several hours or overnight.

Before arranging the salad, make sure all prepared vegetables are well chilled. Line a large platter or individual plates with the lettuce, and attractively place marinated vegetables, drained, and other vegetables on top. Garnish with tiny cooked shrimp, if desired. The salad may be served with *CREAMY CHEESE DRESSING* and picante sauce or other hot sauce.

Makes approximately 4–6 servings

Calories per ¼ recipe (without shrimp or dressing): 105

COUNTRY CLUB SALAD

    2 heads romaine lettuce
    2 cups cut-up chicken pieces, white meat (cook 3–4
        chicken breasts with celery tops in water seasoned
        with a dash of white pepper, onion powder, and a
        bay leaf)
    3 cups cauliflower chunks, cooked tender-crisp
    3 cups broccoli flowerets, cooked tender-crisp
    2 cups zucchini chunks, cooked tender-crisp
    1 cup raw diced celery
    2 tomatoes, cut into wedges
    1¼ cups TANGY FRENCH DRESSING
    4 hard-boiled egg whites, sliced (discard yolks)
    Paprika

Chill all ingredients thoroughly before starting to combine them in salad. Tear the lettuce leaves into bite-sized pieces in a large bowl. In a separate bowl, gently toss the chicken, cooked vegetables, and celery with the *TANGY FRENCH DRESSING*. Place the mixture over the lettuce leaves. Garnish the salad with the tomato wedges and slices of egg white. Sprinkle with paprika. Serve with additional *TANGY FRENCH DRESSING* if desired.

VARIATION: Substitute 2 cups cooked potato cubes for 2 cups of any of the cooked vegetables.

Makes 4–6 servings

Calories per serving (¼ recipe, without additional dressing): 285

TUNA NOODLE SALAD

    2 7-ounce cans water-packed tuna, drained
    1 2-ounce jar pimientos, chopped
    5 stalks celery, chopped
    ½ cup chopped red onions
    ½ green pepper, chopped
    1 dill pickle, chopped
    3 hard-boiled egg whites, chopped (discard yolks)
    1 tablespoon lemon juice
    ¾ teaspoon curry powder
    ¼ teaspoon dill weed

⅛ teaspoon dry mustard
Dash pepper
1 cup MOCK SOUR CREAM
1 cup cooked whole-wheat noodles, rinsed

Break the tuna into small chunks. Add all the other ingredients except the *MOCK SOUR CREAM* and the noodles and mix together well. Add the *MOCK SOUR CREAM* and stir to blend thoroughly. Add the cooked noodles and mix in gently.
Makes 6 cups
Calories per cup: 159

SALADE NIÇOISE

The following recipes are all good individually, and when assembled to make Salade Niçoise they form a very attractive and colorful dish.

Tuna Salad:
    1 10-ounce package frozen French-style green beans
    1 7-ounce can water-packed tuna, drained
    ½ onion, chopped
    2 stalks celery, diced
    1 red apple, sliced unpeeled and tossed with lemon juice
    ½ of a 2-ounce jar of sliced pimientos, drained and chopped
    Vinaigrette dressing to taste (recipe below)

Cook the beans as directed on the package, drain, and cool. Mix with all the other ingredients and refrigerate.

Cauliflower Salad:
    ½ large head cauliflower, broken into flowerets
    1 tablespoon cider vinegar
    1½ teaspoons Spice Islands Salad Herbs
    ¼ teaspoon each garlic powder, dry mustard, and pepper
    1 stalk celery, chopped
    ½ onion, chopped
    ½ cup nonfat yogurt or MOCK SOUR CREAM

Steam the cauliflower until tender-crisp. While still warm, transfer it to a salad bowl and sprinkle the vinegar and spices over it. Then add the celery and onion. Spoon nonfat yogurt or *MOCK SOUR CREAM* over all, toss lightly, and refrigerate.

VARIATION: For potato salad, a more caloric dish, substitute 4 new potatoes, steamed, peeled, and diced, for the cauliflower.

Stuffed Eggs:
>   *4 hard-boiled eggs, cooled*
>   *½ cup cottage cheese (1 percent fat), rinsed and well drained*
>   *1 tablespoon vinaigrette dressing (recipe below)*
>   *Paprika*

Halve the eggs and discard the yolks. Mix the vinaigrette dressing into the cottage cheese. Fill the egg whites with the cheese-dressing mixture and sprinkle with paprika. Chill.

Vinaigrette Dressing:
>   *1⅓ cups rice vinegar or other mild vinegar*
>   *1 cup water*
>   *1 cup dried bell pepper flakes*
>   *1 teaspoon minced fresh or dried garlic*
>   *½ teaspoon Spice Islands Salad Herbs*
>   *1 tablespoon arrowroot*
>   *¼ cup frozen apple juice concentrate*

Place the vinegar, water, bell pepper flakes, garlic, and Salad Herbs in a saucepan and bring to a boil. Turn down the heat and simmer for 5 minutes. In a separate bowl, blend the arrowroot and apple juice concentrate to a smooth paste. Stir it into the simmering liquid and cook 5 minutes more, stirring frequently. Blend the dressing in a blender and refrigerate.

Trimmings:
>   *1 small head red leaf lettuce, washed and chilled*
>   *2–3 tomatoes, cut in wedges*
>   *Green onions*
>   *Vinaigrette dressing*

To assemble the Salade Niçoise, line a large round platter with the lettuce. Arrange the green onions like the spokes of a wheel, forming dividers. Put the cauliflower or potato salad in the center of the platter and fill the spaces between the green onion "spokes" with the tuna salad. Alternate stuffed eggs and tomato wedges around the outer edge of the platter. Serve with a cruet of vinaigrette dressing.

Makes 4 servings
Calories per serving (not including additional dressing): 235
Calories per tablespoon of additional dressing: 5

TROPICAL PINEAPPLE CHICKEN SALAD

  2 cups diced cooked white chicken meat
  1 cup cold cooked long-grain brown rice
  2 cups diced celery
  ½ cup diced fresh pineapple (or canned, unsweetened
      pineapple chunks)
  ½ cup grapes, halved
  1 carrot, chopped
  1 large red or green bell pepper, cut into strips

Dressing:
  1½ cups nonfat yogurt or MOCK SOUR CREAM
  ¼ cup frozen orange juice concentrate
  1½ teaspoons curry powder
  1 teaspoon ground coriander
  1 teaspoon poppy seed
  Juice of ½ lime
  Dash cayenne pepper

  Garnish: romaine or butter lettuce leaves

Place all the salad ingredients in a bowl. Mix together the dressing ingredients and pour over the salad. Toss gently until thoroughly mixed. Serve the salad on a bed of lettuce leaves.

If desired, the salad may be served in pineapple shells from which the fruit has been removed. Fill the shells with the salad mixture and garnish with lettuce leaves placed around the pineapple shells.

Makes 4 servings (approximately 7 cups salad)
Calories per serving: 290

YOGURT WITH CUCUMBER AND MINT

1 clove garlic
2 thin slices onion
1½ tablespoons finely minced parsley
2 cups nonfat yogurt
2 cups thinly sliced cucumbers
½ teaspoon minced fresh mint or ¼ teaspoon dried mint
Dash pepper

Mash the garlic and mix with the onions and parsley. Add the yogurt, cucumbers, mint, and pepper. Marinate a few hours.
Makes 4–6 servings
Calories per serving (¼ recipe): 69

ZESTY BEET MOLD

2 envelopes unflavored gelatin
2 cups water
1 16-ounce can shoestring beets, drained; reserve liquid
1 6-ounce can unsweetened pineapple juice
¼ cup frozen apple juice concentrate
2 tablespoons frozen grapefruit juice concentrate
2 tablespoons lemon juice
1 teaspoon powdered horseradish
⅛ teaspoon pepper
1 cup finely diced celery
1 tablespoon grated onion
Garnish: lettuce leaves

Place the gelatin in a mixing bowl. Add 1 cup of the water and mix well. In a saucepan, heat to a boil the remaining water, beet juice, and fruit juices. Pour the hot liquid over the gelatin mixture, stirring to dissolve it completely. Stir in the powdered horseradish and pepper. Pour the mixture into an appropriate mold and chill until partially thickened. Distribute the beets, celery and onion through the thickened gelatin. Refrigerate until firm. Unmold and garnish with lettuce leaves.

Makes approximately 6–10 servings
Calories per serving (⅛ recipe): 65

ANTIPASTO SALAD

Marinade:
>   ¾ *cup canned tomato juice*
>   ¼ *cup rice vinegar or other mild vinegar*
>   ⅛ *teaspoon cayenne pepper*

Salad:
>   ½ *cup cooked cut green beans*
>   ½ *cup diagonally sliced (½-inch cuts) celery*
>   ½ *cup sliced mushrooms*
>   3 *canned water-packed artichoke hearts, drained and halved*
>   ¼ *cup chopped red or green bell pepper*
>   ½ *cup canned sliced beets*
>   1 *pepperoncini (pepper in vinegar), whole*
>   ⅔ *teaspoon capers*

Combine the marinade ingredients. In a bowl, place all vegetables except the beets, pepperoncini, and capers. Pour the marinade over the vegetables, cover, and refrigerate for several hours, stirring occasionally. With a slotted spoon, remove the vegetables and arrange them on a lettuce-lined platter or bowl. Moisten the beets in the marinade. Remove the beets with the slotted spoon and arrange them with the other vegetables. Garnish with the pepperoncini and capers. Serve chilled.

Makes 2–3 servings
Calories per serving (⅓ recipe): 36

Salad Dressings

ITALIAN DRESSING

¼ cup lemon juice
¼ cup cider vinegar
¼ cup unsweetened apple juice (not concentrate)
½ teaspoon oregano
½ teaspoon dry mustard
½ teaspoon onion powder
½ teaspoon garlic powder
½ teaspoon paprika
⅛ teaspoon thyme
⅛ teaspoon rosemary

Combine all the ingredients in a blender and blend. Chill well.
Makes approximately ¾ cup
Calories per tablespoon: 6

TARRAGON DRESSING

½ cup red wine vinegar
½ cup water
2 teaspoons lemon juice
1 teaspoon frozen apple juice concentrate
1 teaspoon soy sauce or tamari
¼ teaspoon Dijon mustard
1½ teaspoons tarragon
½ teaspoon garlic powder
Dash cayenne pepper

Place all ingredients in a blender and blend well. Chill before serving.
Makes 1 cup
Calories per tablespoon: 3

WINE VINEGAR DRESSING

½ cup wine vinegar
1 cup water
2 teaspoons minced parsley
2 teaspoons capers
1 clove garlic, minced
½ teaspoon dry mustard
½ teaspoon basil
½ teaspoon oregano
¼ teaspoon rosemary (optional)

Combine the wine vinegar and water. Pour about ½ cup of the mixture in a blender and add the seasonings. Blend well. Add the rest of the diluted vinegar to the blender and blend again. Chill before serving.

Makes approximately 1½ cups
Calories per tablespoon: 1

SWEET AND SOUR VINEGAR DRESSING

¼ cup cider vinegar
¼ cup unsweetened apple juice (not concentrate)
1½ cups water
⅓ cup chopped onion
1 tablespoon chopped celery
1 clove garlic, minced
¼ teaspoon dry mustard
⅛ teaspoon paprika
Pinch cayenne pepper

Combine all the ingredients in a blender and blend. Chill before serving.

Makes approximately 2½ cups
Calories per tablespoon: 2

HERB VINEGAR DRESSING

1 cup wine vinegar
⅓ cup snipped fresh mint
¼ cup snipped fresh chives
¼ cup fresh dill or ½ teaspoon dried dill weed
1 clove garlic, finely chopped

Combine all the ingredients. For maximum flavor, refrigerate dressing for at least four days before serving. Strain to remove herbs. Chill before serving.

Makes approximately 1 cup
Calories per tablespoon: 2

ORANGE VINAIGRETTE DRESSING

1 cup rice vinegar or other mild vinegar
2–3 cloves garlic, minced or mashed
2 teaspoons frozen orange juice concentrate
1 teaspoon dry mustard
½ teaspoon white pepper

Place all the ingredients in a blender and blend for 10 seconds. Chill before serving.

Makes approximately 1 cup
Calories per tablespoon: 5

"CAESAR" DRESSING

⅓ cup rice vinegar or other mild vinegar
3 tablespoons water
1 tablespoon frozen apple juice concentrate
1 tablespoon capers, finely chopped
1 tablespoon grated Sapsago cheese, lightly oven-toasted
¼ teaspoon dill weed
⅛ teaspoon paprika
⅛ teaspoon dry mustard
1 clove garlic, minced

Combine all the ingredients and mix well. Chill before serving.

Makes approximately ⅔ cup
Calories per tablespoon: 5

SPICY TOMATO DRESSING

1 cup tomato juice
1 tablespoon frozen apple juice concentrate
1 tablespoon lemon juice
1 tablespoon chopped celery leaves
1 tablespoon chopped parsley
3 cloves garlic, chopped
¼ teaspoon powdered horseradish
Dash each basil and oregano

Place all the ingredients in a blender and blend at high speed for a few minutes. Chill before serving.

Makes approximately 1⅓ cups
Calories per tablespoon: 5

TANGY FRENCH DRESSING

2 cups rice vinegar or other mild vinegar
2 cups V-8 juice
1 cup tomato sauce
⅓ cup lemon juice
3 tablespoons frozen apple juice concentrate
3 tablespoons tomato paste
1 onion, cut in large pieces
½ green pepper, cut in large pieces
1 teaspoon celery seed
1 teaspoon dill weed
½ teaspoon paprika
⅛ teaspoon cayenne pepper
1 tablespoon arrowroot
1 teaspoon finely minced parsley

Combine all but the last 2 ingredients in a saucepan. Heat the mixture to boiling and simmer 5 minutes. Mix the arrowroot with 2 tablespoons water until smooth; stir into the simmering liquid to thicken. Cook, uncovered, 5 more minutes, stirring occasionally. Cool. Transfer the dressing to a blender and blend well. Add parsley and process at "stir." Chill thoroughly before serving.

Makes 6 cups
Calories per tablespoon: 5

CANTONESE DRESSING

> 2½ *cups tomato juice*
> 1⅔ *cups unsweetened pineapple juice*
> 2–3 *cloves garlic*
> ½ *teaspoon dry mustard*
> ¼ *teaspoon pepper*
> 2 *tablespoons diced canned pimientos*
> ¾ *teaspoon capers*

Blend the juices, garlic, and spices in a blender. Stir in the pimientos and capers. Chill before serving.

Makes approximately 4 cups
Calories per tablespoon: 6

SPICY FRUIT DRESSING

> 2 *teaspoons cornstarch*
> ½ *teaspoon paprika*
> ½ *teaspoon dry mustard*
> 1 *cup fresh orange juice*
> ¼ *cup tomato paste*
> ¼ *teaspoon Tabasco (hot pepper sauce)*

Combine the dry ingredients in a saucepan; stir in the orange juice. Bring to a boil over moderate heat, stirring constantly. Boil for 1 minute. Remove from heat and stir in the remaining ingredients. Chill and stir before serving.

Makes approximately 1¼ cups
Calories per tablespoon: 11

CREAMY CAULIFLOWER DRESSING

3⅔ cups chopped cauliflower
1⅔ cups water
¾ cup rice vinegar or other mild vinegar
2–3 cloves garlic, chopped
½ teaspoon dry mustard
¾ teaspoon basil

Cook the cauliflower in the water in a covered saucepan until tender. Transfer the cooked cauliflower and the cooking liquid to a blender. Add other ingredients, except the basil, and blend until the mixture is smooth. Add the basil. Chill before serving.

Makes 1 quart
Calories per tablespoon: 3

RUSSIAN DRESSING

4 cups chopped carrots
¾ cup liquid (broth from cooking the carrots, plus extra water if required)
1¼ cups rice vinegar or other mild vinegar
¼ cup lemon juice
½ cup tomato paste
½ cup chopped onions
1¼ teaspoons paprika

Place the carrots in a saucepan, add sufficient water to cover, and cook until tender. Drain the carrots, reserving the cooking liquid. In a blender, blend the carrots and the ¾ cup liquid with the other ingredients until smooth. Chill before serving.

Makes 1 quart
Calories per tablespoon: 6

CREAMY CHEESE DRESSING

> *1 cup nonfat buttermilk*
> *1/3 cup nonfat yogurt*
> *2 pepperoncinis (peppers in vinegar), stems and seeds removed*
> *2 tablespoons dried minced onion*
> *1 teaspoon garlic powder*
> *1 teaspoon basil*
> *2 cups crumbled hoop cheese or other uncreamed cottage cheese*

Place all the ingredients except the cheese in a blender. Begin blending, adding the cheese a little at a time until the mixture is smoothly blended. Chill before serving.

NOTE: A thinner consistency may be achieved by adding a little more buttermilk; a thicker one by adding a little more cheese.

Makes approximately 2½ cups
Calories per tablespoon: 11

CREAMY ARTICHOKE DRESSING

> *1 cup canned water-packed artichoke hearts, drained*
> *2/3 cup nonfat buttermilk*
> *1½ teaspoons vinegar, or more if desired*
> *1 teaspoon frozen apple juice concentrate*
> *1 tablespoon diced canned green chilies*
> *2 tablespoons chopped green onions (optional)*
> *½ teaspoon basil*
> *½ teaspoon onion powder*
> *1 cup crumbled hoop cheese or other uncreamed cottage cheese*

Place all the ingredients except the cheese in a blender. Begin blending, adding the cheese a little at a time until mixture is smoothly blended. Chill before serving.

NOTE: A thinner consistency may be achieved by adding a little more buttermilk; a thicker one by adding a little more cheese.

Makes approximately 2½ cups
Calories per tablespoon: 6

BUTTERMILK DRESSING

3¼ cups nonfat buttermilk
2½ tablespoons frozen apple juice concentrate
2 tablespoons lemon juice
1 tablespoon dried minced onion
1 teaspoon dill weed
¼–½ teaspoon pepper
¼–½ teaspoon allspice

Blend all the ingredients in a blender. Chill before serving.
Makes approximately 1 quart
Calories per tablespoon: 7

BUTTERMILK-MUSTARD DRESSING

3 cups nonfat buttermilk
1 cup prepared mustard
2 tablespoons frozen apple juice concentrate

Mix all the ingredients in a blender. Chill before serving.
Makes 4 cups
Calories per tablespoon: 9

THOUSAND ISLAND DRESSING

1 cup nonfat yogurt
¼ cup tomato paste
1 teaspoon prepared mustard
½ teaspoon powdered horseradish
½ teaspoon onion powder
1/16 teaspoon pepper
1 hard-boiled egg white, diced (discard yolk)
3 tablespoons chopped dill pickle

Combine the yogurt, tomato paste, mustard, horseradish, onion powder, and pepper, mixing thoroughly. Stir in the diced egg white and pickle. Chill before serving.
Makes 1½ cups
Calories per tablespoon: 8

YOGURT-CHEESE DRESSING

1 cup nonfat yogurt
¼ cup cider vinegar
2 tablespoons frozen apple juice concentrate
2 tablespoons grated Sapsago cheese
1 teaspoon dried parsley
¼ teaspoon garlic powder
¼ teaspoon paprika

Combine all the ingredients and mix until well blended. Chill well. Stir before serving.

Makes approximately 1⅔ cups
Calories per tablespoon: 8

Soups and Stocks

TOMATO BOUILLON

4 tomatoes
5⅓ cups tomato juice
½ chili pepper, chopped
2 tablespoons chopped parsley
¼ teaspoon minced garlic
⅛ teaspoon oregano
⅛ teaspoon dill seed
⅛ teaspoon curry powder
⅛ teaspoon ground cloves
¼ bay leaf

Purée the tomatoes in a blender. Place the puréed tomatoes and all the other ingredients in a large pot. Bring to a boil, then turn down the heat and simmer, covered, for about an hour.

VARIATIONS: This flavorful basic soup can be combined with other ingredients or soups with good results. For *CREAM OF TOMATO SOUP:* Omit the chili pepper, if desired. Combine 1 cup evaporated skimmed milk with 3 cups *TOMATO BOUILLON.* Cook and stir over low heat until the mixture simmers. For *TOMATO-WATERCRESS SOUP:* Combine 1 cup *WATERCRESS AND WATER CHESTNUT SOUP* with ¾ cup *TOMATO BOUILLON.* Serve hot.

Makes 7½ cups
Calories per cup: 48

TOMATO-OKRA SOUP

1 cup chopped fresh or frozen okra
1²/₃ cups diced tomatoes
³/₄ cup chopped carrots
³/₄ cup chopped celery
³/₄ cup chopped onions
½ cup tomato paste
5³/₄ cups water
³/₄ teaspoon basil
³/₄ teaspoon garlic powder
³/₄ teaspoon onion powder
½ teaspoon Italian seasoning

Combine the vegetables, tomato paste, and water in a large pot. Bring to a boil, lower heat, and simmer, covered, until the vegetables are tender. Add the seasonings, mix well, and simmer for a few more minutes.
Makes 8½ cups
Calories per cup: 39

CHINESE TOMATO-VEGETABLE SOUP

4 cups tomato juice
½ cup canned green chili salsa
6 cups chopped bok choy
*4 cups chopped broccoli (peeled stems and heads of
    stalks)*
1 cup chopped onions
2 teaspoons garlic powder
½ teaspoon onion powder
½ teaspoon powdered ginger
Dash chili powder
Dash curry powder
3 cups bean sprouts

Bring 2 cups of water to a boil in a large pot. Add the tomato juice and the green chili salsa. When the mixture returns to a boil, add the bok choy, broccoli, onions, and spices. Return to a boil, lower heat, and simmer, covered, for 10–15 minutes. Add the bean sprouts and continue to simmer, covered, for another 10 minutes.

Makes approximately 10 cups
Calories per cup: 63

GAZPACHO

> 2 cups chopped tomatoes
> 1 cup chopped zucchini
> ¾ cup chopped celery
> 4 cups tomato juice
> 1 cup peeled and chopped cucumber
> ½ cup chopped green onions
> ¼ cup chopped green pepper
> 1 clove garlic, minced
> 1 cup canned green chili salsa
> ¼ teaspoon Tabasco (hot pepper sauce)
> Lime juice to taste
> Garnish: lime slices

Combine chopped tomatoes, zucchini, and celery in a mixing bowl and mix together. Transfer one-third of this mixture to a blender, add some of the tomato juice, and purée. Pour the puréed vegetables back into the bowl and mix in the remaining ingredients. Chill. Serve garnished with lime slices.

Makes approximately 8 cups
Calories per cup: 53

FRESH-BEET BORSCHT

> 6 beets, washed thoroughly
> 1 onion, sliced
> 4 cloves garlic, finely chopped
> 1 cucumber, thinly sliced
> Juice of 1½–2 lemons
> 1–2 tablespoons frozen apple juice concentrate
> ⅛–¼ teaspoon cinnamon

Place the beets in a saucepan with 4 cups of water. Bring to a boil, turn down the heat, cover, and simmer for 30 minutes. Remove the beets and rinse in cold water, then peel the beets and slice thinly or chop into ¼″ pieces. Empty the beet water from the pot. Return the beets to the pot with all the remaining ingredients, and add 8 cups of water. Bring to a boil; cover and simmer for 20 minutes. Chill and serve.

Makes approximately 10 cups
Calories per cup: 26

CABBAGE SOUP

> *5 cups shredded green cabbage (about 1 pound of cabbage)*
> *1 carrot, sliced*
> *1 zucchini, sliced*
> *1 large tomato, coarsely diced*
> *½ green pepper, sliced in rings*
> *1 onion, sliced*
> *2 cloves garlic, finely chopped*
> *2 tablespoons tomato paste*
> *1 tablespoon frozen apple juice concentrate*
> *Juice of ½ lemon*
> *¼ teaspoon basil*
> *¼ teaspoon oregano*
> *Dash cayenne pepper*

Place all the ingredients in a large soup pot with 8 cups of water and bring to a boil. Reduce the heat, cover, and simmer for 30 minutes. Add 4 more cups of water, cover, and simmer for an additional 20 minutes.

Makes approximately 14 cups
Calories per cup: 25

PARSNIP-CARROT SOUP

3 cups water
2 cups defatted stock of choice (see recipes for stocks)
2½ cups coarsely chopped onions
2 cups chopped parsnips
1½ cups chopped carrots
1½ cups coarsely chopped green pepper
1 cup tomato sauce
1 tablespoon soy sauce or tamari
1 tablespoon garlic powder
⅛ teaspoon cayenne pepper
¼ teaspoon celery seed
2 tablespoons chopped chives, fresh or freeze-dried

Place the water and stock in a large pot. Add the onions, parsnips, carrots, and green pepper, and bring to a boil. Turn down the heat and stir in the tomato sauce, soy sauce or tamari, garlic powder, and cayenne pepper. Simmer, covered, until the vegetables are tender. Remove from the heat and purée in a blender in several batches (fill the blender half full for each batch). Return the purée to the pot and reheat. Add celery seed. Garnish with chives.

Makes 7 cups
Calories per cup: 87

ZUCCHINI SOUP

¾ cup water
1½ large onions, sliced
3 pounds zucchini, sliced
1 large green pepper, sliced
1½ cloves garlic, minced
¼ teaspoon pepper
½ cup lightly packed parsley sprigs

In a large pot, add about ¼ cup of the water and the sliced onions. Bring to a boil, then turn down the heat. Cook until soft, stirring often. Add the rest of the water, squash, green pepper, garlic, and pepper. Cover and cook until all are soft, stirring often. Remove from heat and add the parsley. Transfer soup to a blender and blend until smooth. (This is a thick soup, like a thick split pea soup. If desired, it can be thinned by adding liquid left over from vegetable cooking.) Heat and serve.

VARIATION: Substitute crookneck squash for half of the zucchini and purée only half the vegetables, leaving the rest sliced. Add ⅓ cup canned chili salsa, ½ teaspoon basil, ½ teaspoon garlic powder, and ¾ teaspoon curry powder.

Makes approximately 8 cups
Calories per cup: 51

FRENCH ONION SOUP

> *6 onions, sliced*
> *6 cloves garlic, finely chopped*
> *1 green pepper, thinly sliced*
> *1 carrot, thinly sliced*
> *6 cups defatted beef or chicken stock (see recipes for stock) or water*
> *1 tablespoon cornstarch*
> *Soy sauce or tamari to taste (optional)*
> *2 slices acceptable whole-wheat bread*
> *1 clove garlic, finely chopped*
> *1 tablespoon grated Sapsago cheese*

Stir-fry the onions and garlic in a dry nonstick skillet, using the natural juices from the vegetables for liquid. Cook until the onions and garlic are very brown but not charred. Place the onions, garlic, green pepper, and carrot in a pot; add the stock or water. Bring to a boil, then turn down the heat and simmer, covered, for 45 minutes. In a small bowl, mix the cornstarch with ½ cup cold water, and stir into the simmering soup. If desired, add a small amount of soy sauce or tamari.

Cut each slice of bread into 4 squares. Coat the squares with the finely chopped garlic and the Sapsago cheese. Oven-toast the seasoned bread on a nonstick baking tin at 325° for 15 minutes. Just before serving, place one bread square in each soup bowl.

Makes approximately 7 cups
Calories per cup: 73

WHITE BEAN SOUP

1¼ cups uncooked Navy beans or Great Northern beans
11 cups defatted stock of choice (see recipes for stocks)
*   and water in any desired proportion; the more stock*
*   used, the stronger the flavor of the soup*
2 parsley sprigs
1 bay leaf
1 cup chopped onions
1 cup chopped celery
½ cup sliced mushrooms
2 large shallots, minced
2 cloves garlic, minced, then "smashed"
½ cup chopped leeks
1½ teaspoons soy sauce or tamari
½ teaspoon garlic powder
½ teaspoon onion powder
½ teaspoon ground thyme
¼ teaspoon basil
Dash dry mustard
Dash pepper
Garnish: ½ cup snipped chives or minced green onions

Rinse beans and cover with water in a large pot. Bring to a boil, then pour off water. Cover with 8 cups of the liquid, add the parsley sprigs and bay leaf. Bring to a boil, lower heat, cover, and simmer beans until they are three-quarters done. Remove the parsley sprigs and bay leaf. Purée half the beans with the remaining liquid and return to the pot. Add the remaining ingredients except the chives or green onions. Simmer until tender. Just before serving, float the chives or green onions in the soup.

Makes approximately 8 cups
Calories per cup: 132

SNOW PEA SOUP

5 cups defatted chicken or vegetable stock (see recipes
    for stocks)
2 cups snow peas (Chinese pea pods), fresh or frozen
1/2 cup thinly sliced mushrooms
1/4 cup chopped green onions
1/4 cup sliced canned water chestnuts
1/4 cup thinly sliced carrot
1 tablespoon minced fresh ginger or to taste
1 teaspoon soy sauce or tamari
1/8 teaspoon anise
2 egg whites lightly beaten with a fork

Bring the stock to a boil in a large pot. Add the vegetables and
seasonings. When the soup returns to a boil, lower heat, and
simmer, covered, until the vegetables are tender. Bring the soup
to a gentle boil and add the egg whites drop by drop.
Makes approximately 5 cups
Calories per cup: 33

TOFU AND SNOW PEA SOUP

4 cups defatted chicken stock (see recipes for stocks)
1 4-ounce cake tofu, cubed
1/4 cup thinly sliced mushrooms
1/4 cup minced green onions
1/4 cup finely chopped carrot
1 large clove garlic, minced
1 teaspoon minced fresh ginger
Pinch anise
Soy sauce or tamari to taste (optional)
1 cup fresh snow peas (Chinese pea pods)

Place all the ingredients except the snow peas in a large pot.
Bring to a boil, lower heat, and simmer, covered, for 20 minutes
or until the vegetables are tender. Add the snow peas and cook
until just tender. Garnish with additional chopped green onions,
if desired.
Makes 4 cups
Calories per cup: approximately 40

WATERCRESS AND WATER CHESTNUT SOUP

> 4 cups defatted chicken or vegetable stock (see recipes
>   for stocks)
> 2 bunches watercress, cut in short lengths (about 5
>   cups)
> 12 canned water chestnuts, halved
> 1 2-ounce jar pimientos, chopped
> 1 clove garlic, minced
> ½ teaspoon powdered ginger, or more to taste
> Garnish: 1 green onion, sliced

Heat the stock in a saucepan. Add the watercress, water
chestnuts, pimientos, garlic, and ginger. Bring to a boil, lower
heat, and simmer, covered, for 20 minutes. Garnish with green
onion before serving.

Makes approximately 5 cups
Calories per cup: 25

CREAM OF CAULIFLOWER SOUP

> 6 cups coarsely chopped cauliflower
> 1½ cups chopped onions
> ¼ cup chopped carrots
> ⅛ cup chopped green pepper
> 2 cloves garlic, minced
> 1 bay leaf
> ⅛ teaspoon dry mustard
> ⅛ teaspoon curry powder
> ½ cup nonfat dry milk

Place the cauliflower in a pot with 2 cups of water. Bring to a
boil, turn down heat, cover, and cook until tender. Transfer the
cauliflower and cooking liquid to a blender and purée. Return
puréed cauliflower to the pot and add the remaining ingredients,
except the nonfat dry milk. In a separate bowl, mix the nonfat
dry milk with a small amount of water, and then add to the soup.
Bring to a boil, lower heat to moderate, cover, and cook, stirring
occasionally, until all the vegetables are tender. Remove the bay

leaf. Purée half of the soup in a blender; return purée to the pot. Serve hot.

Makes approximately 4 cups
Calories per cup: 107

CREAM OF MUSHROOM SOUP

> 2 cups defatted stock of choice (see recipes for stocks)
> 1 cup sliced fresh mushrooms
> ½ cup finely minced onions
> 1 small carrot, finely chopped
> 1 medium tomato, chopped
> 1 tablespoon minced green pepper
> 1 teaspoon Dijon mustard
> ¼ teaspoon onion powder
> Garlic powder to taste
> Pinch poultry seasoning
> ½ cup nonfat dry milk
> 1 tablespoon cornstarch
> ½ cup nonfat fluid milk or nonfat yogurt
> Garnish: 2 tablespoons finely chopped parsley; lemon
>   slices

Place the stock and all the vegetables in a large saucepan. Bring to a boil, lower heat, and simmer, covered, until the vegetables are tender. Remove the mushrooms, which will float on the top, and purée them in a blender. Return the mushroom purée to the soup. Add the mustard and seasonings, cover, and continue simmering.

In a separate bowl, combine the dry milk and cornstarch. Add the fluid milk or yogurt and mix well. Stir the cornstarch-milk mixture into the soup and simmer for 5 minutes longer. Do not boil, as the soup will curdle. Garnish each serving with parsley and a lemon slice.

Makes approximately 3 cups
Calories per cup: 107

BROCCOLI BISQUE

1 10-ounce package frozen chopped broccoli
1 small onion, sliced
1 teaspoon ground basil
½ teaspoon garlic powder
Pinch ground cloves
Pinch pepper
1 tablespoon sherry
2 cups nonfat milk
1 tablespoon cornstarch
1 teaspoon lemon juice
Garnish: MOCK SOUR CREAM, dill weed

Place the broccoli and onion in a saucepan with ½ cup water. Bring to a boil, then cover the pan, turn down the heat, and cook until the broccoli is very soft. Transfer the broccoli, onion, and cooking liquid to a blender and purée; then return the purée to the saucepan. Add the seasonings and sherry and gently begin to reheat the mixture.

In a separate bowl, combine the nonfat milk and cornstarch to a smooth mixture; stir into the heating broccoli mixture. Continue heating, stirring constantly, until the bisque has thickened slightly. Add the lemon juice and serve at once.

Garnish with a dollop of *MOCK SOUR CREAM* and a sprinkling of dill weed.

Makes approximately 3½ cups
Calories per cup (not including garnish): 91

CARROT BISQUE

1½ tablespoons tomato paste
2¾ cups defatted chicken stock (see recipes for stocks)
5 cups thinly sliced carrots
½ cup chopped onions
½ cup chopped celery
¼ teaspoon curry powder or more to taste
Cayenne pepper to taste
2 cups nonfat milk or more as required
1 tablespoon cornstarch
Garnish: finely chopped parsley, dill weed

Combine the tomato paste and 1 cup of the chicken stock in a nonstick skillet. Add the carrots, onions, and celery and sauté until the liquid has disappeared. Transfer the vegetables to a 3-quart heavy-bottomed saucepan and add the remaining chicken stock, curry powder, and cayenne pepper. Bring to a boil, reduce the heat, and simmer, covered, until the carrots are tender. Remove from heat and cool for 20 minutes.

In a blender, purée the carrot mixture 2 cups at a time. Return the purée to the saucepan and bring to a simmer once again. Add 1½ cups milk to the simmering carrots and stir until the soup has again come to a simmer. Mix the remaining ½ cup milk with the cornstarch, blending well. Add the cornstarch-milk mixture to the soup; stir constantly until the soup thickens slightly. (If a thinner soup is desired, add more milk.) Serve in heated bowls and garnish with parsley and dill weed.

Makes approximately 6 cups
Calories per cup: 76

FISH CHOWDER

> 1½ cups chopped leeks
> 1¼ cups chopped onions
> ¾ cup chopped celery
> 1 clove garlic, finely minced
> ¾ cup chopped carrots
> 1 28-ounce can Italian-style tomatoes, chopped, with juice
> 1 8-ounce can tomato sauce
> 2 tablespoons chopped parsley
> 2 bay leaves
> ¾ teaspoon thyme
> Pepper to taste
> 2 cups water
> ¾ cup sherry
> Juice of 1 lemon
> 2 pounds fish fillets, cut into 1½-inch chunks (sea bass, red snapper, halibut, or other firm-fleshed, low-fat fish)
> 4 cups cooked, peeled, and diced potatoes
> 3 tablespoons cornstarch

Sauté the leeks, onions, celery, and garlic in about ½ cup of water in a large pot. Cook until the vegetables are tender and slightly yellowed. Add the remaining ingredients except the potatoes and cornstarch. Bring to a boil, then cover, turn down the heat, and simmer for about 15 minutes, or until the fish is cooked and the flavors are well blended. Stir in the potatoes. Make a smooth paste of the cornstarch and 3 tablespoons cold water. Stir the cornstarch mixture into the simmering chowder and cook for a few more minutes until thickened.

Makes approximately 14 cups
Calories per cup: approximately 144

CHICKEN AND OKRA GUMBO

Chicken Stock:
> 1 large whole fryer
> 12 cups water
> Vegetable scraps (onion and garlic, celery leaves, green pepper tops, etc.), well washed
> ¾ teaspoon poultry seasoning
> ⅛ teaspoon pepper

Gumbo:
> 2 28-ounce cans whole tomatoes, undrained
> 2 medium onions, chopped
> 1 green pepper, chopped
> 2 cloves garlic, finely minced or pressed
> ½ cup chopped green onion bottoms
> ⅓ cup whole-wheat pastry flour
> Defatted chicken stock (from first step)
> 2 tablespoons soy sauce or tamari
> 1 tablespoon gumbo filé
> 1½ teaspoons ground celery seed
> ½ teaspoon basil
> ½ teaspoon Tabasco (hot pepper sauce)
> Pinch cayenne pepper
> 3 cups sliced okra
> 2 cups diced white chicken meat (from first step)
> Garnish: 1 cup chopped green onion tops, ½ cup finely chopped parsley

Chicken Stock: A day in advance, skin the chicken and place it in a large pot with the water, vegetable scraps, and seasonings. Bring to a boil, then turn down the heat and simmer partially covered until the chicken is tender. Remove the chicken and cool. Bone the chicken and dice (cutting across the grain) enough white meat to make 2 cups. Refrigerate. Strain the stock and refrigerate overnight, or until the fat has congealed. (The stock may be placed in the freezer to hasten the process.) Remove congealed fat before using the stock in the gumbo.

Gumbo: Quarter the tomatoes. Place the tomatoes, tomato liquid, onions, green pepper, garlic, and green onion bottoms in a skillet. Bring to a boil, cover, turn down the heat and simmer for about 10 minutes, stirring occasionally. Remove from the heat and set aside. Brown the flour in a nonstick skillet over moderate heat, stirring constantly until flour is browned but not too dark. Make a paste of the flour with ½ cup of the chicken stock.

Bring the remaining chicken stock to a boil in a large pot; reduce the heat and simmer. Slowly add the flour paste, stirring to blend well. Add the seasonings and the cooked vegetables. Cook slowly for 1 hour partially covered, stirring occasionally. Sauté the okra in a skillet with a little water or broth from the cooking pot; cook until somewhat dry and less slick in texture. Add the okra and the diced chicken to the soup pot; cook for 30 minutes longer.

Garnish with chopped green onion tops and parsley and serve in bowls.

Makes approximately 4 quarts (8–10 servings)
Calories per serving (⅛ recipe): 160

STOCKS

The following stocks are useful for many of the recipes in this book. Some recipes specify which stock to use; other recipes give you a choice, and in these cases, use whichever stock appeals to you. Keep in mind also that leftover liquid from cooking vegetables can often be substituted for vegetable stock.

The beef and chicken stocks should be defatted before using them in recipes. To defat stock, chill the stock liquid in the refrigerator overnight or until the fat has completely congealed at the top (using the freezer will accelerate this process). Carefully remove as much of the congealed fat as you can, then if necessary strain the stock through several layers of cheesecloth to remove any remaining fat particles.

No caloric values are given for the stock recipes, since the calories are negligible if all the fat has been removed.

Stocks can be frozen for later use in premeasured amounts in small plastic containers or zip-lock baggies.

CHICKEN STOCK

>   *16 cups water*
>   *1½–2 pounds chicken, or equivalent inexpensive chick-*
>   *en parts; if you have a butcher bone chicken breasts*
>   *for some of the other recipes, take the bones and*
>   *attached meat scraps, which are very good in mak-*
>   *ing stock*
>   *4 stalks celery, cut in large pieces*
>   *2 carrots, cut in large pieces*
>   *1–2 onions, quartered*
>   *2 cloves garlic, pressed or crushed*
>   *1 bay leaf*
>   *Sprig parsley*
>   *Dash pepper*
>   *2 cups well-washed vegetable scraps (celery tops and*
>   *bottoms, onion and garlic skins, bell pepper bot-*
>   *toms, etc.) (optional)*

Place all the ingredients in a large pot. Bring to a boil, turn down the heat, and simmer, partially covered, for 1½ to 2½ hours (the longer the stock cooks, the more flavorful it will be.) Strain the stock to remove the chicken, vegetables, and whole spices. Defat the stock, following the directions given on pages 240–41.

Makes approximately 2 quarts

BEEF STOCK No. 1

> *2 pounds packaged beef shanks*
> *4 pounds veal and/or beef knuckle bones, cracked*
> *6 large carrots, cut into 1-inch rounds*
> *2 large leeks, cut into 1-inch lengths*
> *2 stalks celery with leaves, cut into 1-inch lengths*
> *1 large onion, coarsely chopped*
> *1 cup chopped parsley*
> *2 whole cloves*
> *3 large bay leaves*
> *1 tablespoon thyme*
> *1 tablespoon whole peppercorns*
> *2 large cloves garlic*
> *3 quarts boiling water.*

Combine all the ingredients except water in a large heavy casserole or roasting pan and place in a 425° oven. Brown slowly, stirring occasionally. When the meat, bones, and vegetables are nicely browned, add the boiling water. Bring to a boil in the oven, skimming off any foam that may appear during the first part of the boil. Lower the oven temperature to 300° and simmer, covered, for 3 hours. Strain the stock to remove the meat bones, vegetables, and whole spices. Defat the stock, following the directions on pages 240–41.

Makes approximately 6 cups

BEEF STOCK No. 2

> *5 pounds beef bones*
> *1 clove garlic*
> *1 bay leaf*
> *¼ teaspoon each thyme, tarragon, dill weed, oregano, and basil*

Place all the ingredients in a large pot with 12 cups of water. Bring to a boil, reduce the heat, and simmer, partially covered, for 2 hours. Strain the stock to remove the meat bones and whole spices. Defat the stock, following the directions given on pages 240–41.

Makes approximately 6 cups

VEGETABLE STOCK No. 1

Use this stock when a delicate flavor and color are suitable, as in white sauces and most cream soups.

> 4 stalks celery, cut in half
> 2 large onions, quartered
> 3 leeks, cut in half
> 2 carrots, cut in large chunks
> Well-washed vegetable scraps (onion skins, celery tops, bell pepper tops, etc.)
> 2 parsley sprigs
> About 10 cloves garlic
> 1 bay leaf
> 3 quarts water

Place all the ingredients in a large pot. Bring to a boil, then turn down heat and simmer, covered, for an hour or more. Strain the stock to remove the vegetables and whole spices.

Makes approximately 3 quarts

VEGETABLE STOCK No. 2

This vegetable stock is heartier than the preceding one, and is appropriate for soups, stews, and entrées, especially those that contain tomatoes and tomato products.

> 3 stalks celery with leaves
> 2 carrots
> ½ bunch broccoli
> ¼ head cauliflower
> 2 small zucchini
> 2 cups green beans
> ¼ pound mushrooms
> ½ bunch green onions, coarsely chopped
> ¼ bunch parsley
> ½ bunch cilantro (optional)
> 3 cloves garlic
> 1 teaspoon coarsely minced ginger
> 1 tablespoon basil

Cut or break up the celery, carrots, broccoli, cauliflower, and zucchini into large pieces. Place all the ingredients in a large pot with 12 cups of water. Bring to a boil, then cover, turn down the heat, and simmer for about an hour. Strain the stock to remove the vegetables and whole spices.

NOTE: Some of the cooked vegetables can be used as snacks or as vegetable dishes at a meal.

Makes approximately 11 cups

Poultry / Fish / Meat
Entrées

STUFFED BREAST OF CHICKEN
WITH LEMON-WINE SAUCE

6 7–8 ounce chicken breast halves, skinned and boned
  (dressed weight, about 4 ounces each)
Approximately 2 cups coarsely chopped assorted vege-
  tables (carrots, cauliflower, turnips, zucchini)
Dash pepper
Dash oregano
Dash thyme
Dash ground rosemary

Lemon-Wine Sauce:
  2 teaspoons nonfat dry milk
  2 cups nonfat fluid milk
  2 cups defatted chicken or vegetable stock (see recipes
    for stocks)
  ¼ teaspoon garlic powder
  ⅛ teaspoon white pepper
  ⅛ teaspoon nutmeg
  Cayenne pepper to taste
  2 tablespoons cornstarch
  2–3 tablespoons white wine
  2 tablespoons lemon juice

Garnish:
  ½ cup chopped mushrooms, lightly sautéed in 2 table-
    spoons stock
  Capers
  18 thin lemon slices
  6 thin slices canned pimiento
  Parsley, finely chopped

Pound the chicken breasts flat and trim the ends. Place the vegetables in a steamer basket or pot and lightly steam for a few minutes. Drain and dice the vegetables. Place about ¼ cup of the diced vegetables in the center of each chicken breast and roll up. Set aside while preparing sauce.

Lemon-Wine Sauce: Stir the nonfat dry milk into the fluid milk to dissolve. Add the stock, garlic powder, white pepper, nutmeg, and cayenne pepper. Heat the mixture in a saucepan almost to a boil, then turn down the heat so it simmers. Make a paste of cornstarch and a little water and stir into the simmering liquid. Simmer, stirring constantly, until thickened. Add the white wine. Remove from the heat and add the lemon juice. (Makes 4 cups)

Spread ⅓ cup of the Lemon-Wine Sauce on the bottom of a casserole dish and place the rolled chicken breasts seam-side-down in the sauce. Top each chicken breast with a little sauce.
Cover the casserole and bake at 450° for 15 minutes. Remove from oven and spread a little more sauce over each chicken breast. Garnish as follows: sprinkle cooked mushrooms over each breast and attractively arrange on each 3–4 capers, 3 lemon slices, 1 slice pimiento, and some parsley. Return to the oven and bake, uncovered, for another 20–25 minutes. Serve with additional Lemon-Wine Sauce.

Makes 6 servings
Calories per serving (with additional sauce): 193

CHICKEN BREASTS AUX CHAMPIGNONS

> 1 cup fine whole-wheat breadcrumbs (from acceptable
>   bread)
> 4 7–8-ounce chicken breast halves, skinned and boned
>   (dressed weight, about 4 ounces each)
> ½ cup evaporated skimmed milk
> 2 cups sliced fresh mushrooms
> 2 tablespoons diced shallots
> ½ cup dry white wine
> 1 teaspoon lemon juice
> ⅛ teaspoon thyme
> ⅛ teaspoon marjoram
> MUSHROOM CREAM SAUCE

Prepare the breadcrumbs by processing bread in a food processor or blender. Pound the chicken breasts flat with a meat mallet. Dip each breast in the milk and then in the breadcrumbs, covering well. Roll up each breast and arrange seam-side-down in a nonstick baking pan, cover, and bake at 350° for 25 minutes.

Meanwhile, sauté the mushrooms and shallots in the wine and lemon juice, stirring in the seasonings as the vegetables cook. Uncover the chicken and spoon some of the sautéed vegetables over each chicken breast. Bake uncovered 10 minutes longer, or until the chicken is tender and brown.

Just before serving, ladle *MUSHROOM CREAM SAUCE* over each chicken breast.

Makes 4 servings
Calories per serving (without sauce): 210

MALAYSIAN CHICKEN

> 6 7–8 ounce chicken breast halves, skinned
> 1 cup defatted chicken or vegetable stock (see recipes for stocks)
> 1 cup tomato sauce
> ½ cup red wine vinegar
> 2 tablespoons red burgundy wine
> 2 tablespoons frozen apple juice concentrate
> 2 teaspoons soy sauce or tamari
> Juice of 1 lemon
> 2 cloves garlic
> 2 teaspoons each curry powder, powdered ginger, cardamom
> 1 teaspoon each ground cumin, onion powder
> ½ teaspoon each garlic powder, red pepper flakes, dry mustard
> 1 cup nonfat yogurt
> Garnish: 1 orange, sliced; ½ cup finely chopped parsley

Place the chicken pieces in a large bowl or pan. Place all the remaining ingredients, except the yogurt, in a blender, and blend. Pour the mixture over the chicken, turning to coat well. Cover and marinate overnight in the refrigerator.

About 1 hour before serving, transfer the chicken and marinade to a baking dish. Cover and bake at 350° for 50 minutes, or until chicken is nearly done. Remove from the oven and spoon some of the chicken sauce into a small bowl. Allow sauce to cool slightly, then add the yogurt to the bowl and mix with the sauce. Pour the mixture over the chicken. Cover and return to the oven for 20 minutes, or until the chicken is tender. (The sauce may curdle slightly, but this will not affect the taste or quality of the dish.) Garnish with orange slices and parsley.

VARIATION: Sprinkle 1½ cups hot cooked peas over the chicken breasts just before serving.

Makes 6 servings

Calories per serving: 209; with peas, 236

CHICKEN CURRY

> 5 cups defatted chicken stock (see recipes for stocks)
> 1 cup finely chopped onions
> 2 stalks celery with leaves, finely chopped
> 3 large cloves garlic, finely chopped
> 1 large apple, peeled and coarsely grated
> 2 tablespoons finely chopped ginger
> 2 tablespoons curry powder, or to taste
> ½ teaspoon mace
> ½ teaspoon cardamom
> 3 tablespoons tomato paste
> ½ cup white vermouth
> 2 tablespoons frozen apple juice concentrate
> Juice of 1 lime
> 2 tablespoons cornstarch
> 3 cups poached, skinned, and diced chicken breast
> Garnishes as suggested below

Place 1 cup of the chicken stock in a large pot. Add the onions, celery, garlic, apple, and ginger; sauté over medium heat, stirring constantly, until the liquid has almost evaporated. Stir in the spices and tomato paste. Add the remaining chicken stock and bring to a boil; then cover, turn down the heat, and simmer for 30 minutes.

Make a smooth mixture of the vermouth, apple juice concentrate, lime juice, and cornstarch. Add this mixture to the simmering sauce and continue simmering for a few minutes until slightly thickened. Stir in the diced chicken just before serving; heat thoroughly.

Serve accompanied by assorted garnishes: suggested are sliced papaya and strawberries; diced red and green bell peppers; chopped, cooked egg whites; *YOGURT WITH CUCUMBER AND MINT; INDONESIAN RELISH; FRUIT CHUTNEY.*

Makes 6 servings
Calories per serving (without garnishes): 186

CHICKEN RATATOUILLE

> 2 cups defatted chicken or vegetable stock (see recipes
>   for stocks), or more if required
> 1 small eggplant, chopped
> 2 green peppers, chopped
> 1 onion, chopped
> 2–3 cloves garlic, minced
> 1 small red pepper, whole or seeded and finely minced
>   (optional)
> 3 medium zucchini, chopped
> 1 small cucumber, peeled and chopped
> 1 tablespoon basil or oregano
> 3 tomatoes, chopped
> 1⅔ cups cooked chicken cut into chunks
> ⅔ cup tomato paste

In a large skillet, bring 1 cup of the stock to a boil. Sauté the eggplant, green peppers, onion, garlic, and red pepper, if used, over moderate heat. When the vegetables are half-cooked, add the zucchini, cucumber, and basil or oregano. Continue cooking and stirring gently. After a few minutes, add the tomatoes and chicken chunks. Mix the tomato paste with the remaining stock, stirring to blend well. Pour this mixture over the ratatouille; continue cooking, stirring gently, until tender. Add more stock to the skillet if necessary.

Makes 4 servings
Calories per serving: 235

CHICKEN AND VEGETABLE TETRAZZINI

3½ cups defatted chicken stock (see recipes for stocks)
¼ cup dry white wine
1 cup diced onions
1 cup diced celery
2 tablespoons minced garlic
1 teaspoon basil
½ teaspoon thyme
⅛ teaspoon pepper
⅛ teaspoon saffron (optional)
Dash cayenne pepper
Dash salt
1 cup frozen baby carrots
2 cups halved fresh mushrooms
2 tablespoons diced canned pimientos
2 cups diced, cooked chicken breasts
1 cup evaporated skimmed milk
¼ cup whey powder (available in health-food stores)
¼ cup cornstarch
1 tablespoon grated Sapsago cheese, lightly oven-toasted
1½ tablespoons minced parsley
2 cups cooked whole-wheat spaghetti, well drained
Paprika

In a large skillet, heat ½ cup chicken stock and white wine, and sauté the onion, celery, and garlic. Add the spices and remaining stock and heat to a boil. Add the carrots, turn down the heat, and simmer, covered, until nearly tender. Add the mushrooms, pimientos, and chicken, and simmer for 5 minutes.

In a blender, blend the milk, whey powder, cornstarch, and cheese. Add the mixture to the simmering vegetables. Stir constantly until thickened. Stir in the parsley. Place the cooked spaghetti in a casserole and ladle the vegetable-chicken mixture over the spaghetti. Sprinkle with paprika. Bake at 350° for 20 minutes.

Makes 4–5 servings
Calories per serving (⅕ recipe): 285

STIR-FRIED CHINESE VEGETABLES
WITH CHICKEN

2⅓ cups defatted chicken stock (see recipes for stocks)
2½ tablespoons soy sauce or tamari
1 tablespoon curry powder
2½ teaspoons garlic powder
Dash pepper
4 tablespoons cornstarch
3 7–8-ounce chicken breast halves, skinned and boned
  (dressed weight, about 4 ounces each)
1 carrot, diagonally cut
3 stalks celery, diagonally cut
1 onion, diced or cut in chunks
2 green peppers, cut in large chunks
1 rounded tablespoon finely chopped ginger
1 medium head bok choy, diagonally cut
1 medium napa cabbage, shredded
1 8-ounce can water chestnuts, sliced
1 8-ounce can bamboo shoots
1 bunch green onions, cut in 1½-inch lengths
1 pound bean sprouts

In a bowl, make a marinade of ½ cup of the chicken stock, the soy sauce, curry powder, garlic powder, pepper, and 1 tablespoon of the cornstarch. Cut the chicken in strips and coat thoroughly with the marinade. Marinate the chicken for at least 1 hour. Stir the chicken and marinade, then transfer to a nonstick skillet or wok. Bring the liquid to a boil, lower the heat, and stir-fry the chicken for about 3 minutes, or until tender. Transfer the chicken and marinade to a covered container and set aside.

Use the remaining 2 cups of stock, about ½ cup at a time, as needed, to stir-fry the vegetables. Add the carrots first, followed by the celery, onions, peppers, and ginger, and cook about 5 minutes. Add the bok choy, cabbage, water chestnuts, bamboo shoots, green onions and bean sprouts; cook another 5 minutes.

Make a paste of the remaining cornstarch mixed with 3 tablespoons stock or water. Add the cornstarch paste to the simmering vegetables and stir constantly until thickened. Return the cooked chicken and marinade sauce to the skillet, mix gently with the vegetables, and heat thoroughly. Serve at once.

Makes 6–8 servings (16 cups)
Calories per cup: 71

CHICKEN OR TURKEY ENCHILADAS

> 1 cup defatted stock of choice (see recipes for stocks) or water
> 1½ cups chopped onions
> 1½ cups chopped green pepper
> 4 cloves garlic, minced
> 2 16-ounce cans diced tomatoes in purée or substitute 1½ 15-ounce cans of tomato sauce plus 1½ 1-pound cans of whole tomatoes, drained and chopped
> ½ cup diced canned green chilies
> 2 teaspoons cumin
> 2 shallots, minced (optional)
> 2 cups diced cooked chicken or turkey
> 1 teaspoon oregano
> 1 teaspoon onion powder
> 1 teaspoon dried or fresh cilantro (optional)
> 8 corn tortillas
> Garnish: shredded lettuce; minced green onions; MOCK SOUR CREAM or nonfat yogurt

Sauce: In a skillet, bring ½ cup of the stock or water to a boil. Add half the onion, half the green pepper, and half the garlic. Sauté, stirring as needed, until tender. Mix in the tomatoes, half the chilies, and 1 teaspoon of the cumin. Simmer the sauce for several minutes. Set aside and reheat before use.

Filling: Heat the remaining stock or water to a boil in another skillet. Add the remaining onion, green pepper, and garlic, and the shallots if used. Sauté the vegetables, stirring as required, until tender. Add the chicken or turkey and the rest of the spices and chilies and continue to heat and stir until the ingredients are well blended.

Oven-warm each tortilla briefly and fill with about ⅓ cup of the chicken or turkey mixture; roll and lay the enchiladas seam-side-down in a nonstick baking dish. Ladle a little of the reheated sauce over each enchilada and bake at 350° for 10–15 minutes.

To serve, place each enchilada on a bed of shredded lettuce, ladle more sauce over each, and garnish with a sprinkling of green onions and a dollop of *MOCK SOUR CREAM* or nonfat yogurt.

Makes 8 enchiladas
Calories per enchilada (without garnish): 187

TURKEY CHILI

1 small turkey breast, skinned
Celery tops
1 onion, sliced
Poultry seasoning to taste
1 cup chopped onions
½ cup chopped celery
⅓ cup chopped green pepper
3 cloves garlic, minced
1½ cups broth from cooking the turkey breast (if there
*   is not enough, add water to equal 1½ cups)*
1 28-ounce can crushed tomatoes in purée
1 15-ounce can tomato sauce
1 tablespoon onion powder
1 tablespoon chili powder, or more to taste
2 teaspoons cumin
1 teaspoon garlic powder
1 teaspoon oregano
1 teaspoon soy sauce or tamari
Dash cayenne pepper
1 cup cooked kidney beans

Place the turkey breast in a nonstick baking dish with 1½ cups of water. Add the celery tops and sliced onion and sprinkle with poultry seasoning. Cover and bake at 350° until tender, about 1½ hours. Remove the turkey breast. Defat the broth by chilling it in the freezer until the fat rises to the top. Discard the fat, then pour the broth through cheesecloth.

Sauté the chopped onion, celery, green pepper, and garlic in ½ cup of the turkey broth. Add the remaining ingredients except the turkey breast and beans. Simmer the sauce for 45 minutes uncovered, stirring occasionally.

Meanwhile, dice the turkey breast and grind in a meat grinder or in a blender or food processor. Add 1 cup of the ground turkey (leftover ground turkey may be frozen) and the beans to the chili. Cook and stir about 5 more minutes.

Makes 6–8 servings
Calories per serving (⅙ recipe): 175

TURKEY-MUSHROOM PATTIES

2 cups ground raw turkey breast
2 cups chopped fresh mushrooms
1 cup chopped canned water chestnuts
¼ cup finely chopped onions
¼ cup finely chopped celery
1 canned chili pepper, finely chopped
2 teaspoons Dijon mustard
2 teaspoons poultry seasoning
3 egg whites

Combine all the ingredients except the egg whites. Beat the egg whites until stiff; fold into the other ingredients. Shape into patties and broil on a nonstick pan, turning once.

These patties are good served hot with Dijon mustard, lettuce leaves, sliced tomtoes, sliced onion, pickles, and bread or crackers. Refrigerate leftover patties and reheat for sandwiches, or eat them cold.

Makes approximately 16 patties
Calories per patty: 36

VERA CRUZ RED SNAPPER

1 large onion, chopped
2 cloves garlic, finely minced
1 28-ounce can Italian plum tomatoes, undrained
1 teaspoon garlic powder
1 teaspoon thyme
1 teaspoon ground cloves
1 tablespoon lemon juice
1 tablespoon frozen apple juice concentrate
1 tablespoon soy sauce or tamari
1 tablespoon cornstarch
2 tablespoons capers
1 small fresh jalapeño pepper, seeded and finely chopped
1 whole red snapper, about 2½ pounds, head removed, scaled, and cleaned; or 2½ pounds red snapper fillets
Garnish: pimiento strips, lemon slices, 3 tablespoons finely chopped parsley

Water-sauté the onion and garlic in a large skillet. Chop the tomatoes and add them, including juice, to the skillet. Add the spices and cook over high heat, stirring frequently, for 8–10 minutes. Blend together the lemon juice, apple juice concentrate, soy sauce or tamari, and cornstarch, and stir into the tomato mixture. Simmer until the mixture is thickened and clear. Remove the skillet from the heat and stir in the capers and jalapeño pepper.

Rinse the fish and pat dry. Spread some of the sauce in a baking pan, lay the fish in the pan, and cover with the remaining sauce. Bake uncovered at 400° for 35 minutes, or until the fish flakes in the thickest part; if red snapper fillets are used, cooking time may be reduced. Baste often with the sauce during the last 10–15 minutes of baking. When the fish is nearly done, arrange the pimiento strips over the top and bake a few more minutes. Before serving, stir the sauce to blend. Complete the garnish with a row of slightly overlapping lemon slices and a sprinkling of chopped parsley.

Makes 10–12 servings
Calories per serving (¹⁄₁₀ recipe): 146

BREADED FISH

2 *large fish fillets (about 1 pound each), cut into 8 individual serving pieces*

Marinade:
  2 *tablespoons Sauternes*
  2 *tablespoons lemon juice*
  2 *tablespoons soy sauce or tamari*
  2 *tablespoons onion powder*
  1 *teaspoon fines herbes*
  ¼ *teaspoon sage*
  ¼ *teaspoon pepper*
  ¼ *teaspoon paprika*

Breading:
  ¼ *cup whole-wheat pastry flour*
  ¼ *cup yellow cornmeal*
  2 *tablespoons matzo meal*
  2 *egg whites, whisked until foamy*

Rinse the fish and pat dry. Combine the marinade ingredients and marinate the fish for at least 30 minutes.

Combine the breading ingredients. Coat the fish on both sides with the breading. Dab the fish with the egg whites and any leftover marinade. Place the fish in a nonstick baking pan, cover, and bake at 400° for 30 minutes. Remove the cover for browning the last 10 minutes. Do not turn fish. If greater browning is desired, place the pan briefly on the middle rack under the broiler.

Makes 8 servings
Calories per serving: 149

POACHED FISH

Poaching liquid:
  2 *cups water, or as required*
  3 *tablespoons lemon juice*
  1 *onion, sliced*
  6 *peppercorns*

2 whole allspice
1 bay leaf
2 sprigs parsley
½ cup white wine (optional)

Fish for poaching:
14 ounces lean fish such as halibut, red snapper, sea bass, etc.

Combine all the ingredients for the poaching liquid in a large pot and bring to a simmer. Lower the fish into the hot liquid, cover, and continue to simmer over low heat. Cook about 8–10 minutes, or until the fish flakes when tested with a fork. Lift the fish fillets carefully from the liquid with a large spatula. Serve hot, with or without a sauce, or chilled and flaked for use in salads, sandwiches, and appetizers. To use the poaching liquid as a flavorful base for a sauce, boil it down to about half volume.

NOTE: More delicate fish should be wrapped in cheesecloth or romaine lettuce leaves before poaching. To poach fish in romaine lettuce leaves, parboil the leaves in 1 inch of boiling water in a skillet until they are wilted and bright green (about 1 minute). Place a piece of fish on each leaf, fold the sides in, and roll up, piecing with another leaf if necessary.

Makes 4 servings
Calories per serving: 100

HALIBUT CREOLE

1 cup vegetable stock (see recipes for stocks)
2 cups coarsely diced red and/or brown onions
1 cup coarsely diced green pepper
1 cup diagonally sliced celery
2 cloves garlic, minced
2 shallots, minced
½ cup chopped leeks
1 cup diced tomatoes
1 15-ounce can tomato sauce
1 16-ounce can diced tomatoes in purée or substitute
    ¾ of a 15-ounce can of tomato sauce plus ¾ of a
    1-pound can of whole tomatoes, drained and chopped

> ¼ *cup tomato paste*
> ¼ *cup white vermouth or dry sherry*
> 2 *tablespoons chopped parsley*
> 2 *teaspoons gumbo filé*
> ½ *teaspoon thyme*
> 1 *bay leaf*
> *Cayenne pepper or Tabasco (hot pepper sauce) to taste*
> 1 *pound halibut or other firm-fleshed lean white fish,*
>   *cut into bite-sized pieces with bones removed*

In a large skillet, heat ½ cup of the stock to a boil. Sauté the onion, green pepper, celery, garlic, shallots, and leeks in the stock. Add the remaining stock and all the other ingredients except the fish. Bring to a boil, then turn down the heat and simmer uncovered for 5 minutes. Add the fish and simmer uncovered for 10 minutes longer or until the fish is cooked. Remove the bay leaf before serving.

Makes 5–5 servings
Calories per serving (⅕ recipe): 226

MARINATED SWORDFISH KABOBS

Marinade:

> 1 *cup pineapple juice from pineapple chunks used in*
>   *making kabobs, below*
> 1 *tablespoon soy sauce or tamari*
> 1 *tablespoon Sauternes*
> 1 *tablespoon garlic powder*
> 1 *tablespoon fresh grated ginger*

Kabobs:

> 1⅓ *pounds swordfish, cut into 1½-inch-square chunks*
> 2 *large green peppers, cut into 2-inch squares*
> 12 *large mushrooms, cut lengthwise into thirds*
> 8 *small tomatoes, quartered, or about 1⅓ boxes cherry*
>   *tomatoes*
> 3 *medium onions, cut into quarters and each quarter*
>   *cut lengthwise into 2–3 wedges*
> 1 *20-ounce can unsweetened pineapple chunks, juice-*
>   *packed, drained*
> *Bamboo skewers, as required*

Combine all the marinade ingredients. Place the swordfish chunks and the marinade in a shallow dish and turn the fish to make sure all sides are coated with the marinade. Marinate for several hours or overnight.

Alternate the marinated swordfish and the other ingredients on the bamboo skewers. Place the kabobs on 2 broiling pans and brush with the marinade. Broil for 10–15 minutes, turning once. Serve on a bed of shredded lettuce.

Makes 6 servings (using 10-inch skewers, about 17 kabobs)
Calories per serving (about 3 kabobs): 236

CRAB OR CHICKEN CRÊPES WITH WHITE SAUCE

Sauce:
> *1 cup evaporated skimmed milk*
> *2 cups defatted chicken or vegetable stock (see recipes for stocks)*
> *¼ cup whey powder (available in health-food stores)*
> *2½ tablespoons cornstarch*
> *1 tablespoon dry white wine*
> *½ cup diced red bell pepper or canned pimientos, rinsed*
> *⅛ teaspoon curry powder*

Filling:
> *½ cup defatted chicken or vegetable stock (see recipes for stocks)*
> *1 tablespoon dry white wine*
> *2 cups chopped celery*
> *1½ cups chopped onions*
> *½ cup minced shallots*
> *¼ teaspoon curry powder*
> *⅛ teaspoon fennel seeds, soaked in 1 tablespoon water and drained*
> *10 ounces cooked crab meat (about 1⅞ cups) or 1⅞ cups diced cooked chicken breast*

Crêpes:
> *1½ cups nonfat milk*
> *¾ cup nonfat buttermilk*
> *1½ cups whole-wheat pastry flour*
> *1 tablespoon baking powder*
> *4 egg whites*

Sauce: Pour the milk and 1 cup of the stock into a saucepan and heat to a simmer. In a bowl, stir together the whey powder, cornstarch, and remaining stock. Add the whey-cornstarch mixture to the simmering liquid and stir constantly until the sauce is smooth and thickened. Stir in the wine, red bell pepper, and curry powder. Remove from heat and set aside

Filling: In a skillet, bring the stock and wine to a boil. Add the vegetables and sauté over moderate heat until the vegetables are nearly tender. Stir in the curry powder, fennel seeds, and crab or chicken. Set aside.

Crêpes: In a blender, add the milks, flour, and baking powder, and blend until very smooth. Transfer to a large mixing bowl. Beat the egg whites until stiff peaks form; stir well into the batter. If necessary to prevent sticking, prepare a nonstick skillet or crêpe pan by dabbing a little oil on a paper towel or Handi-Wipe, rinsing the towel in water and wringing it out, then wiping over the skillet or crêpe pan surface. Use this towel whenever sticking is a problem, but do not add more oil to it. Place the pan over moderate heat. Pour about ½ cup of batter into the pan, spreading it around evenly, and brown on one side. Turn the crêpe and lightly brown the other side.

Carefully remove each crêpe to a plate and fill with about ⅓ cup of filling. Tuck the corners in, if desired, and roll. Lay the filled crêpe seam-side-down on a nonstick baking pan. Repeat this procedure until all the crêpes have been filled and arranged in the pan. Spoon some white sauce over the crêpes, cover, and bake at 375° for 15–20 minutes. Reheat the remaining white sauce and serve with the crêpes.

Makes approximately 12 filled crêpes and 3 cups sauce
Calories per filled crêpe with sauce: 142 (crab); 156 (chicken)

FISH BALLS WITH SAUCE

¾ pound cod, cleaned and patted dry
½ pound halibut, cleaned and patted dry
2 large onions, quartered
4 teaspoons lemon juice
1 tablespoon chopped parsley
1 teaspoon marjoram
⅛ teaspoon pepper
⅔ cup matzo meal
2 egg whites, stiffly beaten
1 tablespoon soy sauce or tamari
1 carrot, cut into strips
1 stalk celery
1 bay leaf

Sauce:
Cooking broth from fish balls
1 tablespoon lemon juice
1 tablespoon cornstarch
¼ cup minced green onions

Place the fish, 1 of the quartered onions, 3 teaspoons of the lemon juice, the parsley, and spices in a food processor, meat grinder, or blender; grind fine. Transfer the mixture to a bowl. Add the matzo meal, mixing well, and fold in the egg whites. Refrigerate about 25 minutes. Form the mixture into balls approximately 1 inch in diameter.

Bring 6 cups of water to a boil in a large pot; add the remaining onion and lemon juice, soy sauce or tamari, carrot, celery, and bay leaf. Reduce the heat, then drop in about half of the fish balls. Simmer for 15 minutes, stirring occasionally to prevent the fish balls from sticking to the bottom of the pot. Remove the fish balls with a slotted spoon and place in a casserole dish. Cook the remaining fish balls and add them to the casserole dish.

Ladle some of the cooking broth over the fish balls, or prepare fish sauce and ladle it over the fish balls.

Sauce: Strain the fish broth through a colander to remove the vegetables. Measure out ⅓ cup of the broth and set aside to cool.

Heat the remaining broth in a saucepan to a simmer; add the lemon juice. Blend the cornstarch with the ⅓ cup cooled fish broth. Add the cornstarch mixture to the simmering liquid, and stir until thickened. Stir in the minced green onions.

Serve with *HORSERADISH*, if desired. May be served hot or cold.

Makes 50–60 fish balls
Calories per fish ball: approximately 15
Calories per ⅙ recipe (including sauce): 146

SALMON SOUFFLÉ

> *1 7¾-ounce can pink salmon, drained*
> *1 4-ounce jar pimientos, drained*
> *1 chili pepper, seeds removed*
> *¼ onion*
> *1 teaspoon chopped dill or ½ teaspoon dried dill*
> *½ teaspoon grated lemon peel*
> *½ teaspoon chopped mint*
> *¼ teaspoon garlic powder*
> *¼ teaspoon dry mustard*
> *1 cup crumbled hoop cheese or other uncreamed cottage cheese*
> *4 egg whites, stiffly beaten*
> *Garnish: WHITE SAUCE No. 2 or nonfat yogurt and chopped cucumbers*

Bone the salmon and remove the skin and fat. Place the salmon in, preferably, a food processor, or a blender, adding all the ingredients except the cheese and egg whites. Blend for several minutes until smooth. Transfer to a mixing bowl. Add cheese to the processor (if using a blender, leave some of the salmon mixture in the blender to provide some liquid for blending the cheese) and blend to a smooth paste. Return salmon mixture to the food processor and blend with the cheese. Transfer to a mixing bowl and fold in the beaten egg whites. Use a nonstick baking dish or prepare a soufflé dish by dabbing a little oil on a paper towel or Handi-Wipe, rinsing the towel in water and wringing it out, then wiping over the soufflé dish surface. Sprinkle flour sparingly over the dish, and shake to remove excess flour. Fill the soufflé dish or baking pan ¾ full to allow room for rising. Bake at 400° until set and brown, about 20–25 minutes. Serve with *WHITE SAUCE* No. 2 or nonfat yogurt and chopped cucumbers.

Makes 4 servings
Calories per serving (without garnish): 146

TUNA LOAF

2½ cans chunk-style tuna (6½-ounce cans, water-packed)
    or 2⅓ cans solid-pack tuna (7-ounce cans, water-
    packed)
1 cup sourdough breadcrumbs, freshly made in a
    blender
½ cup cooked long-grain brown rice
½ cup finely chopped onions
½ cup finely chopped celery with leaves
½ green or red bell pepper, finely chopped
1 large clove garlic, minced
2 egg whites, beaten with a wire whisk
½ of a 6-ounce can tomato paste
2 tablespoons evaporated skimmed milk
¼ cup finely chopped parsley
1 tablespoon basil or marjoram
1½ teaspoons thyme
1½ teaspoons oregano
1½ teaspoons paprika
⅛ teaspoon curry powder
⅛ teaspoon pepper
Dash cayenne pepper
SPICY TOMATO SAUCE or WHITE SAUCE No. 1 or
    No. 2

Place all the ingredients in a large mixing bowl. Using both hands or a large spoon, mix the ingredients thoroughly until well blended. On a large nonstick pan, mold the mixture to form a rounded oblong loaf, or use a nonstick loaf pan. Cover with foil and bake at 325° for 50 minutes. Remove the foil, turn up the heat to 350°, and continue baking for about 10 minutes more to brown the top. Serve with *SPICY TOMATO SAUCE* or *WHITE SAUCE* No. 1 or No. 2.

VARIATION: For *LONDON MEAT LOAF,* substitute 1 pound leanest ground beef (flank steak preferred) for the tuna. Omit the milk and curry powder. Increase the pepper to ½ teaspoon and the cayenne pepper to ⅛ teaspoon. Bake uncovered at 325° for 1¼ hours. Serve with *SPICY TOMATO SAUCE.*

Makes 6 servings

Calories per serving (without sauce): 170 (TUNA LOAF); 177 (LONDON MEAT LOAF)

TUNA PUFFS

1½ cups breadcrumbs (from acceptable bread)
1 7-ounce can water-packed tuna, drained and mashed
½ cup nonfat milk
2 tablespoons grated onion
1 tablespoon lemon juice
1 tablespoon dried parsley
¼ teaspoon pepper
¼ teaspoon paprika
3 egg whites

Prepare the breadcrumbs by processing bread in a food processor or blender. Mix together all the ingredients except the egg whites. Beat the egg whites to soft peaks and stir into the tuna mixture. Distribute the tuna-egg white mixture in a 12-muffin tin. Place the muffin tin in a pan of hot water and bake at 350° for 45 minutes.

Makes 12 puffs
Calories per puff: 46

STIR-FRIED STEAK AND GREEN PEPPERS

1 pound flank steak, trimmed of all visible fat
2 tablespoons cornstarch
1 tablespoon powdered ginger
2 tablespoons frozen apple juice concentrate
2 tablespoons soy sauce or tamari
¼ cup dry sherry or wine vinegar
¾ cup defatted stock of choice (see recipes for stocks)
4 large green peppers, cut into thin strips
1 large carrot, thinly sliced on the diagonal
½ red onion, sliced

Place flank steak in the freezer until partially frozen. Slice diagonally into very thin strips, cutting across the grain. In a mixing bowl, combine the cornstarch, ginger, apple juice concentrate, soy sauce, sherry, and ¼ cup of the stock. Marinate the meat strips in the mixture for at least 30 minutes, stirring occasionally. (If the meat can be marinated longer, it will be even better.)

In a large skillet or wok, heat the remaining stock over high heat. Add the vegetables and stir-fry quickly, no more than 2–3 minutes. Push the vegetables to the sides of the pan, leaving the center empty. Remove the meat from the marinade and stir-fry quickly. Add any remaining marinade, stir until thickened, and then stir in the vegetables.

Makes 4–5 servings
Calories per serving (⅕ recipe): 203

TOMATO BEEF CURRY

1 pound flank steak, trimmed of all visible fat

Marinade:

¼ cup rice vinegar or other mild vinegar
1 tablespoon soy sauce or tamari
1 tablespoon frozen apple juice concentrate
1 tablespoon cornstarch
1 clove garlic, minced
Dash cayenne pepper

> *½ cup defatted stock of choice (see recipes for stocks)
>   or water*
> *2 medium tomatoes, cut in wedges*
> *1 onion, diced*
> *1 green pepper, cut into strips*
> *1 tablespoon frozen apple juice concentrate*
> *1 tablespoon curry powder or more to taste*
> *1 teaspoon onion powder*
> *¼ cup tomato paste*

Slice the flank steak ⅛-inch thick across the grain. Combine all the marinade ingredients in a bowl and mix well. Marinate the steak strips for at least 30 minutes.

Heat the stock or water in a nonstick skillet or wok. Add the tomatoes, onion, and green pepper; sauté for about 3 minutes. Stir in the apple juice concentrate, curry powder, and onion powder. Remove the vegetables from the skillet and set aside. Add the flank steak and the marinade to the skillet; sauté until the meat is almost done, about 5 minutes. Add the tomato paste and additional stock or water if needed. Return the vegetables to the skillet and stir-fry for about 1 minute longer.

Makes 4–5 servings
Calories per serving (⅕ recipe): 201

BEEF CHOP SUEY

> *1¼ pounds flank steak, trimmed of all visible fat, and
>   cut against the grain in thin slices*

Marinade:
> *⅓ cup rice vinegar or other mild vinegar*
> *¼ cup Sauternes*
> *2 tablespoons red wine vinegar*
> *1 tablespoon soy sauce or tamari*
> *1½ teaspoons garlic powder*
> *1½ teaspoons onion powder*

Breading:
> ½ cup flour
> 2 tablespoons cornstarch
> 1 tablespoon paprika

Chop Suey:
> 4 cups defatted stock of choice (see recipes for stocks)
>   or water
> 1 head bok choy, coarsely chopped
> 4 stalks celery, diagonally cut
> 1 onion, diagonally cut
> 1 green pepper, diagonally cut
> 1 tablespoon minced ginger
> 1 small napa cabbage, shredded
> 3 cups bean sprouts
> 2 cups fresh snow peas (Chinese pea pods), trimmed
> 2 cups sliced mushrooms
> 1 bunch green onions, coarsely chopped
> 1 small can water chestnuts or bamboo shoots, drained
> 2 tablespoons cornstarch
> 1 tablespoon soy sauce or tamari
> 1 teaspoon curry powder
> ⅛ teaspoon pepper

Combine the marinade ingredients in a mixing bowl. Place the meat slices in the marinade and refrigerate for at least 2 hours. Mix together the breading ingredients. Remove the meat from the marinade and coat with the breading. In a large skillet, heat 2 cups of the stock or water to a boil. Add the meat and any remaining marinade liquid and stir-fry for 3–4 minutes, or until the meat is just tender. Transfer meat and gravy to a covered container and set aside.

Bring the remaining stock or water to a boil. Add the bok choy, celery, onion, green pepper, and ginger, and cook for about 5 minutes, stirring rapidly. Add the remaining vegetables and cook for about 3 more minutes. In a separate bowl, make a paste of the cornstarch, soy sauce or tamari, spices, and a little water. Add the cornstarch mixture to the simmering vegetables and stir constantly until thickened. Add the reserved meat and gravy to the vegetables and heat thoroughly. Serve at once.

Makes 8–10 servings
Calories per serving (⅛ recipe): 236

NATCHITOCHES MEAT PIE

Pastry:
> 2 teaspoons active dry yeast
> ¾ cup defatted stock of choice (see recipes for stocks)
> 3 cups whole-wheat pastry flour
> 1½ teaspoons baking powder

Filling:
> 1 pound lean flank steak, trimmed of all visible fat and
>   ground
> 2 cups chopped onion
> 1 green pepper, chopped
> 3 cloves garlic, minced
> 1 bunch green onions, chopped
> 1½ tablespoons soy sauce or tamari
> 1 tablespoon thyme
> ½ teaspoon cardamom
> ½ teaspoon pepper
> Cayenne pepper to taste
> 2 tablespoons flour
> Additional stock or water as required
> 2 egg whites, fork-beaten

In a small bowl, dissolve the yeast in ¼ cup warm water. Add the ¾ cup stock or water and stir to blend well. Mix 1½ cups of the flour with the baking powder in a large mixing bowl; stir in the yeast-liquid mixture. Add the remaining flour and mix well. Turn out the dough onto a floured breadboard. Brush 2 tablespoons of water over the dough and knead until pliant. Transfer the dough to a large bowl which has been lined with waxed paper to prevent sticking. Cover and place in a warm spot until the dough has doubled in volume (about 1½ hours at 80°). Punch down the dough and turn it out again on the floured breadboard. Divide the dough in half. With a rolling pin, roll each half very thin. Using a saucer for a guide, cut the dough into approximately 14 rounds. Reroll and cut leftover dough as necessary.

Brown the meat in a nonstick skillet; cover and cook until ⅔ done. Add the remaining filling ingredients except the flour. Cook until the meat and vegetables are tender. Transfer the cooked meat and vegetables to a mixing bowl and sprinkle with flour. Stir well. Fill each dough round with about ¼ cup of the filling. Fold dough over and crimp the edges with a fork.

Add stock or water to a large pot until the liquid is deep enough to submerge the meat pies in. Bring to a boil, and add the meat pies. When the liquid returns to a gentle boil, turn down the heat and simmer for about 1 minute. Carefully remove the pies with a slotted spoon and place them on a nonstick baking pan. Brush the tops with the egg whites and bake at 400° for 15 minutes, or until nicely browned. Cover with foil to keep the pies moist.

NOTE: The beautiful town of Natchitoches, Louisiana, gained national prominence in 1980 because of their involvement as a community with the Pritikin Diet.

Makes 14 meat pies
Calories per meat pie: 162

BEEF STEW

1½ pounds leanest stewing beef, cut into 1-inch cubes
2 large cloves garlic, chopped
1 cup dry red wine
½ cup beet juice from canned beets
3 cups defatted stock of choice (see recipes for stocks)
  or water
2 tablespoons tomato paste
½ cup finely chopped parsley
1 teaspoon thyme
2 bay leaves
4 large carrots, cut into 1-inch lengths
¾ pound fresh green beans
12 large mushrooms, quartered
12 small white boiling onions, blanched for 1 minute in
  boiling water and skinned
¼ cup cornstarch
¼ cup cold water

Using a heavy nonstick skillet, sear the meat on all sides over moderate heat, adding the garlic near the end. Transfer the meat to a heavy stew pot. Place the red wine and the beet juice in the skillet; turn up the heat and deglaze the encrusted meat juices from the skillet with a wooden spoon. Pour the juice over the meat. Add the stock or water, tomato paste, parsley, thyme, and bay leaves, and bring to a very low simmer. Cover tightly and cook until the meat is nearly tender. Add the carrots and beans, cover and continue cooking until the vegetables are nearly tender. Add the mushrooms and onions, simmering for a few more minutes. Mix the cornstarch and water to a smooth paste, add to the stew, and stir gently until well blended. Simmer the stew uncovered for an additional 10 minutes.

Makes 6 servings
Calories per serving: 285

SWEET AND SOUR COCKTAIL MEATBALLS

Meatballs:

> ¼ cup fine dry whole-wheat breadcrumbs (from acceptable bread)
> ½ pound flank steak, trimmed of all visible fat and ground
> 1 cup finely grated carrots
> ¾ cup finely chopped onions
> ¼ cup finely chopped green pepper
> ¼ cup finely chopped celery
> 1 teaspoon soy sauce or tamari
> ¼ teaspoon garlic powder
> Dash pepper
> 2 egg whites, slightly beaten

Sauce:

> 1 cup tomato sauce
> ⅔ cup cider vinegar
> ⅓ cup frozen apple juice concentrate
> 1 8-ounce can unsweetened crushed pineapple or pineapple chunks, drained (or the equivalent in fresh pineapple chunks)
> 2 tablespoons unsweetened grapefruit juice

Prepare the breadcrumbs by processing oven-toasted bread in a food processor or blender.

Mix the meatball ingredients together and chill. Form into small balls. Place on a nonstick pan in the broiler and broil until browned.

In a large skillet, combine the sauce ingredients and bring to a boil, whisking constantly. Add the meatballs. When mixture returns to a boil, turn down the heat and simmer for about 10 minutes. Serve hot in a chafing dish.

Makes 40–50 meatballs
Calories per meatball (¹⁄₅₀ recipe): 19

STUFFED EGGPLANT

> ¼ cup whole-wheat breadcrumbs (from acceptable bread)
> ¼ pound leanest beef (flank steak preferred), ground
> 1 small eggplant
> ½ cup chopped onions
> 1½ cups diced yellow and green summer squash
> ½ cup defatted stock of choice (see recipes for stocks) or water
> ½ cup canned green chili salsa
> 1 tablespoon basil
> 1 tablespoon thyme
> 1 teaspoon onion powder
> 1 teaspoon garlic powder
> 1½ teaspoons grated Sapsago cheese

Prepare the breadcrumbs by processing bread in a food processor or blender; set aside. Brown the beef in a skillet, stirring as necessary until the pink color is gone. Cover and simmer for about 5 minutes, stirring as needed. Drain the beef in a fine colander; set aside.

Cut the eggplant in half, then cut around the edges. Scoop out the eggplant, taking care to keep the shells intact. Dice the eggplant. In another skillet, cook the eggplant, onions, and squash in the stock over medium heat until tender, adding the chili salsa and spices after a few minutes.

Mix the browned beef into the cooked vegetables and fill the eggplant shells with this mixture. Sprinkle Sapsago cheese and the breadcrumbs over the tops. Bake at 400° for about 25 minutes, or until the tops are lightly browned. (For a more tender version, cover with foil for the last 10 minutes of baking.)

Makes 2 servings

Calories per serving: 204

Vegetarian Entrées

VEGETABLE STEW

4 turnips, peeled and quartered
4 carrots, cut in chunks
3 medium white rose potatoes, peeled and quartered
1 rutabaga, peeled and quartered
4 cloves garlic, finely chopped
5 stalks celery, sliced
3 onions, quartered
1 red or green bell pepper, cut into small squares
3 shallots, chopped
5 tomatoes, quartered
1 cup canned green chili salsa
¼ cup soy sauce or tamari
⅔ cup chopped parsley
1 tablespoon garlic powder
¼ cup cornstarch mixed with ¼ cup water to a smooth
   paste

Bring 3 cups water to a boil in a large pot. Add the turnips, carrots, potatoes, rutabaga, and garlic. When the water returns to a boil, lower heat, cover, and simmer for about 15 minutes or until vegetables are nearly tender. Add the celery, onions, pepper, and shallots; cook until tender, about 10 minutes. Add the remaining ingredients except the cornstarch, and simmer for 2–3 minutes, adding more water if necessary. Mix in the cornstarch paste, stirring very gently, and cook until the stew is thickened.

Makes approximately 16 cups or 8 servings
Calories per serving: 172

273

VEGETABLE CUTLET

> 1 cup finely diced mushrooms
> ⅔ cup chopped green beans (½-inch lengths)
> ⅔ cup chopped asparagus (½-inch lengths)
> ½ cup finely diced celery
> ¼ cup frozen corn
> 1¼ cups grated carrot
> ¾ cup finely diced onion
> ⅓ cup frozen peas, thawed under warm running water
> 1 teaspoon frozen apple juice concentrate
> ¾ teaspoon Dijon mustard
> ¾ teaspoon minced ginger, puréed in a blender
> 1¼ cups matzo meal
> 2 egg whites, stiffly beaten
> *TANGY SAUCE*

Place the mushrooms, green beans, asparagus, celery, and corn in a steamer basket or saucepan with a little water. Bring to a boil, cover, turn down the heat and steam the vegetables for 5–10 minutes, or until lightly cooked. Transfer to a mixing bowl. Add the remaining ingredients and mix together carefully to avoid mashing the vegetables. Form the mixture into patties and place the patties on a nonstick baking sheet. Cover with aluminum foil. Bake at 350° for 20 minutes. Uncover and bake for another 15 minutes, or until lightly browned. Serve with *TANGY SAUCE*.

Makes 6–8 servings (15 cutlets)
Calories per cutlet (without sauce): 44

STUFFED CABBAGE ROLLS

> 2 large cabbages

Filling:
> 2 large eggplants
> 1 large onion, chopped
> 1 cup chopped leeks
> 1 medium green pepper, chopped
> 2 shallots, minced
> 2 cloves garlic, minced

½ cup defatted stock of choice (see recipes for stocks)
or water
1 7-ounce can green chili salsa, drained
1 16-ounce can diced tomtoes in purée drained, or
substitute ¾ cup drained and chopped canned tomatoes
2 cups tomato sauce
2 tablespoons dry Sauternes
½ teaspoon soy sauce or tamari
1 tablespoon basil
1 teaspoon oregano
1 teaspoon ground coriander
2½ cups cooked long-grain brown rice
2 egg whites

Sauce:
1 28-ounce can crushed tomatoes in purée
1 15-ounce can tomato sauce
¼ cup tomato paste
2 tablespoons frozen apple juice concentrate
1 tablespoon garlic powder
1 tablespoon basil

Cut around the stem of each cabbage, but leave the cabbages whole. Parboil in water for 5 minutes; then let steep for another 5 minutes. Remove from the water and drain. Carefully remove the leaves one by one. Place the leaves, one at a time, on a cutting board with the outer side up. Level a knife blade against the outer side of each leaf and cut off the excess portion of the thick center vein without cutting into the leaf. Set leaves aside.

Filling: Pierce the eggplant skins with a fork and bake the eggplants at 400° until soft. Peel and chop the eggplants and press out the excess water. In a large skillet, sauté the onion, leeks, green pepper, shallots, and garlic in the stock. Stir in the chopped eggplant, salsa, and tomato products. Add the Sauternes, soy sauce or tamari, and spices. Cook until fairly thick. Remove from heat and cool. Transfer the vegetable mixture to a large mixing bowl and combine with the rice. Beat the egg whites until stiff and fold into the filling.

Sauce: Combine the sauce ingredients in a saucepan. Bring to a boil, turn down the heat, and simmer for about 15 minutes.

To assemble the cabbage rolls, spoon about ½ cup of the filling onto each cabbage leaf, in the center near the bottom. Fold the bottom up, tuck in the sides, and roll up. Place the rolls seam-side-down in a shallow nonstick baking pan. Pour the sauce over the cabbage rolls. Cover and bake at 350° for 1 hour.

Makes approximately 12 cabbage rolls
Calories per serving: 179

EGGPLANT STEAKS

½ cup whole-wheat breadcrumbs (from acceptable bread)
½ cup tomato sauce
1 large eggplant, sliced about 1 inch thick
½ cup tomato paste
1 16-ounce can diced tomatoes in purée or substitute ¾ of a 15-ounce can of tomato sauce plus ¾ of a 1-pound can of whole tomatoes, drained and chopped
1 tablespoon soy sauce or tamari
1½ teaspoons garlic powder
⅛ teaspoon pepper
1 large onion, cut in half, sliced twice, and separated into pieces
1 large green pepper, cut into strips
2 large canned green chilies, chopped
2 tablespoons grated Sapsago cheese
1 tablespoon basil
1½ teaspoons oregano

Prepare the breadcrumbs by processing bread in a food processor or blender. Pour the tomato sauce into a large nonstick baking pan and spread evenly. Sprinkle the breadcrumbs over the sauce. Place the eggplant slices in the pan, forming a single layer. Mix together the tomato paste, diced tomatoes, soy sauce or tamari, garlic powder, and pepper. Spoon about ¼ cup of this mixture onto each eggplant slice. Decorate each eggplant slice with onion pieces, green pepper strips, and chopped green chilies. Sprinkle with the Sapsago cheese, basil and oregano.

Cover the pan tightly (if using foil, make a dome to avoid contact with the tomato products). Bake at 375° for 40 minutes.

Increase the temperature to 400° and bake for an additional 20 minutes. Remove the cover for the last 5–10 minutes of baking.

Makes 4–6 servings
Calories per serving (¼ recipe): 194

BOK CHOY CAKES

> 4 cups finely chopped bok choy
> 1 cup chopped mushrooms
> ½ cup chopped onions
> 4 egg whites
> 1 teaspoon soy sauce or tamari
> ½ teaspoon onion powder
> ¼ teaspoon garlic powder
> ⅜ cup matzo meal
> Garnish: chopped lettuce, tomato slices, hot mustard

Place the bok choy, mushrooms, and onions in a steamer basket or saucepan, with a little water. Bring to a boil, cover, turn down the heat, and steam the vegetables for 5–10 minutes or until tender. Set aside to cool for a few minutes. Beat the egg whites and soy sauce or tamari with a wire whisk until foamy, then mix in the steamed vegetables, onion powder, garlic powder, and matzo meal. Heat a large nonstick skillet and, using a large mixing spoon, drop large spoonfuls of the vegetable batter onto the hot surface. The cakes should be about as large as medium-size pancakes. Let the cakes cook for a few minutes over moderate heat until nicely browned, then turn them over and cook until the other side browns sufficiently.

To serve, garnish a serving platter with chopped lettuce, arrange the cakes on top of the lettuce, place a large slice of fresh tomato on top of each cake, and finish with a dollop of hot mustard in the center of each tomato slice.

Makes 8 cakes
Calories per cake (without garnish): 36

CANNELONI CRÊPES WITH RED SAUCE

Sauce:
>   1 16-ounce can diced tomatoes in purée or substitute
>   ¾ of a 15-ounce can of tomato sauce plus ¾ of a
>   1-pound can of whole tomatoes, drained and chopped
>   1 15-ounce can tomato sauce
>   1 zucchini, coarsely diced
>   1 onion, coarsely diced
>   1 clove garlic, coarsely chopped
>   1 tablespoon frozen apple juice concentrate
>   1 teaspoon basil
>   1 teaspoon oregano
>   ⅛ teaspoon cayenne pepper
>   2 tablespoons grated Sapsago cheese
>   6 mushrooms, thinly sliced

Filling:
>   2 cups crumbled hoop cheese, or other uncreamed
>   cottage cheese
>   ¼ cup nonfat milk
>   1 cup YOGURT "CREAM CHEESE"
>   1 tablespoon lemon juice
>   2 tablespoons minced parsley
>   2 egg whites

Crêpes:
>   1½ cups nonfat milk
>   ¾ cup nonfat buttermilk
>   1½ cups whole-wheat pastry flour
>   1 tablespoon baking powder
>   4 egg whites

Sauce: Place all the sauce ingredients except the mushrooms in a saucepan. Bring to a boil, then turn down the heat and simmer about 30 minutes, stirring occasionally. Pour the sauce into a blender; blend only until smooth (not to a fine purée). Transfer sauce to a bowl. In a small skillet, water-sauté the mushrooms, stirring as needed. Drain the mushrooms and add them to the sauce. Set aside.

Filling: Place the hoop cheese in a food processor with the milk. (If a food processor is not available, use a blender, or mash by hand, adding a minimum of extra milk if necessary.) Process for several minutes until the cheese is thick and smooth. Transfer the mixture to a bowl. Stir in the *YOGURT "CREAM CHEESE,"* lemon juice, and parsley. Beat the egg whites until stiff peaks form and fold into filling. Set aside.

Crêpes: In a blender, add the milks, flour, and baking powder, and blend until very smooth. Transfer to a mixing bowl. Beat the egg whites until stiff peaks form and stir well into the batter. If necessary to prevent sticking, prepare a nonstick skillet or crêpe pan by dabbing a little oil on a paper towel or Handi-Wipe, rinsing the towel in water and wringing it out, and wiping over the skillet or crêpe pan surface. Use the towel whenever sticking is a problem, but do not add more oil to it. Place the pan over moderate heat. Pour a thin layer of batter (about ½ cup) into the pan, spreading it around evenly, and brown one side. Turn the crêpe and lightly brown the other side.

Carefully transfer the crêpes to a plate and fill with a large spoonful of the cheese filling. Tuck the corners in, if desired, and roll. Lay the filled crêpe seam-side-down on a nonstick baking pan. Repeat this procedure until all the crêpes have been filled and arranged in the pan. Spoon some red sauce over the crêpes, cover, and bake at 375° until heated through, about 25 minutes. Serve with extra grated Sapsago cheese.

Makes approximately 12 crêpes
Calories per crêpe: 156

CHEESE QUICHE

1 cup fine whole-wheat breadcrumbs (from acceptable
    bread)
2 tablespoons tomato juice
1 carrot, sliced
1 green pepper, cut into small squares
5 mushrooms, sliced
1 large clove garlic
⅓–½ cup nonfat milk, as required
¼ cup frozen apple juice concentrate
3 cups crumbled hoop cheese or other uncreamed
    cottage cheese (dry curd cottage cheese is excellent)
4 egg whites
WHITE SAUCE No. 2 (optional)

Prepare the breadcrumbs by processing bread in a food processor or blender. Mix the tomato juice with the breadcrumbs. Press the breadcrumbs into a 9-inch pie pan, forming a crust approximately ¼-inch thick. Bake the crust at 350° for 10–15 minutes.

Steam the carrots, bell pepper, mushrooms, and garlic for 10 minutes in a little water in a covered pan or steamer basket. Remove the garlic and place in a blender with the milk, apple juice concentrate, and cheese; blend until smooth but still thick. If ½ cup milk is not enough to obtain a good consistency, add milk 1 tablespoon at a time until the desired consistency is achieved. Transfer the cheese mixture to a bowl. Stir in the steamed vegetables. Beat the egg whites until stiff peaks form; fold into cheese-vegetable mixture. Pour the quiche batter into the prepared crust. Bake at 350° for 20–25 minutes. Allow the quiche to set at room temperature for about 15 minutes. Serve with *WHITE SAUCE No. 2*, if desired.

Makes 6–8 servings
Calories per serving (⅙ recipe): 135

JEANNE'S GARDEN "PASTA" WITH SAUCE

Sauce:
>   2 29-ounce cans tomato sauce
>   4 cups water
>   1 large onion, finely chopped
>   3 cloves garlic, minced
>   1½ teaspoons oregano
>   1½ teaspoons basil
>   Dash cayenne pepper
>
>   1 large spaghetti squash (about 5 pounds)
>   ½ cup crumbled hoop cheese or other uncreamed cottage cheese
>   8 sprigs parsley

Combine all the sauce ingredients in a large saucepan. Bring to a boil, then reduce the heat and simmer uncovered for at least 2 hours.

Cut the squash in half with a heavy knife. (The squash can be cut crosswise or lengthwise; cutting it lengthwise produces longer strands.) Remove and discard the seeds. Place the squash halves, cut side down, in nonstick baking dishes. Bake at 350° for 1 hour, or until fork-tender. Using a fork, pull the cooked squash in strands from the skin.

Put 1 cup of the "spaghetti" on each plate. Pour ¾ cup sauce over each serving (the sauce should be hot). Sprinkle 1 tablespoon hoop cheese on each serving and garnish with a parsley sprig.

Makes 8 servings
Calories per serving (including sauce): 170

POTATO GNOCCHI

> *1½ pounds white rose potatoes, peeled*
> *1 cup whole-wheat pastry flour*
> *1 cup unbleached white pastry flour*
> *Additional flour as required for kneading (about ½ cup)*

Optional Fillings:
> *1⅓ cups minced onions*
> *½ cup grated Sapsago cheese, lightly oven-toasted*

Sauce:
> *1 28-ounce can crushed tomatoes in purée*
> *1 15-ounce can tomato sauce*
> *1 tablespoon ground oregano*
> *1 tablespoon garlic powder*

Cook the potatoes in boiling water until tender but still firm. While the potatoes are cooking, prepare the sauce. Combine the sauce ingredients in a saucepan. Bring to a boil, then turn down the heat and simmer gently for about 10 minutes. Set aside.

Drain the cooked potatoes, and transfer to a bowl; mash the potatoes while still hot. In a small bowl, blend together the whole-wheat and unbleached white pastry flours. Mix the flours into the potatoes, a little at a time, blending well. The dough should be firm. Transfer the dough to a floured breadboard and knead gently for about 4 minutes, adding more flour as required to prevent sticking. Sprinkle the dough with more flour, and cut into 4 equal pieces. Roll each piece into a long cylinder about ½-inch in diameter. (If a filling is used, flatten the cylinders, and sprinkle ⅓ cup onions and/or 2 tablespoons Sapsago cheese on each cylinder, distributing evenly on the flattened surface; then reroll the cylinders.) Cut each cylinder into 1-inch pieces; press around the cut edges with the tines of a fork.

Cook the gnocchi in approximately 3 batches in a large pot of boiling water. Drop them in carefully, a few at a time. Stir with a spoon to prevent sticking and to enable the gnocchi to float freely (they will rise to the surface). Cook each batch for 10 minutes, then remove with a slotted spoon and place in a nonstick baking dish. Reheat the sauce and spoon it over the gnocchi. Bake at 350° for 15–20 minutes.

Makes approximately 9 servings (12 gnocchi/serving with sauce)

Calories per serving (without optional fillings): 224

CHINESE EGG ROLLS

> ⅔ cup bean sprouts
> ⅔ cup canned sliced water chestnuts
> ⅔ cup chopped green onions
> ⅔ cup diced green or red bell peppers
> ⅔ cup chopped bok choy
> ⅔ cup coarsely chopped snow peas (Chinese pea pods)
> 1 tablespoon soy sauce or tamari
> 1 tablespoon onion powder
> ¼ teaspoon garlic powder
> ¼ teaspoon thyme
> ¼ teaspoon poultry seasoning
> Pinch turmeric
> Defatted chicken or vegetable stock (see recipes for stocks) or water, as required
> 6 chapatis (whole-wheat tortillas sold in health food stores) or CHAPATIS (see recipe)
> 2 egg whites, beaten with a fork

In a large skillet, sauté the vegetables and seasonings in a small amount of stock or water until tender. Divide the vegetable mixture into 6 portions. Place 1 portion in the center of each chapati, and roll up the chapati. Place seam-side-down on a nonstick baking sheet and brush with the egg whites. Bake uncovered at 375° for 20 minutes. Serve with prepared hot mustard, if desired.

NOTE: In the 14-day menu plan, the serving size for this recipe is based on store-bought chapatis.

Makes 6 servings

Calories per serving: 135 (store-bought chapatis); 99 (chapatis made from recipe)

EGGPLANT ENCHILADAS

1 large onion, chopped
1 large green pepper, chopped
3 cloves garlic, minced
5 cups peeled eggplant chunks (about 1 large eggplant)
1 15-ounce can whole tomatoes, drained and chopped
1 15-ounce can tomato sauce
3 tablespoons cider vinegar
1 tablespoon canned diced green chilies
1 tablespoon mild chili powder
1 teaspoon ground cumin
1 teaspoon ground coriander
⅛ teaspoon black mustard seeds
12 corn tortillas
Additional tomato sauce if required
Garnish: nonfat yogurt or GREEN GODDESS TOP-
PING, chopped green onions

In a skillet, water-sauté the onion, green pepper, and garlic. Stir in the eggplant chunks and tomatoes. Cook over low heat until most of the liquid has evaporated. Add the tomato sauce, vinegar, chilies, and spices; stir to mix. Bring to a boil, then cover, turn down the heat, and simmer until the eggplant is tender.

Warm each tortilla briefly in the oven. Using a slotted spoon, fill each tortilla with eggplant mixture. Roll and lay the enchiladas seam-side-down in a nonstick baking dish. As a topping for the enchiladas, use 1 cup of the sauce remaining in the skillet. (If the sauce in the skillet is not sufficient, add additional tomato sauce to equal 1 cup.) Pour the sauce over the enchiladas and cover the baking pan. If using foil, make a dome to avoid contact with the tomato products. Bake at 350° for 30 minutes. Serve the enchiladas garnished with nonfat yogurt or *GREEN GODDESS TOPPING* and chopped green onions.

VARIATIONS: Instead of baking the enchiladas, simply fill the warmed tortillas with the eggplant mixture, add a dollop of nonfat yogurt or *GREEN GODDESS TOPPING*, and serve. For enchiladas with more bulk and texture, mix 1 cup cooked millet with ½ cup tomato juice. When the eggplant filling is cooked, use a slotted spoon to transfer the eggplant and vegetables from the skillet to a bowl. Add the millet mixture to the eggplant and mix before filling the tortillas. You may wish to increase the amount of the spices in this version.

Makes 12 enchiladas
Calories per enchilada (without garnish): 104

SCRAMBLED TOFU OLÉ

> *1 4-ounce cake firm tofu*
> *2 egg whites*
> *¼ cup minced green onions*
> *¼ cup sliced mushrooms*
> *1 clove garlic, minced*
> *1/16 teaspoon ground cumin*
> *1/16 teaspoon cayenne pepper*
> *Chili powder to taste*
> *Garnish: SALSA*

Combine all the ingredients in a bowl, using a wire whisk to blend the mixture. Heat a nonstick skillet and add the mixture. Cook rapidly over moderate heat, stirring constantly. Garnish with *SALSA*.

VARIATION: Use ¼ cup chopped canned artichoke hearts (water-packed) instead of the sliced mushrooms.

Makes 1–2 servings
Calories per serving (without garnish, ½ recipe): 72

OMELET

> *¼ cup defatted chicken or vegetable stock (see recipe*
> *for stocks) or water*
> *1 cup chopped onions*
> *½ teaspoon curry powder*
> *½ cup nonfat buttermilk*

½ cup evaporated skimmed milk
⅓ cup whole-wheat pastry flour
1 teaspoon baking powder
6 egg whites
1 cup chopped green onions (chopped chives may be
    substituted for ½ cup of the green onions, if desired)
Garlic powder to taste
Pepper to taste
SPANISH SAUCE, optional

Heat the stock or water in a small skillet and sauté the onions, sprinkling with the curry powder. Set aside. Blend the milks, flour, and baking powder in a blender. In a large mixing bowl, beat the egg whites until soft peaks form. Gently fold the blender mixture into the beaten egg whites. Mix the sautéed onions, green onions, and spices into the omelet batter.

If necessary to prevent sticking, prepare a nonstick skillet or crêpe pan by dabbing a little oil on a paper towel or Handi-Wipe, rinsing the towel in water and wringing it out, then wiping over the skillet or crêpe pan surface. Use the towel whenever sticking is a problem, but do not add more oil to it. Place the pan over moderate heat. When the pan is hot, pour about ¾ cup omelet batter into the pan, spreading it around evenly, and cook on one side. When the edges brown, turn the omelet, using an extra-wide spatula, and brown the other side. Carefully fold the omelet in half and place in a covered baking dish. Keep the dish in a warm oven, adding the other omelets as they are cooked. Serve hot with SPANISH SAUCE if desired.

Makes 5 servings
Calories per serving (not including sauce): 99

EGG WHITE SCRAMBLE

½ cup chopped green pepper
½ cup chopped onions
4 egg whites
¼ cup evaporated skimmed milk
1 tablespoon canned diced green chilies
¼ teaspoon chili powder or more to taste
Pinch oregano
Onion powder and garlic powder to taste (optional)

Heat a nonstick skillet over moderate heat. Add the green pepper and onions to the skillet and stir-fry the vegetables for a few minutes over the dry heat until they are slightly yellowed and partially cooked. Beat the egg whites with a wire whisk until foamy, then beat in the milk. Pour this mixture over the green pepper and onions and continue to cook, stirring occasionally, for a few minutes. Stir in the chilies and spices and continue cooking, stirring occasionally, for a few more minutes, until the eggs are almost completely cooked. Cover the skillet and leave over the heat for a few minutes to dry out the eggs a little more, if desired.

Makes 1–2 servings
Calories per recipe: 173

HONG KONG EGG WHITE SCRAMBLE

1 cup sliced mushrooms
¼ cup chopped onions
¼ cup chopped green onions
¼ cup chopped green pepper
½ teaspoon soy sauce or tamari
4 egg whites
¼ teaspoon curry powder
¼ cup nonfat dry milk mixed with 2 tablespoons cold water
1 cup bean sprouts
⅛ teaspoon paprika
Pinch pepper

Heat a nonstick skillet over moderate heat. Add the mushrooms, onions, green onions, green pepper, and soy sauce or tamari to the skillet and stir-fry the vegetables for a few minutes over the dry heat until they are slightly yellowed and partially cooked. Beat the egg whites with a wire whisk until foamy. Stir the curry powder into the dry milk mixture and add to the beaten egg whites. Pour this mixture over the vegetables and continue to cook, stirring occasionally, for a few minutes. Stir in the bean

prouts and spices and continue cooking, stirring occasionally,
or a few more minutes, until the eggs are almost completely
ooked. Cover the skillet and leave over the heat for a few
minutes to dry out the eggs a little more, if desired.

Makes 1–2 servings
Calories per recipe: 221

Vegetables

VEGETABLE COMBINATION No. 1

> 4 cups cut-up broccoli stalks
> 2 cups sliced cauliflower
> 1 cup sliced carrots
> Curry powder and lemon juice to taste

Place the vegetables in a steamer basket or pot with a little water. Steam, covered, until tender-crisp. Sprinkle curry powder and lemon juice to taste over the hot vegetables.

Makes 4–5 servings
Calories per serving (¼ recipe): 64

VEGETABLE COMBINATION No. 2

> 4 cups coarsely chopped broccoli
> 2 cups diagonally sliced celery
> 1 cup coarsely diced onions
> ½ cup diced red bell pepper or 1 2-ounce jar pimientos, rinsed and diced
> Dill weed and thyme or marjoram to taste

Place the vegetables in a steamer basket or pot with a little water. Steam, covered, until tender-crisp. Season to taste with the spices.

Makes 4–5 servings
Calories per serving (¼ recipe): 73

VEGETABLE COMBINATION No. 3

> 2 cups sliced green beans
> 2 cups sliced zucchini
> 2 cups sliced yellow squash
> 1 cup coarsely diced onions
> 2 large tomatoes, diced
> Italian seasoning to taste

In a skillet, cook the green beans in a small amount of water until they are half done. Add the zucchini, squash and onions and cook until tender-crisp, stirring occasionally. Add tomatoes and Italian seasoning near the end of the cooking period.

Makes 4–6 servings
Calories per serving (¼ recipe): 77

VEGETABLE COMBINATION No. 4

4 cups sliced celery
3 cups coarsely diced green pepper
1 cup coarsely diced onions
2 large tomatoes, diced
¼ cup frozen corn
Cumin, garlic powder, onion powder, and pepper to taste

Sauté the celery, green pepper, and onions in a little water in a skillet until almost done, stirring occasionally. Add the tomatoes, corn, and seasonings, and continue cooking and stirring occasionally until done.

Makes 4–6 servings
Calories per serving (¼ recipe): 89

VEGETABLE COMBINATION No. 5

1 medium head cabbage, cut in wedges
8 large stalks celery, cut in large pieces
2 onions, quartered
2 carrots, halved
1 red or green bell pepper, sliced in strips or coarsely diced
Garlic powder, powdered ginger, lemon juice, and pepper to taste

Place the cabbage wedges, celery, onions, and carrots in a large skillet with a small amount of boiling water. Cover, lower heat, and steam until almost done. Add the red pepper and seasonings and continue cooking until done. Serve with hot prepared mustard if desired.

Makes 4–6 servings
Calories per serving (⅕ recipe): 91

BOUQUET OF GARDEN VEGETABLES

> 2 large stalks broccoli (chop stems and cut heads into flowerets)
> 2 carrots, sliced
> 2 tomatoes, quartered
> 2 stalks celery, sliced
> 1 onion, sliced
> 1 green pepper, sliced in rings
> ¼ head cauliflower, cut into flowerets
> 12 green beans, broken in half, with the ends removed
> 4 cloves garlic, finely chopped
> ½ bunch parsley, finely chopped
> Juice of ½ lemon (optional)

Place all the ingredients except the lemon juice in a large pot; add 3 cups water. Bring to a boil, lower heat, cover, and simmer over low heat for about 15 minutes. If desired, add the lemon juice before serving.

NOTE: This preparation results in very tender vegetables and a relatively large amount of left-over cooking liquid, which may be enjoyed as a broth or reserved for use in other recipes as a vegetable stock.

Makes 4 servings
Calories per serving: 128

RATATOUILLE No. 1

> ½ cup defatted stock of choice (see recipes for stocks) or water
> 1 cup cubed eggplant
> 1 cup diced tomatoes
> 2 cloves garlic, minced
> 1 teaspoon fresh oregano or ½ teaspoon dried oregano
> 1 teaspoon fresh basil or ½ teaspoon dried basil

1 cup diced onions
1 cup diced celery
1 cup finely chopped green pepper
2/3 cup thinly sliced zucchini
2/3 cup diced mushrooms

Sauce:
1 cup tomato sauce
1 tablespoon frozen apple juice concentrate
1 tablespoon vinegar
1 tablespoon cornstarch

In a skillet, sauté the eggplant, tomatoes, garlic, and herbs together in the stock or water until the eggplant is ¼ done. Add the other vegetables and cook until almost done.

Using a wire whisk, combine the sauce ingredients and pour over the vegetables. Mix well and cook, covered, until slightly thickened.

Makes 4 servings
Calories per serving: 98

RATATOUILLE No. 2

*1 cup defatted stock of choice (see recipes for stocks)
    or water*
2 cups coarsely chopped celery with leaves
5 cloves garlic, minced
4 tomatoes, cut into chunks
*1 large eggplant, peeled and cut up (cut eggplant in
    half and then cut each half lengthwise into 6 pieces;
    slice each piece diagonally)*
2 medium zucchini, sliced about 1 inch thick
2 large parsnips, sliced about 1 inch thick
*2 medium red or green bell peppers, cut lengthwise
    into 4 pieces*
1 large onion, cut into large chunks
2 cups chopped green onions
*1 16-ounce can diced tomatoes in purée or substitute
    ¾ of a 15-ounce can of tomato sauce plus ¾ of a
    1-pound can of whole tomatoes, drained and chopped*
1 15-ounce can tomato sauce

½ cup tomato paste
¼ cup frozen apple juice concentrate
1 tablespoon rice vinegar or other mild vinegar
1 tablespoon basil
1 teaspoon tarragon
2 tablespoons cornstarch
3 tablespoons water

Heat the stock or water in a large pot. Add the celery and garlic and cook for a few minutes. Add the rest of the vegetables except for the canned tomato products. Bring to a boil, lower heat, cover, and simmer for 30 minutes, stirring occasionally. Add the canned diced tomatoes, tomato sauce, and tomato paste. Cook for another 20 minutes. Stir in the apple juice concentrate, vinegar, basil, and tarragon. In a separate bowl, combine the cornstarch and water, and mix well. Add the cornstarch mixture to the vegetables and cook until thickened, stirring constantly.
Makes 14–16 cups
Calories per cup: approximately 96

CHINESE VEGETABLE STEW

1 onion, sliced
1 green pepper, sliced
½ 8-ounce can bamboo shoots, drained
½ 8-ounce can water chestnuts, drained and thinly sliced
1 tomato, cut in 8 wedges
2 green onions, finely chopped
1 1-inch piece of ginger, peeled and finely chopped
4 cloves garlic, finely chopped
Pinch poultry seasoning
½ pound fresh snow peas (Chinese pea pods) or ½ package frozen pea pods
½ pound bean sprouts or 1 16-ounce can bean sprouts, drained
Soy sauce or tamari (optional)

Place all the ingredients except the snow peas and bean sprouts in a pot with 1 cup water. Bring to a boil, lower heat and simmer, covered, for 15 minutes. Add the snow peas and bean sprouts; simmer 5–10 minutes longer. At serving time, season with a little soy sauce or tamari if desired.

Makes 3–4 servings (approximately 5 cups)
Calories per serving (⅓ recipe): 103

CHINESE STIR-FRIED VEGETABLES

½ cup defatted stock of choice (see recipes for stocks)
1 cup chopped onions
4 cups chopped bok choy
4 cups bean sprouts
2 tomatoes, quartered
1 tablespoon soy sauce or tamari
½–1 teaspoon powdered ginger
½ teaspoon garlic powder
½ teaspoon onion powder

Heat the stock in a large skillet. Add the onions and then the bok choy and cook over moderate heat, stirring occasionally. After about 5 minutes, add the bean sprouts, tomatoes, and seasonings. Continue to cook, stirring as necessary, until the vegetables are tender.

Makes 6 cups (4 servings)
Calories per serving: 83

STIR-FRIED CAULIFLOWER COMBINATION

1 head cauliflower, broken into flowerets
2 cloves garlic, mashed
1 slice ginger the size of a quarter, minced
1 yellow squash, cut into ½-inch pieces
1 red or green bell pepper, cut into ¼-inch strips
3 tomatoes, cut into wedges
½ teaspoon oregano
½ teaspoon basil
½ cup green peas, fresh or frozen

Precook the cauliflower in a covered steamer basket or in a pot with a little water until partially cooked. Drain the cauliflower and reserve the cooking liquid. In a large skillet, sauté the garlic and ginger for 1 minute in a few tablespoons of water. Add the cauliflower and a few tablespoons of the reserved cooking liquid and stir-fry the cauliflower for 2 minutes. Add the squash, peppers, and a few more tablespoons of the reserved cooking liquid if necessary and stir-fry for 2 more minutes. Add the tomatoes, seasonings, and about ½ cup of the reserved cooking liquid and cover and steam for 5 minutes. Remove the cover, add the peas, and cook for 3–4 minutes or until vegetables are tender.

Makes 8 servings
Calories per serving: 56

VEGETABLE MEDLEY

>   *2 cups sliced carrots*
>   *2 cups sliced zucchini*
>   *2 cups broccoli flowerets*
>   *2 cups cauliflower flowerets*
>   *1 cup diced red bell pepper*
>   *1 cup diced green bell pepper*
>   *¼ cup chopped parsley*
>   *¼ cup chopped chives or green onion tops*
>   *2 teaspoons basil, crushed*

Steam the vegetables in a steamer basket or pot with a little water, covered, until just tender-crisp. Drain the vegetables and set aside, reserving the cooking liquid. Heat ½ cup of the cooking liquid in a large skillet. Add the parsley, chives, and basil and mix thoroughly. Add the drained vegetables and heat through, stirring occasionally.

Makes 6–8 servings
Calories per serving (⅛ recipe): 45

ARTICHOKES WITH FRESH TOMATO SAUCE

>   *4 medium artichokes*
>   *1 lemon, sliced*
>   *1 cup chopped onions*

4 cloves garlic, minced
6 cups chopped tomatoes (8–10 tomatoes, peeled if
    desired)
½ cup chopped parsley
¼ cup lemon juice
1 teaspoon basil
½ teaspoon rosemary

Rinse the artichokes. Cut off the stems close to the base and cut 1 inch off the tops. In a large pot, bring 2 inches of water to a boil and add the lemon slices and artichokes. Cover, turn down the heat, and simmer 25–30 minutes or until tender. Remove the artichokes from the pot and turn upside down to drain.

Place the onion, garlic, and a few tablespoons of water in a large skillet and sauté until the vegetables are soft. If the tomatoes are to be peeled, plunge them briefly in boiling water and then skin them. Stir in the chopped tomatoes and the remaining ingredients and simmer over low heat for 15 minutes, stirring occasionally.

Place the artichokes on individual serving dishes and spoon the tomato sauce around them. To eat, pull off leaf, dip into sauce, and draw the fleshy portion off between the teeth; discard the remainder of the leaf. When you reach the center, remove the fuzzy section and eat the artichoke heart with sauce.

VARIATION: To make artichoke bowls to hold the tomato sauce, remove the center leaves and spread the artichokes open carefully. The fuzzy choke can be pulled out a little at a time, using a teaspoon (a serrated one works best) to remove the last bits. If desired, the bowls may be used to hold salads, jellied soups, or other sauces, or to hold dips for party buffets.

Makes 4 servings
Calories per serving: 149

STIR-FRIED ASPARAGUS

1½ pounds asparagus or 2 packages frozen asparagus
½ cup defatted stock of choice (see recipes for stocks)
    or water
1 teaspoon soy sauce or tamari
1 teaspoon lemon juice or ½ lemon cut in slices

Cut the asparagus into thick diagonal slices. Heat the stock or water and soy sauce or tamari in a skillet. Add the asparagus and stir-fry rapidly for a few minutes. Add the lemon juice or lemon slices just before serving.

Makes 4–6 servings
Calories per serving (¼ recipe): 46

ONIONED GREEN BEANS

3½ cups green beans, fresh or frozen
1 cup sliced onions
2 teaspoons dried minced onion

Cook the green beans in a few inches of water until tender. Drain, reserving the liquid. In a skillet, heat a few tablespoons of water to a boil. Add the sliced onions and dried onion and cook, stirring constantly, until the onions have yellowed and the water has evaporated. Add the green beans and a little of their cooking liquid. Heat through.

Makes 4–6 servings
Calories per serving (¼ recipe): 50

GREEN BEANS AND TOMATOES OREGANO

1 pound fresh green beans, trimmed and sliced
2 tomatoes, chopped
1 small onion, diced
½ teaspoon oregano
⅛ teaspoon pepper

Place the ingredients in a saucepan with 1 cup of water. Bring to a boil, lower heat and simmer, covered, until the beans are tender-crisp, about 10 minutes. Drain and serve.

Makes 6 servings
Calories per serving: 37

SWEET-AND-SOUR RED CABBAGE

1 cup defatted stock of choice (see recipes for stocks)
1 16-ounce can diced tomatoes in purée or substitute
   ¾ of a 15-ounce can of tomato sauce plus ¾ of a
   1-pound can of whole tomatoes, drained and chopped
1 15-ounce can tomato sauce
3 tablespoons lemon juice
2 tablespoons vinegar
1 medium-sized red cabbage, shredded
1 red onion, cut in thin strips
3 shallots, sliced
1 tablespoon pickling spices tied in cheesecloth or in a
   tea infuser
1 teaspoon curry powder
⅛ teaspoon cayenne pepper
Allspice to taste
1 tablespoon arrowroot
¼ cup frozen apple juice concentrate

Place the stock, tomatoes, tomato sauce, lemon juice, and vinegar in a large skillet. Add the raw vegetables, pickling spices, curry powder, cayenne pepper, and allspice. Heat to a boil, turn down the heat, cover, and simmer for 20 minutes, stirring occasionally. In a separate bowl, combine the arrowroot and apple juice concentrate and mix well. Stir into the cabbage mixture and simmer for another 10 minutes, stirring occasionally. Remove the pickling spices before serving.
Makes 8 cups
Calories per ½ cup: 57

PICKLED BEETS

½ cup cider vinegar
½ cup beet juice (liquid from can of beets)
1 tablespoon frozen apple juice concentrate
2 whole cloves
3 peppercorns
¼ bay leaf
2½ cups canned sliced beets
2 small green onions, sliced

Boil the vinegar and beet juice together for a few minutes. Add the apple juice concentrate, cloves, peppercorns, and bay leaf. Heat to boiling. Pour the liquid with seasonings over the sliced beets and green onions. Chill before serving.

NOTE: If you prefer using fresh beets, see the recipe for *FRESH-BEET BORSCHT* for a method of preparing beets and juice.

Makes 6–8 servings
Calories per serving (⅛ recipe): 28

STEAMED YOUNG GREENS

Mustard or turnip greens, collards, romaine lettuce or butter lettuce, or other suitable greens (beet greens and spinach are not recommended for frequent use because of their high content of a calcium-binding substance)
Lemon juice (optional)

If the greens are young and fresh, they may be cooked in the water that clings to them after they have been thoroughly washed and drained. Place the greens in a skillet with a close-fitting lid and simmer for a few minutes, up to about 10 minutes if necessary, until tender. If the greens are not particularly young, place a little water in the bottom of the skillet, bring to a boil, and add the washed greens. Turn down heat to a simmer, and continue cooking until tender. Sprinkle with lemon juice if desired.

Calories per cup: 32 (mustard greens); 29 (turnip greens); 63 (collard greens)

HERBED GREENS

8 cups coarsely chopped greens (mustard or turnip
greens, collards, or other suitable greens; beet
greens and spinach are not recommended for frequent use because of their high content of a calcium-
binding substance)
2 cups defatted chicken or vegetable stock (see recipes
for stocks) or more if desired
1 tablespoon soy sauce or tamari
1 tablespoon frozen apple juice concentrate
1 tablespoon dried minced onion
¾ teaspoon garlic powder
½ teaspoon Italian seasoning or rosemary

Wash the greens thoroughly and remove the stems below the
leaves. Bring the stock and an additional 1 cup water to a boil in
a pot and add the greens and the remaining ingredients. Turn
down the heat to a simmer, cover, and cook about 1½ hours. (If
frozen greens are used, the cooking time may be reduced by
about half.) Drain the greens before serving and allow ¼ cup
cooking liquid to be mixed with each serving of greens.

Makes 2 servings (approximately 2 cups drained greens)
Calories per serving: 47 (mustard or turnip greens); 80
(collard greens)

STUFFED MUSHROOMS

½ cup whole-wheat breadcrumbs (from acceptable bread)
18 large mushrooms
¼ cup finely chopped parsley
¼ cup chopped shallots or onions
1½ teaspoons basil
⅛ teaspoon garlic powder
⅛ teaspoon onion powder
⅛ teaspoon celery seed
Cayenne pepper to taste
⅓ cup defatted stock of choice (see recipes for stocks)
or water
2 tablespoons white wine
½ teaspoon soy sauce or tamari
2 tablespoons tomato sauce

Prepare the breadcrumbs by processing bread in a food processor or blender. Cut the stems from the mushrooms and set aside the mushroom caps. Chop the mushroom stems finely and combine them with the parsley, onions, and seasonings. Heat the stock, wine, and soy sauce or tamari in a skillet. Sauté the vegetable mixture in the simmering liquid for about 10 minutes, stirring occasionally. (If more liquid is required, add more stock or water.) Remove the skillet from the heat and drain off any excess liquid. Mix the breadcrumbs and the tomato sauce with the vegetables.

Stuff the mushroom caps with the prepared filling. Place them in a baking pan with a slight amount of water or stock in the bottom. Cover and bake at 325° for 20 minutes.

Makes 9 servings (2 mushrooms each)
Calories per serving: 26

ONION RINGS

> 2 cups fine whole-wheat breadcrumbs (from acceptable
>   bread), or matzo meal
> 3 shallots, minced (optional)
> ½ teaspoon garlic powder
> 2 large onions, sliced into rings
> 3 cups nonfat milk
> 1 cup rice flour
> 4 egg whites, whisked until foamy

If breadcrumbs are to be used, prepare them by processing in a food processor or blender. Mix the breadcrumbs or matzo meal with the shallots and garlic powder in a small bowl. Dip the onion rings in nonfat milk and then in rice flour, coating them thoroughly. Dip the coated rings in the egg whites and then in the breadcrumbs or matzo meal, again coating them thoroughly. Bake on a nonstick cookie sheet at 350° for about 25 minutes until golden brown.

Makes 7–8 servings
Calories per serving (⅛ recipe): 75

GINGERED PEPPERS

¼ cup wine vinegar
2 tablespoons Sauternes
1 tablespoon frozen apple juice concentrate
¼ teaspoon minced fresh ginger
1 green pepper, sliced or cut into small squares

Place the vinegar, Sauternes, apple juice concentrate, and ginger in a small skillet and bring to a boil. Add the green pepper and cook until tender-crisp, stirring frequently.

Makes 1–2 servings
Calories per serving (½ recipe): 35

POTATOES WITH CREAM SAUCE

10–12 small red potatoes
2 cups chopped onions
1½ cups nonfat milk
3 tablespoons flour
⅛ teaspoon pepper
1 cup defatted stock of choice (see recipes for stocks)
Paprika
Dried parsley

Place the potatoes in a pot of boiling water and simmer until nearly tender. Drain and cool the potatoes, then peel and halve lengthwise. Soak the onions in 1 cup of the milk for about 30 minutes. Blend the remaining milk with the flour and pepper. In a saucepan, heat the onion-milk mixture and the stock to a boil. Stir in the flour paste, and continue stirring until mixture is thickened.

Spread a thin layer of the cream sauce in a nonstick baking dish. Arrange the potatoes flat-side-down over the sauce. Spoon the remaining sauce over the potatoes and sprinkle with paprika and parsley. Cover and bake at 375° for about 30 minutes.

Makes 6–8 servings
Calories per serving (⅛ recipe): 172

OVEN-ROASTED POTATOES

> *6 round potatoes, peeled and sliced in half lengthwis*
> *1 cup chopped onions*
> *2 tablespoons soy sauce or tamari*
> *1 teaspoon dried parsley*
> *1 teaspoon paprika*

Cut the potatoes into ¼-inch slices and line them up on
nonstick baking pan. Sprinkle with the onions, soy sauce
tamari, and the parsley and paprika. Bake covered at 400° f
one hour.
Makes 6–9 servings
Calories per serving (⅑ recipe): 69

HASH BROWN POTATOES

> *2 cups chopped onions*
> *4 russet potatoes, cooked until almost done, peele*
> *and cut shoestring style*
> *¾ cup whole-wheat pastry flour or more as required*
> *1½ cups defatted stock of choice (see recipes for stock*
> *or more as required*
> *1 tablespoon soy sauce or tamari*
> *Pepper to taste*
> *SPANISH SAUCE (optional)*

Brown the onions in a large nonstick skillet over low hea
adding a little stock if too dry. Remove from the heat. Separat
the onions and the potatoes into three portions of roughly equa
size, as three batches will be prepared.
For each batch, coat the potatoes with flour. Add ½ cup stoc
and 1 teaspoon soy sauce or tamari to the skillet and heat unt
simmering. Add one portion each of the onions and potatoe
Lightly sprinkle with pepper. Cook until the potatoes are glaze
and tender, adding a little more stock if needed. Transfer to
covered casserole to keep warm while the other batches ar
prepared.
Serve with *SPANISH SAUCE* if desired.
Makes 4 servings
Calories per serving: 284

PARSLIED POTATOES

8 small red or white rose potatoes
1 cup defatted stock of choice (see recipes for stocks)
  or more if needed
1 tablespoon soy sauce or tamari
1 tablespoon dry white wine
1 tablespoon dried parsley
1 tablespoon paprika
¼ teaspoon each: pepper, onion powder, garlic powder

Boil the potatoes until about ⅔ cooked. Cool; peel and halve lengthwise. In a skillet, heat the stock, soy sauce or tamari, and wine to a boil. Add the potato halves and cook, basting constantly for 2–3 minutes.

Pour the remaining liquid from the skillet into a nonstick baking dish and arrange the potatoes, flat side down. Mix the parsley flakes, paprika, pepper, and onion and garlic powders together and sprinkle over potatoes. Bake uncovered at 350° for 20 minutes. (If the bottom of the dish becomes too dry, add more stock.)

Makes 6–8 servings
Calories per serving (⅛ recipe): 83

BAKED STUFFED POTATOES

3 potatoes (Idaho or other baking variety)
⅓ cup chopped onions
1 cup nonfat buttermilk
1 tablespoon grated Sapsago cheese
½ teaspoon onion powder
½ teaspoon garlic powder
½–1½ teaspoons dried or fresh parsley
¼–½ teaspoon paprika
⅛–¼ teaspoon dill weed
⅛–¼ teaspoon prepared mustard
1 egg white, stiffly beaten
MOCK SOUR CREAM (optional)

Bake the potatoes at 350° for 1–1½ hours, or until tender. Cut them in half lengthwise. With a spoon, scoop the potato into a mixing bowl, keeping the skins intact for stuffing. Sauté the chopped onions in a few tablespoons of water in a skillet until tender. Add the onions and all the remaining ingredients except the egg white to the potatoes, and whip together. Fold in the egg white.

Stuff the potato skins with the mashed potato mixture and place them on nonstick baking sheets. Sprinkle the potatoes with additional paprika and parsley. Bake at 350° until hot and browned.

May be served with *MOCK SOUR CREAM*.

Makes 6 servings
Calories per serving: 98

SPINACH PUFF

> *1 10–ounce package frozen chopped spinach*
> *½ cup nonfat milk*
> *1½ teaspoons unbleached all-purpose flour*
> *½ teaspoon onion powder*
> *⅛ teaspoon pepper*
> *2 tablespoons grated Sapsago cheese*
> *4 egg whites*

Cook spinach according to package directions; drain well. Stir together the spinach, milk, flour, onion powder, pepper, and cheese. Beat the egg whites until stiff peaks form. Gently fold the whites through the spinach mixture. Pour into an 8-inch-square nonstick pan or a nonstick muffin pan. Bake at 350° for 30 minutes, or until a knife inserted in the center comes out clean.

Makes 4 servings
Calories per serving: 53

BAKED BANANA SQUASH

> *1½ pounds Hubbard or banana squash*
> *1 tablespoon grated lemon rind*
> *¼–½ teaspoon nutmeg*

Scrub, rinse, and drain the squash and cut into individual serving pieces. Arrange the pieces in a baking pan with about 1 cup water. Distribute the lemon rind over the squash cavity and sprinkle with nutmeg. Cover and bake at 400° until fork-tender, about 45 minutes.

VARIATION: To serve with *BURGUNDY SAUCE*, pour off ⅓ cup of the cooked squash liquid into a saucepan, add ¼ cup burgundy wine, and heat to a simmer. Blend ¼ cup frozen apple juice concentrate with 1 tablespoon arrowroot and ¼ teaspoon allspice to a smooth paste. Add to the simmering liquid and thicken, stirring constantly. Spoon the sauce over the squash and return to a slow oven for a short time before serving.

Makes 4 servings
Calories per serving: 45 (without sauce); 84 (with sauce)

SQUASH SOUFFLÉ

> 4 cups cooked, mashed banana or butternut squash
>   (steamed or boiled squash has fewer calories than
>   baked squash)
> 2 tablespoons frozen apple juice concentrate
> 1½ teaspoons cinnamon
> 1½ teaspoons pumpkin pie spice
> 1 teaspoon grated orange rind
> ⅛ teaspoon cayenne pepper
> 3 egg whites

Purée the squash in a blender. Add all the other ingredients except the egg whites and blend again; transfer to a mixing bowl. Beat the egg whites until stiff peaks form and fold into the squash mixture. Use a nonstick pan or prepare a soufflé dish by dabbing a little oil on a paper towel or Handi-Wipe, rinsing the towel in water and wringing it out, then wiping over the dish. Bake at 400° for about 25 minutes until top begins to brown.

Makes 6–8 servings
Calories per serving (⅙ recipe): 84

SPICY SPROUTS

1 cup water or defatted stock of choice (see recipes for stocks)
1½ cups tomato sauce
⅓ cup tomato paste
⅓ cup rice vinegar or other mild vinegar
3 tablespoons frozen apple juice concentrate
1 tablespoon soy sauce or tamari
1 tablespoon garlic powder
1 teaspoon celery seed
7 cups fresh bean sprouts
1 tablespoon cornstarch mixed with 1½ tablespoons water to a smooth paste

Combine all the ingredients, except the bean sprouts and cornstarch, and bring to a boil in a pot. Add the bean sprouts, reduce the heat, and simmer, covered, for 3 minutes. Add the cornstarch paste and stir mixture constantly until thickened.

Makes 6 cups
Calories per cup: 105

REFRIED BEANS

2 cups small red beans
4 small carrots, cut in chunks
2 onions, quartered
2 cloves garlic, minced
4 teaspoons cumin
½ cup canned green chili salsa
¼ cup tomato sauce
2 teaspoons lemon juice
1 tablespoon chili powder or to taste
2½ teaspoons garlic powder
2 teaspoons chopped shallots
2 teaspoons chopped fresh cilantro (optional)

Soak the beans in water overnight or soak for several hours in water that has been preheated to a boil. Drain the beans and place in a large saucepan with 8 cups water. Add the carrots, onions, garlic, and 2 teaspoons of the cumin. Bring to a boil, turn down the heat, and simmer partially covered until the beans are tender, about 1–2 hours. Drain and mash the cooked beans and vegetables. Mix in the chili salsa, tomato sauce, lemon juice, chili powder, garlic powder, and the remaining 2 teaspoons cumin. In a small skillet, sauté the shallots and cilantro in 2 tablespoons water or defatted stock for a few minutes; mix in with the beans. Transfer the beans to a casserole and bake in a moderate oven until very hot.

VARIATION: To serve as a dip, stir in additional canned green chili salsa to achieve a thinner consistency and add 2–3 teaspoons additional chopped fresh cilantro (not sautéed). Garnish with additional cilantro or parsley.

Makes 7 cups
Calories per ½ cup: 110

BAKED TOMATOES

> *3 large tomatoes, halved*
> *2 tablespoons dried parsley*
> *2 tablespoons dried minced onion*
> *1 tablespoon basil*
> *2 tablespoons grated Sapsago cheese*

Place the halved tomatoes cut side up in a shallow nonstick baking pan. Sprinkle the parsley, onion, basil, and cheese over the tomatoes. Bake at 325° until tender, about 15–20 minutes.

Makes 6 servings
Calories per serving: 31

CHERRY TOMATO GARNISH

> *12 cherry tomatoes*
> *Liquid, as required: for example, equal parts of de-*
> *fatted stock of choice (see recipes for stocks) and*
> *white wine*
> *⅓ cup finely chopped parsley*
> *Dash white pepper*

Bring a small amount of liquid to a boil in a saucepan. Reduce the heat and add tomatoes. Toss them in the hot liquid, just long enough to heat them and give them a gloss. Sprinkle with parsley and white pepper. Serve immediately.

Makes 4 servings

Calories per serving: 14

Sauces, Gravies, Relishes

MUSHROOM CREAM SAUCE

1½ cups defatted chicken or vegetable stock (see recipes for stocks)
½ cup sliced mushrooms
1 teaspoon diced shallots
½ teaspoon finely minced parsley
1 tablespoon tomato paste
1 teaspoon minced canned pimientos
1 teaspoon soy sauce or tamari
2 tablespoons cornstarch
¼ cup evaporated skimmed milk
2 tablespoons dry white wine

Put all the ingredients except the cornstarch, milk, and wine in a saucepan. Bring to a boil. Turn down the heat and simmer covered until the mushrooms are tender. In a separate bowl, mix the cornstarch, milk, and wine, blending well. Add the cornstarch mixture to the simmering sauce and stir constantly until thickened.

This sauce is excellent with vegetables, potatoes, chicken, or beef, and noodles.

Makes approximately 2 cups
Calories per ¼ cup: 17

WHITE SAUCE No. 1

2 cups defatted chicken or vegetable stock (see recipes
  for stocks)
2 cups nonfat dry milk
1 tablespoon dry white wine
2½ tablespoons cornstarch
1 teaspoon rosemary or other seasoning as desired
⅛ teaspoon curry powder
1 cup water

Heat the stock to a boil in a saucepan. In a bowl, blend the remaining ingredients to make a smooth mixture. Add slowly to the simmering stock, stirring constantly until the sauce is thickened and smooth.

Makes approximately 3 cups
Calories per ¼ cup: 47

WHITE SAUCE No. 2

> 1⅓ cups nonfat milk
> ⅓ cup nonfat dry milk
> 1 tablespoon arrowroot
> 2½ tablespoons Sauternes
> 1 teaspoon soy sauce or tamari
> 1 tablespoon onion powder
> 1 teaspoon garlic powder
> Dash dill weed

Heat 1 cup of the nonfat milk in a small saucepan, stirring occasionally. Combine the remaining milk and all the other ingredients, mixing to a smooth paste. When the milk in the saucepan simmers, add the thickening mixture and stir constantly until thickened.

Makes approximately 1½ cups
Calories per ¼ cup: 43

WHITE CHEESE SAUCE

> 2½ cups nonfat milk
> 3–4 tablespoons cornstarch
> 3 tablespoons grated Sapsago cheese, lightly oven-toasted
> 2 teaspoons whey powder (available in health-food stores), lightly oven-toasted
> 2 tablespoons dried minced onion
> ¼ teaspoon white pepper
> 1 2-ounce can whole pimientos, rinsed, coarsely diced

Blend the milk with the cornstarch and mix in the remaining ingredients. Cook over low heat, stirring frequently, until thickened.

Makes approximately 2⅔ cups
Calories per ¼ cup: 39

LEMON-GINGER SAUCE

2 cups defatted chicken or vegetable stock (see recipes for stocks)
1/4 cup nonfat dry milk
2 tablespoons whole-wheat pastry flour or rice flour
2 tablespoons cornstarch
1 cup nonfat fluid milk
1/4 cup frozen apple juice concentrate
3 tablespoons lemon juice
1 tablespoon finely chopped parsley
1 tablespoon curry powder
1/2 teaspoon powdered ginger
1/2 teaspoon garlic powder

Heat the stock in a saucepan to a boil, then turn down the heat to a simmer. Combine the dry milk, flour, and cornstarch in a bowl and stir in the fluid milk, apple juice concentrate, and lemon juice to make a smooth paste. Slowly add the paste to the simmering stock, stirring until thickened. Add the seasonings and continue stirring. Serve hot over crêpes, vegetables, etc.
Makes approximately 2 1/2 cups
Calories per 1/4 cup: 42

EGG-MUSTARD SAUCE

1/4 cup nonfat dry milk
1 tablespoon whole-wheat pastry flour
1 teaspoon onion powder
1/4 teaspoon garlic powder
1/4 teaspoon dry mustard
Dash cayenne pepper
2/3 cup water
1/3 cup rice vinegar or other mild vinegar
1 teaspoon frozen apple juice concentrate
1 egg white
Capers, horseradish, nonfat yogurt (optional)

Place the dry milk, flour and spices in a bowl. Stir in the water until smooth. Heat the vinegar and apple juice concentrate to a boil in a saucepan; add the milk-flour mixture and simmer, stirring constantly, until thickened.

Beat the egg white until foamy. (The sauce will be frothy.) Using a wire whisk, blend the egg white into the cooked sauce. If desired, add capers, horseradish, and/or nonfat yogurt. This sauce is especially good with fish.

Makes approximately 1¼ cups
Calories per ¼ cup (without optional ingredients): 27

CAULIFLOWER SAUCE

⅓ *medium cauliflower*
⅓ *leftover baked or boiled potato, peeled and quartered*
1 *cup nonfat buttermilk*
2 *tablespoons stoneground mustard (Inglehoffer's)*
1 *teaspoon dill weed*
¼ *teaspoon garlic powder*
⅛ *teaspoon curry powder*
⅛ *teaspoon pepper*

Place cauliflower in a steamer basket or pot with water and steam, covered, until well done. Drain, then transfer cauliflower to a blender; add the potato and purée. Pour puréed mixture into a saucepan together with the other ingredients. Stir continuously over low heat to mix well and heat thoroughly. Serve hot over vegetables (this sauce is especially good with broccoli or Brussels sprouts).

Makes approximately 3 cups
Calories per ¼ cup: 22

SPANISH SAUCE

½ *cup vegetable stock (see recipes for stocks) or water*
1 *16-ounce can diced tomatoes in purée or substitute*
     ¾ *of a 15-ounce can of tomato sauce plus ¾ of a*
     1-pound can of whole tomatoes, drained and chopped
¼ *cup picante sauce*
⅓ *cup chopped green onions*
1 *tablespoon frozen apple juice concentrate*
¼ *teaspoon garlic powder*
1 *tablespoon flour*

In a saucepan, combine ⅓ cup of the stock or water with all other ingredients except the flour. Heat the mixture to a gentle boil, then turn down the heat to a simmer. In a small bowl, mix the remaining stock or water and the flour to form a smooth paste, and stir it into the simmering mixture in the saucepan. Continue stirring until the sauce is thickened. Simmer covered several minutes longer.

Makes approximately 2 cups
Calories per ¼ cup: 33

ITALIAN SAUCE

2 onions, chopped
3 cloves garlic, minced
⅓ cup chopped parsley
1 carrot, grated
2 large tomatoes, chopped
1 28-ounce can crushed tomatoes in purée
2 15-ounce cans tomato sauce
⅓ cup red burgundy
2 tablespoons frozen apple juice concentrate
1 tablespoon basil
⅛ teaspoon thyme
⅛ teaspoon crushed dried red pepper
1 bay leaf

In a saucepan, sauté the onion, garlic, parsley, and carrot in ½ cup water. When the water has nearly evaporated, add the remaining ingredients and simmer uncovered for 30 minutes, stirring occasionally. Remove the bay leaf. If a smoother consistency is desired, purée all or part of the sauce in a blender, a few cups at a time.

Makes approximately 9 cups
Calories per ½ cup: 49

BARBECUE SAUCE

> 1 24-ounce can V-8 juice
> 1 tablespoon garlic powder
> 1 tablespoon onion powder
> 1 teaspoon curry powder
> 1 teaspoon powdered ginger
> 1 teaspoon Italian seasoning
> 1 teaspoon dried parsley

Mix together all the ingredients in a saucepan. Heat to a boil then simmer, stirring occasionally, until enough moisture has evaporated that the sauce is thickened sufficiently. If possible, refrigerate overnight before using.

Makes approximately 1½ cups
Calories per ¼ cup: 34

SPICY TOMATO SAUCE

> ½ cup dry vermouth or vegetable stock (see recipes for
>   stocks)
> 1 large onion, finely chopped
> 2 stalks celery with leaves, finely chopped
> 3 large cloves garlic, minced
> ½ cup finely chopped carrot
> ½ cup chopped parsley
> 1 16-ounce can diced tomatoes in purée or substitute
>   ¾ of a 15-ounce can of tomato sauce plus ¾ of a
>   1-pound can of whole tomatoes, drained and chopped
> 2 large tomatoes, chopped
> 1 tablespoon basil
> 1 tablespoon marjoram
> 1 tablespoon thyme
> 1 teaspoon pepper
> 1 teaspoon paprika
> 1 large bay leaf

In a nonstick skillet, sauté the onion, celery, garlic, and carrot in the dry vermouth or stock until the liquid has evaporated. Add the remaining ingredients and bring the mixture to a boil. Reduce the heat and simmer, covered, for one hour. Remove cover and continue simmering for 30 minutes, stirring occasionally.

Makes approximately 1½ quarts
Calories per ½ cup: 40

TANGY SAUCE

2 cups tomato sauce or crushed tomatoes in purée
1 tablespoon prepared mustard
1 tablespoon frozen apple juice concentrate
1 teaspoon coriander
1 teaspoon garlic powder
1 teaspoon onion powder
⅛ teaspoon allspice
Pinch cayenne pepper
½–1 whole green chili, minced

Combine all the ingredients in a saucepan and bring to a boil. Reduce the heat, cover, and simmer for one hour.

Makes 2 cups
Calories per ¼ cup: 29

ALL-PURPOSE SWEET-AND-SOUR COOKERY

1 cup rice vinegar or other mild vinegar
1 cup defatted stock of choice (see recipes for stocks) or water
¼ cup frozen apple juice concentrate
2 teaspoons soy sauce or tamari
1 teaspoon powdered ginger
1 teaspoon garlic powder
Onion powder to taste
Dry mustard to taste
2 tablespoons cornstarch

Marinade: Mix together all the ingredients except the cornstarch and use as a marinade for vegetables, chicken, beef, and fish.

VARIATION: Add tomato juice, unsweetened pineapple juice, and/or dry sherry or white wine.

Sauce: Mix together all the ingredients, including the cornstarch, and heat in a saucepan. Simmer for a few minutes, stirring constantly, until thickened. Serve as a sauce for stir-fried or steamed vegetable combinations.

NOTE: If additional liquid ingredients are used, such as those suggested in the marinade variation, a greater amount of cornstarch will be required for thickening.

Sweet-and-Sour Stir-Fry Cookery: Pour about ½ cup of the marinade into a skillet or wok and bring to a boil. Add selected vegetables and stir-fry until tender-crisp, using more marinade as required. Thinly sliced raw chicken or flank steak can also be cooked in this manner: the meat should be cooked separately before the vegetables, and then combined with them.

Mix the cornstarch and the remaining marinade, with additional liquid if necessary, to make a smooth paste. Add this mixture to the simmering vegetables and/or meat and stir constantly until thickened.

NOTE: Some basic ingredients in a good sweet-and-sour vegetable dish are quartered onions, fresh tomato wedges, and green pepper strips or squares, all cooked tender-crisp. Add pineapple chunks, either fresh or unsweetened canned, for a contrasting sweet flavor.

Makes approximately 2⅓ cups marinade or sauce
Calories per ⅓ cup sauce: 34

INDONESIAN RELISH

> *1 basket cherry tomatoes*
> *3 canned chili peppers, diced*
> *1 bunch green onions, thinly sliced*
> *½ cup chopped parsley*
> *¼ cup lemon juice*
> *¼ cup chopped cilantro (optional)*

Slice the tomatoes in half. Combine all the ingredients in a bowl and chill before serving.

Makes 6–8 servings
Calories per serving (⅛ recipe): 26

FRUIT CHUTNEY

8–10 large ripe mangoes or 3 pounds apples, apricots,
  or other fruit
2 large dried chilies
1 cup rice vinegar
2 cloves garlic
1 teaspoon chopped fresh ginger
1 teaspoon garam masala (Indian spice available at
  specialty food stores)
1 cup unsweetened apple juice (not concentrate)
1 cup raisins, chopped
Grated lemon or orange rind (optional)

Peel the mangoes or other fruit and slice thickly, discarding the seeds. Remove the stems and seeds from the chilies and soak them in a little of the vinegar for 10 minutes. Put the chilies, undrained, in a blender with the garlic, ginger, and garam masala and blend. Transfer the blended mixture to a saucepan and add the remaining vinegar and apple juice and bring to a boil. Simmer, uncovered, for 15 minutes. Add the mangoes or other fruit, the raisins, and the lemon or orange rind, if used, and simmer until thick and syrupy. Chill before serving; use sparingly!
Makes approximately 5 cups
Calories per tablespoon: 19

CHICKEN GRAVY

¼ cup nonfat milk
2 tablespoons flour
⅛ teaspoon pepper
⅛ teaspoon poultry seasoning
1 cup defatted chicken stock (see recipes for stocks)

Combine the milk, flour, and spices in a blender and blend until smooth. Add the chicken stock and blend again. Transfer to a saucepan and cook over medium heat, stirring constantly, until thickened.
Makes 1 cup
Calories per ¼ cup: 18

BEEF GRAVY

> 2 tablespoons flour
> 1/8 teaspoon onion powder
> 1/8 teaspoon pepper
> 1 cup defatted beef stock (see recipes for stocks)

To add color and flavor to the gravy, brown the flour by spreading it in a large skillet and cooking over low heat, stirring constantly, until lightly colored. Transfer the browned flour to a blender and add seasonings and beef stock. Blend until thoroughly mixed. Pour into a saucepan and cook over moderate heat, stirring constantly, until thickened.

VARIATIONS: Add chopped mushrooms or chopped cooked onions to the saucepan and cook with the beef stock-flour mixture.

Makes 1 cup
Calories per 1/4 cup: 13

GRAVY JARDINIÈRE

> 1/2 cup chopped celery
> 1/2 cup chopped carrots
> 1/4 cup chopped onions
> 2 tablespoons chopped parsley
> 1/4 teaspoon thyme
> 1/4 teaspoon pepper
> 1/8 teaspoon poultry seasoning
> Pinch basil
> 1 1/4 cups defatted stock of choice (see recipes for stocks)

Combine all the other ingredients with 1/2 cup of the stock. Bring to a boil, lower heat, and simmer, covered, until the vegetables are cooked. Transfer to a blender, add the remaining stock, and blend until smooth. Reheat before serving.

Makes approximately 1 1/3 cups
Calories per 1/4 cup: 11

Cereals, Pancakes, Breads, Rice

The recipes in this section are relatively high in calories, as you will see from the calorie data. Except for some basic recipes, such as the hot cereals and a few others, they are meant for your maintenance diet after you have reached your optimum weight.

HOT CORNMEAL

½ cup yellow cornmeal, whole-grain preferred
2½ cups cold water
Cinnamon

Stir the cornmeal into the cold water in a saucepan. Over moderate heat, bring the mixture to a boil, stirring constantly. Turn down heat to a simmer and continue cooking and stirring until the mixture thickens. Cook for approximately 10 minutes longer, stirring frequently to avoid sticking. Serve with a sprinkling of cinnamon.
Makes 2 cups
Calories per cup: 108

HOT CRACKED WHEAT

½ cup cracked wheat
2½ cups boiling water
Cinnamon

Stir the cracked wheat into boiling water in a saucepan. Turn down heat to a simmer and continue cooking for approximately 20 minutes, stirring from time to time, until the mixture thickens sufficiently. (Cover near end of cooking time if a softer texture is desired.) Serve with a sprinkling of cinnamon.
Makes approximately 2 cups
Calories per cup: 106

HOT OATMEAL

1 cup "old-fashioned" rolled oats
3¼ cups boiling water
Cinnamon

Stir the oats into boiling water in a saucepan. Turn down heat to a simmer and continue cooking for 15–20 minutes, stirring occasionally, until the oats are cooked through and the mixture is thickened and not too watery. (Decreasing the amount of water to 2 cups makes a thicker oatmeal but increases the calories per cup.) Serve with a sprinkling of cinnamon.
Makes 2⅓ cups
Calories per cup: 132

GRANOLA

⅓ cup raisins or currants
1 cup water
4 cups rolled oats
¼ cup frozen apple juice concentrate
1 tablespoon vanilla extract
2 tablespoons whole-wheat pastry flour
2 tablespoons nonfat dry milk
1½ teaspoons cinnamon
⅛ teaspoon nutmeg

Soak the raisins or currants in the water for 20 minutes; drain the raisins, reserving the water. Place the oats in a colander. Pour the water reserved from soaking the fruit over the oats. Place the moistened oats in a mixing bowl and add all of the remaining ingredients except the fruit. Mix well.

Spread the granola in a thin layer on nonstick baking sheets. Bake at 325° for 30 minutes. Add the raisins or currants to the granola for the last few minutes of baking.
Makes 5 cups
Calories per ½ cup: 160

VANILLA-SESAME FRENCH TOAST

2 egg whites
2 tablespoons nonfat milk
1 teaspoon vanilla extract
¼ teaspoon sesame seeds
Dash cinnamon

3 slices sourdough bread, cut in half

Beat the egg whites until smooth and fluffy. Stir in the remaining ingredients. Soak each piece of bread thoroughly in the mixture. Heat a nonstick skillet until a drop of water steams or "dances." Cook the bread in the skillet for 2½ minutes on each side, or until lightly browned.
Makes 6 pieces
Calories per piece: 45

BUTTERMILK PANCAKES

1 cup nonfat buttermilk
1 cup whole-wheat pastry flour
2 egg whites
2 teaspoons baking powder

Pour the buttermilk into a blender. Add the flour and blend to make a smooth mixture, using a spatula to mix in any flour on the blender sides. Transfer to a mixing bowl. Beat the egg whites until stiff peaks form; fold into the batter. Mix in the baking powder.

Heat a nonstick skillet or crêpe pan to a moderate temperature. Pour the batter into the skillet to make pancakes of desired size (⅔ cup batter makes a large pancake). Cook covered. When bubbles appear and the underside is nicely browned, flip the pancake over, cover, and brown the other side. To avoid any problems with sticking, clean the skillet with a damp towel between batches.
Makes 4 large pancakes
Calories per ¼ recipe: 136

VANILLA BRAN CRÊPES

2½ cups nonfat milk
½ cup unprocessed bran flakes
1½ cups whole-wheat pastry flour
¼ cup rice flour
1 tablespoon vanilla extract
1 tablespoon frozen apple juice concentrate
3 egg whites

Place all the ingredients except the egg whites in a mixing bowl and whisk until they are thoroughly blended. Beat the egg whites until stiff peaks form. Fold the egg whites into the batter.

Heat a nonstick skillet or crêpe pan to a moderate temperature. (If necessary to prevent sticking, prepare a skillet or crêpe pan by dabbing a little oil on a paper towel or Handi-Wipe, rinsing the towel in water and wringing it out, and wiping the skillet or crêpe pan surface. Use the towel whenever sticking is a problem, but do not add more oil to it.) Pour a thin layer of batter into the skillet (about ½ cup batter per crêpe), spreading it around evenly; brown on one side. Turn the crêpe over and lightly brown the second side.

Makes approximately 12 crêpes
Calories per crêpe: 94

CHEESE BLINTZES

¼ cup frozen apple juice concentrate
1 tablespoon vanilla extract
¼ teaspoon cinnamon
1½ bananas
2⅓ cups crumbled hoop cheese or other uncreamed cottage cheese
1–2 tablespoons nonfat milk or nonfat buttermilk, if required to blend the cheese
4 egg whites
VANILLA BRAN CRÊPES

Place the apple juice concentrate, vanilla, cinnamon, bananas, and cheese in a blender and blend until smooth. (The consistency will be thick. Due to variations in cheese moisture and banana size, some additional liquid may be needed to blend the cheese. The cheese mixture, however, will be further thinned out by the addition of the beaten egg whites.) Beat the egg whites until stiff peaks form. Fold the egg whites into the cheese mixture.

Place ⅓ cup of the blintz filling in each crêpe. Roll the crêpes and place seam-side-down in a nonstick pan. Cover with foil and bake at 325° for 20–25 minutes, or until heated through. Garnish with sliced fresh fruit.

Makes approximately 12 blintzes
Calories per blint: 145

BROCCOLI SPOONBREAD

2 small bunches broccoli
3 cups nonfat buttermilk
1 cup yellow cornmeal, whole-grain preferred
1 tablespoon baking powder
1 teaspoon baking soda
2 tablespoons frozen apple juice concentrate
6 egg whites
WHITE CHEESE SAUCE (optional)

Cut the broccoli in chunks and cook in a covered saucepan with a small amount of boiling water until tender-crisp, about 5 minutes. Drain and set aside. Stir the buttermilk into the cornmeal in a large skillet and cook over low heat until thickened. Add the baking powder, baking soda, and apple juice concentrate. Remove from heat and cool slightly. Beat the egg whites until stiff peaks form; fold into cornmeal mixture. Put about half the broccoli on the bottom of a nonstick casserole or large soufflé dish, then add a layer of the cornmeal mixture. (If an appropriate nonstick baking dish is not available, lightly oil a baking dish as follows: dab a little oil on a paper towel or Handi-Wipe; rinse the towel in water and wring it out, then wipe over the baking dish.) Layer the remaining broccoli and cornmeal. Cover and bake at 375° for 45–50 minutes, or until cooked through.

Serve with *WHITE CHEESE SAUCE,* if desired.
NOTE: BROCCOLI SPOONBREAD freezes well.
Makes 16 servings
Calories per serving (without sauce): 76

SPOONBREAD MUFFINS

3 cups nonfat buttermilk
2 tablespoons frozen apple juice concentrate
1 cup yellow cornmeal, whole-grain preferred
1 tablespoon baking powder
½ teaspoon baking soda
1 teaspoon onion powder (optional)
6 egg whites, beaten to stiff peaks

In a skillet, stir the buttermilk and apple juice concentrate into the cornmeal. Heat the mixture to a simmer, stirring constantly as it thickens. Turn off heat and allow to sit for a couple of minutes. Add the baking powder, baking soda, and onion powder if used. Gently stir in the egg whites.

Using a ¼-cup measure, pour the batter into nonstick muffin tins. Bake at 350° for 35 minutes. Cover the muffins during the first 10 minutes of baking. Place muffins briefly under the broiler to brown if the tops are not browned sufficiently. Store covered.

Makes 24 muffins
Calories per muffin: 38

BLUEBERRY MUFFINS

1 12-ounce package frozen blueberries, unthawed
1½ cups whole-wheat pastry flour
1 cup unbleached white pastry flour
½ cup unprocessed bran flakes
1 tablespoon baking powder
1½ teaspoons baking soda
⅔ cup nonfat milk
½ cup nonfat yogurt
¼ cup frozen apple juice concentrate
1 tablespoon vanilla extract
4 egg whites, beaten to stiff peaks

Toss the blueberries with ½ cup of the whole-wheat pastry flour; set aside. Combine the remaining dry ingredients in a large bowl. Stir the milk, yogurt, apple juice concentrate, and vanilla extract into the dry ingredients. Fold the egg whites into the batter, then fold in the blueberries. Pour the batter into nonstick muffin tins, lined with paper cupcake wrappers if desired. Cover with a dome of aluminum foil. Bake at 425° for 25 minutes, removing the foil cover for the last 5 minutes. Cool the muffins, replacing the foil cover to keep them moist. Store in an airtight container.

Makes 24 muffins
Calories per muffin: 68

CORN PANCAKES

1 cup yellow cornmeal, whole-grain preferred
1 teaspoon baking powder
¼ teaspoon baking soda
1 cup nonfat buttermilk
4 egg whites

Mix the dry ingredients. Stir in the buttermilk slowly. Beat the egg whites with a wire whisk until foamy, then gently fold them into the batter. Heat a nonstick skillet over moderate heat. Using a large spoon, drop the batter into the skillet to make individual pancakes. Cook for a few minutes until brown, then turn with a spatula to brown the other side. To avoid any problems with sticking, clean the skillet with a damp towel between batches.

VARIATION: To make *CORN MUFFINS*, drop the batter by spoonfuls into a nonstick muffin tin. Bake at 450° for approximately 10 minutes.

Makes 14 pancakes or 12 muffins
Calories per pancake: 44
Calories per muffin: 51

ROBIN'S WHOLE-WHEAT BREAD

¾ cup warm water
2 tablespoons active dry yeast (2 packages)
1 cup nonfat buttermilk (preferred) or nonfat milk, at room temperature
¼ cup frozen apple juice concentrate, at room temperature
4–6 cups whole wheat flour
1–2 tablespoons soy sauce or tamari (optional)

Place the warm water in a mixing bowl. Sprinkle the yeast into it and stir until the yeast is dissolved. Cover the bowl and let it sit for 5 minutes. Stir the buttermilk or milk and the apple juice concentrate into the mixture. Mix in 2 cups flour, beating for about 1 minute. Cover the bowl with a towel and let it sit for 20 minutes. (After this period, the mixture should look thick and bubbly.) Stir in the soy sauce or tamari if desired.

Mix in the remaining flour, one cup at a time, using enough flour so that the dough won't stick to the board when you knead it, but not so much as to make it heavy. A heavy dough produces a heavy bread. Turn out the dough onto a lightly floured board and knead it for 10 minutes. Add more flour if the dough sticks to the board. Put the dough back into the bowl, cover it with a towel, and let it sit in a warm place for 40 minutes or until the dough has doubled in bulk. (An unlit gas oven heated only by the pilot light or an electric oven with the light turned on are suitably warm.)

Punch down the dough, turn it out onto the breadboard, and knead for 3 minutes. Divide the dough in half and shape into loaves. Place the loaves in nonstick loaf pans, cover the pans with a towel, and let them sit in a warm place until the dough has again doubled in volume. Bake at 350° for about 35–40 minutes. Let the bread cool after it comes out of the oven. Remove from pans. (Wrapping the bread in aluminum foil will keep the crust soft.) This bread is especially delicious toasted.

Makes 2 loaves
Calories per slice (1/20 loaf): 60

NAN'S WHOLE-WHEAT BREAD

3 cups water
1 tablespoon frozen apple juice concentrate
1 tablespoon active dry yeast (1 package)
1/3 cup dried minced onion
2 tablespoons soy sauce or tamari
2 tablespoons caraway seeds
6 1/2–7 cups whole-wheat flour

All ingredients should be at room temperature. Heat the water until it is lukewarm. Pour the water into a large bowl and stir in the apple juice concentrate. Sprinkle the yeast over the water and apple juice concentrate. Stir in the onion, soy sauce or tamari, and caraway seeds, and then add 6 cups of flour.

Turn the dough out onto a floured breadboard or countertop. Knead the dough for 5 minutes and return it to the bowl. Cover with a towel and let the dough rise in a warm place. When the dough has doubled in size, punch it down and turn it out onto the breadboard. Knead again for a few minutes, adding more flour if the dough becomes sticky.

Divide the dough in half and shape into 2 ovals. Put the dough into nonstick loaf pans, drape with a towel, and put it in a warm place for the final rising. When the dough has doubled in size, put the pans in a preheated 375° oven and bake for 45 minutes. Remove the bread from the pans and cool on a rack. The cooler the bread, the easier it will be to slice. This bread is good sliced thin and toasted.

VARIATION: Shape the dough into rolls rather than loaves.
Makes 2 loaves
Calories per slice (1/20 loaf): 72

CHAPATIS

> *1 cup whole-wheat pastry flour*
> *Pinch salt*
> *1/2 cup water*

Combine the flour and salt in a bowl. Add the water gradually, stirring to form a firm dough. Transfer the dough to a floured breadboard and knead for 5 minutes. Roll the dough into a ball and cover with a damp cloth. Set aside to rest for 30 minutes (this will make the dough easier to roll out).

Divide the dough into 6 pieces and shape each piece into a ball. Cover again with a damp cloth. Take out 1 piece at a time. Flatten each piece into a circle and roll out with a rolling pin on a surface that has been dusted with whole-wheat pastry flour. Roll from the center of the circle to the edges, applying equal pressure on all sides, to form a thin circle about 8 inches in diameter. Place a nonstick griddle or skillet over medium heat. Cook the chapatis quickly on both sides. Place them on aluminum foil and slide under the broiler for a minute to crisp them and make them puff up. (Omit the last step if *CHAPATIS* are to be filled and rolled, as in *CHINESE EGG ROLLS*.)

Makes 6 chapatis
Calories per chapati: 66

HERBED RICE PILAF

 2 cups long-grain brown rice
 3 cups defatted stock of choice (see recipes for stocks)
 1²/₃ cups water
 1 teaspoon soy sauce or tamari
 2 tablespoons onion powder
 2 teaspoons gumbo filé
 1 teaspoon garlic powder
 ¼ teaspoon rosemary
 1 cup frozen peas, rinsed in warm water to thaw
 ½ cup diced canned pimientos
 1 tablespoon lemon juice

Oven-toast the rice in a large pan until it is lightly browned. In a saucepan, bring the stock, water, soy sauce or tamari, and spices to a boil. Add the rice and bring to a boil again. Reduce the heat and simmer covered for 45–50 minutes or until the liquid is absorbed. Turn off the heat and let the rice steam for 10–15 minutes without lifting the lid.

Gently stir the peas, pimientos, and lemon juice into the cooked rice. Transfer to a casserole dish, if desired; serve hot.

VARIATION: For *CURRIED RICE PILAF,* substitute 1 tablespoon curry powder for the 2 teaspoons gumbo filé.

Makes 10 or more servings (approximately 10 cups)
Calories per ½ cup: 77

SPANISH RICE

 1 cup long-grain brown rice
 2¹/₃ cups water
 ½ cup chopped onions
 ½ cup chopped celery
 ½ cup chopped red or green bell pepper
 ¼ cup canned diced green chilies

2 cloves garlic, minced
2 tablespoons minced shallots (optional)
½ cup water or defatted stock of choice (see recipes for
    stocks)
¾ cup tomato sauce
1 teaspoon soy sauce or tamari
1 teaspoon lemon juice
Scant tablespoon cumin
1 teaspoon mild chili powder
¼ teaspoon garlic powder
Garnish: cilantro or parsley

Lightly brown the rice in a large pan in the oven. Bring the 2⅓ cups water to a boil in a saucepan and add the rice. Bring to a boil again, lower heat, cover, and simmer for 45–50 minutes or until the liquid is absorbed. Turn off the heat, but leave the pot on the burner, covered, to steam for approximately 10 minutes. Do not stir the rice.

Meanwhile, sauté the vegetables in the ½ cup water or stock in a skillet. Add the tomato sauce, soy sauce or tamari, lemon juice, and seasonings; heat and stir to blend flavors. Combine the seasoned vegetables with 3 cups of the cooked rice (there will be some rice left over), and mix thoroughly. Serve immediately or transfer to a casserole and keep warm in a slow oven. Serve garnished with cilantro or parsley.

Makes 4 or more servings (approximately 4 cups)
Calories per ½ cup: 99

BROWN RICE

1½ cups long-grain brown rice
3½ cups defatted stock of choice (see recipes for stocks)
    or water, or combine the liquids in desired propor-
    tions
Pinch powdered saffron or seasoning of choice (op-
    tional)

In a large nonstick skillet, stir the rice over medium heat to toast evenly. In a saucepan, bring the stock and/or water to a boil; add the rice and mix well. If a seasoning is used, mix it in now also. Bring to a boil, then turn down the heat as low as possible, cover the saucepan tightly, and cook for 45–50 minutes or until the liquid is absorbed. Turn off the heat and let the rice steam for 10–15 minutes without lifting the lid.

Makes 5 or more servings (approximately 5 cups)
Calories per ½ cup: 100

Sweet Toppings,
Desserts, Snacks

Some of the recipes in this section are intended for use *after* you have reached your optimum weight. The calorie data will guide you to those that are appropriate for you, and to suitable serving sizes.

BLUEBERRY SYRUP

¾ cup water
½ cup frozen apple juice concentrate
1¼ cups frozen unsweetened blueberries (broken apart to measure)
2 tablespoons vanilla extract
⅛ teaspoon lemon extract
Dash nutmeg
1 tablespoon cornstarch blended with 2 tablespoons nonfat milk

Bring the water and apple juice concentrate to a boil in a saucepan. Add 1 cup of the berries. Add the vanilla and lemon extracts and nutmeg. Cook over low heat until the berries soften. Transfer the mixture to a blender and process at "blend." Return the mixture to the saucepan and heat to a simmer. Add cornstarch paste and simmer, stirring constantly, until thickened. Stir in the remaining ¼ cup of berries and simmer just until the berries are thawed. Serve hot over pancakes or crêpes.

Makes approximately 1½ cups
Calories per tablespoon: 16

STRAWBERRY PRESERVES

> 1 tablespoon arrowroot
> 1/3 cup frozen apple juice concentrate
> 2 tablespoons lemon juice
> 3 tablespoons Sauternes
> 1 16-ounce package frozen strawberries, thawed (or
>   equivalent in fresh strawberries)
> 1 tablespoon vanilla extract

Mix the arrowroot with 2 tablespoons of apple juice concentrate in a small bowl. Combine the lemon juice, the remaining apple juice, and the Sauternes in a saucepan over low heat. Add the strawberries and cook for five minutes. Stir in the arrowroot mixture and the vanilla extract and simmer until thickened, stirring constantly. Chill and serve with bread or pancakes.

Makes 2½ cups
Calories per tablespoon: 9

BANANA-GINGER TOPPING

> ½ cup nonfat buttermilk
> 1/3 cup frozen apple juice concentrate
> 1 rounded teaspoon frozen orange juice concentrate
> 1 tablespoon vanilla extract
> ¼ cup nonfat dry milk
> 1 ripe banana
> 1 tablespoon finely grated fresh ginger
> 2 cups crumbled hoop cheese or other uncreamed
>   cottage cheese

Put the liquids in a blender and add the dry milk, banana, and ginger. Add hoop cheese, a little at a time, blending until mixture is velvety smooth. Chill several hours to thicken slightly. Use as cake frosting or fruit topping.

NOTE: A thinner consistency may be achieved by adding more liquid; a thicker one by adding a little more cheese.

Makes approximately 2⅔ cups
Calories per tablespoon: approximately 15

APPLE SYRUP

¾ cup frozen apple juice concentrate
¾ cup water
2 tablespoons vanilla extract
Pumpkin pie spice to taste
1 tablespoon cornstarch mixed with 1½ tablespoons
*   water to a smooth paste*

In a saucepan, heat the apple juice concentrate, water, vanilla extract, and pumpkin pie spice. Simmer, covered, for 5 minutes. Stir the cornstarch paste into the juice mixture and simmer, stirring constantly, until the syrup is thickened and clear. Serve hot over crêpes or pancakes.

Makes 1⅓ cups
Calories per tablespoon: 18

BANANA PURÉE

1 ripe banana
1 teaspoon vanilla extract
Pinch cinnamon

Place all the ingredients in a blender and blend briefly, or mash with a fork in a dish. Use as a spread on bread or pancakes.

Makes approximately ½ cup
Calories per tablespoon: 12

APPLE PURÉE

4 apples
Pinch cinnamon and/or nutmeg

Peel and core the apples and wrap them in aluminum foil. Place them in a 350° oven for 40 minutes. Blend them in a blender briefly or mash them in a bowl with a potato masher. Add seasonings as desired. Use as a spread on bread or pancakes.

Makes approximately 2½ cups
Calories per tablespoon: 8

JEANNE'S PINEAPPLE BOATS
WITH VANILLA SAUCE

2 fresh pineapples
2 cups VANILLA SAUCE
Cinnamon

Cut the pineapples lengthwise into quarters, carefully cutting through the green leaves at the top to leave a section of leaves on each quarter. Using a small, sharp paring knife, carefully cut the fruit from its shell (cut down both sides of the pineapple sections, beginning at the corners). Cut off the tough portion of the center core of each pineapple quarter and discard it. Cut each pineapple quarter as it rests on its shell in half lengthwise; then cut it horizontally into bite-sized pieces.

To serve, top each pineapple boat with ¼ cup *VANILLA SAUCE* and sprinkle lightly with cinnamon.

Makes 8 servings
Calories per serving (without sauce): 92

VANILLA SAUCE

2¼ teaspoons unflavored gelatin
2 tablespoons frozen apple juice concentrate
¼ cup boiling water
2 cups nonfat milk
1 tablespoon vanilla extract

Soften the gelatin in the apple juice concentrate. Add the boiling water and stir until the gelatin is completely dissolved. Add 1 cup of the milk and mix well. Place the mixture in a covered container and refrigerate until it is jelled. Put the jelled mixture in a blender and add the remaining milk and the vanilla extract. Blend briefly to a smooth, thick consistency. Serve over *PINEAPPLE BOATS* or other fresh fruit.

Makes 2 cups
Calories per ¼ cup: 31

STEWED APPLES

1¼ cups water
¼ cup frozen apple juice concentrate
Juice of 1 orange
Juice of ½ lemon
½ cup raisins
½ teaspoon cinnamon
¼ teaspoon nutmeg
6 large Golden Delicious apples, peeled, cored, and
    cut into thick slices
2 tablespoons cornstarch
1 teaspoon grated orange rind
3 tablespoons water
2 teaspoons vanilla extract
Garnish: nonfat yogurt or MOCK SOUR CREAM

Place the water, juices, raisins, cinnamon, and nutmeg in a saucepan and bring to a boil. Reduce the heat, cover, and simmer the mixture for 5 minutes. Add the apples and gently stir to coat them thoroughly with the liquid. Cover the saucepan and simmer until the apples are just tender, about 10 minutes.

Mix the remaining ingredients to a smooth paste and pour over the apples. Again, coat the apples with the sauce and stir gently as the sauce thickens. Continue to simmer the apples, uncovered, for 5 minutes.

Cool the stewed apples to room temperature and serve in glass custard dishes or in stemmed glasses. Top with a dollop of nonfat yogurt or MOCK SOUR CREAM if desired.

Makes 6 servings
Calories per serving: 159

BAKED APPLES WITH RAISIN GLAZE

4 baking apples
½ cup water
⅓ cup frozen apple juice concentrate
½ cup raisins
1 tablespoon cornstarch
½ cup nonfat milk
1 tablespoon vanilla extract
Cinnamon

Wash and core the apples. Cut a thin slice from the apple tops to make a flat surface. Place apples on a nonstick pan with 2 tablespoons water on the bottom. Bake uncovered at 350° for 35 minutes.

Meanwhile, heat the ½ cup water, juice, and raisins in a saucepan. Blend the cornstarch with the milk and vanilla extract to a smooth paste. When the saucepan liquid is simmering, add the cornstarch paste gradually, stirring constantly until thickened and clear. Sprinkle the baked apples with cinnamon and spoon the raisin glaze over them. Return apples to oven for 5 minutes. Serve hot or cold.

Makes 4 servings
Calories per serving: 200

PINEAPPLE MERINGUE

> 1 20-ounce can unsweetened crushed pineapple, juice-
>   packed
> 1 tablespoon frozen apple juice concentrate
> 1 teaspoon lemon juice
> 1 tablespoon vanilla extract
> 8 egg whites

Drain the pineapple, reserving the juice. Combine the pineapple juice, apple juice concentrate, and lemon juice in a saucepan and bring to a boil. Remove from heat, transfer to a mixing bowl, and add the pineapple and vanilla. Beat the egg whites until stiff peaks form; carefully fold them into the mixture. Pour into a large nonstick baking dish or pan. Set the pan in a large baking pan filled halfway with hot water. Bake at 350° for 40 minutes, or until a knife inserted near the center comes out clean. When the meringue has browned sufficiently on top, cover the pan for the remainder of the baking. If some liquid remains in the bottom of the meringue after baking, remove the pan of water and bake the meringue until it is sufficiently dry (about 5–10 minutes).

Makes 12 servings
Calories per serving: 43

TAPIOCA PUDDING

⅓ cup small pearl tapioca, quick-cooking
2½ cups nonfat milk
1 cup evaporated skimmed milk
¾ cup frozen apple juice concentrate
2½ teaspoons frozen orange juice concentrate
3 egg whites, stiffly beaten
2 tablespoons vanilla extract

Cover the tapioca with warm water and soak 20 minutes; drain well. In a saucepan or a double boiler, heat both milks until just simmering, stirring as needed to avoid scorching. Stir in the tapioca, blending well, and bring the mixture to a gentle simmer. Simmer 5 minutes or until tapioca is cooked. Add the juices. Mix a little hot tapioca into the beaten egg whites. Whip the egg whites into the tapioca with a wire whisk. Cook several minutes over low heat, until a good consistency is obtained (tapioca will thicken further when chilled). Stir in the vanilla extract. Serve warm or chilled.

Makes approximately 8 cups
Calories per half cup: 65

TAPIOCA CREAM PARFAIT

TAPIOCA PUDDING
½ cup Grape-Nuts cereal
1 tablespoon frozen apple juice concentrate
⅛ teaspoon cinnamon
2½ bananas, sliced
Nutmeg to taste

Prepare *TAPIOCA PUDDING* and chill. Grind Grape-Nuts in a blender. Mix in the juice and cinnamon. To assemble parfaits, layer pudding, banana, and crumbs in desired arrangement in parfait glasses. Top with a light sprinkling of nutmeg. Chill thoroughly.

Makes approximately 10 parfaits
Calories per parfait: 153

CAROB-MINT MOUSSE

2 envelopes unflavored gelatin
2½ tablespoons unsweetened carob powder
1 cup frozen apple juice concentrate
2½ tablespoons vanilla extract
3¼ cups nonfat fluid milk
⅓ cup nonfat dry milk
¼ teaspoon mint flakes

Place the gelatin and carob powder in a mixing bowl. Add ¼ cup of the apple juice concentrate and mix well. Heat the remaining apple juice concentrate and vanilla extract to a boil in a saucepan, then turn down the heat. Add gelatin-carob mixture and stir constantly, over low heat, for about 5 minutes. Refrigerate until cool.

Place milks, mint, and gelatin mixture in a blender. (The mousse liquid may overflow a bit when blended in a 5-cup capacity blender. To avoid this, first blend only part of the fluid milk with the other ingredients. Pour some of the blended mixture into a bowl, then add remaining milk to the blender and blend.) Mix at low speed, then switch to "blend" for 3–4 minutes. Transfer to a mixing bowl and chill in the freezer until cold and thickened. Whip mousse with electric mixer until light and fluffy, then return to the freezer until icy cold. (Do not allow mousse to freeze.) Before serving, whip again with electric mixer or wire whisk. Pile mousse into dessert glasses, garnished with fruit slices, if desired.

Makes approximately 5 cups
Calories per ½ cup: 93

VARIATION: For *FUDGESICLES,* follow the procedure above for making the gelatin mixture. Cool. In a blender, combine the gelatin mixture with mint and nonfat fluid milk, and substitute ⅓ cup evaporated skimmed milk for the nonfat dry milk. Blend 3–4 minutes. Heat the mixture in a double boiler until bubbling; cook about 10 minutes. Transfer to a mixing bowl and chill in the freezer until icy cold (do not freeze). Whip with an electric mixer until light and fluffy. Pour into popsicle molds and insert ice cream sticks, or use ice cube molds and insert toothpicks. Freeze until firm.

ORANGE WHIP

1½ envelopes unflavored gelatin
3½ cups orange juice
2 tablespoons frozen apple juice concentrate
2 teaspoons lemon juice

Soften gelatin in ½ cup of the orange juice in a small mixing bowl. Heat the remaining orange juice to a boil. Add this to the gelatin mixture and stir until gelatin is thoroughly dissolved. Add the apple juice and lemon juice. Chill until the mixture begins to thicken. Beat with an electric mixer at high speed until fluffy and doubled in volume. Chill again, then mound into 6 sherbet glasses.

Makes 6 servings
Calories per serving: 82

PINEAPPLE-LEMON CHEESECAKE

2 8-ounce cans unsweetened crushed pineapple, juice-packed
¾ cup nonfat buttermilk
2 cups crumbled hoop cheese or other uncreamed cottage cheese
2 envelopes unflavored gelatin
¾ cup frozen apple juice concentrate
¼ cup lemon juice
1 tablespoon vanilla extract
1 egg white
⅛ cup Grape-Nuts cereal, ground fine in blender

Drain the pineapple and reserve juice. Put the buttermilk and the drained pineapple into a blender. Add the cheese and blend for about 5 minutes, stirring occasionally, until very smooth.

In a large bowl, mix the gelatin with the juice from the canned pineapple. Heat the apple juice concentrate and lemon juice to a boil. Pour the boiling liquid over the gelatin mixture; stir well to dissolve. Place in the refrigerator to cool. Remove the cooled gelatin mixture from the refrigerator and add the cheese mixture and vanilla. Beat the egg white until stiff peaks form, and fold it into the cheese mixture. Sprinkle the ground Grape-Nuts evenly into a 10-inch pie pan. Spoon the cheese filling into the pan. Refrigerate for several hours until set.

Makes 8 servings
Calories per serving: 136

PUMPKIN MOUSSE PIE

1 cup canned pumpkin
½ cup evaporated skimmed milk
1 teaspoon cinnamon
¼ teaspoon nutmeg
⅛ teaspoon powdered ginger
2 teaspoons vanilla extract
1 envelope unflavored gelatin
½ cup boiling water
¼ cup frozen apple juice concentrate
3 egg whites

Combine the pumpkin, milk, cinnamon, nutmeg, ginger, and vanilla extract. Stir the gelatin in the boiling water until it is completely dissolved, then add the apple juice concentrate and stir again. Stir this mixture into the pumpkin mixture and chill for 20 minutes. Beat the egg whites until stiff peaks form; fold into the pumpkin mixture. Mound the mousse into a pie pan and chill until firm.

Makes 6–8 servings
Calories per serving (⅛ recipe): 48

VANILLA CUSTARD FREEZE

½ cup frozen apple juice concentrate
1 envelope unflavored gelatin
1 teaspoon cornstarch
1½ cups nonfat milk
¾ cup evaporated skimmed milk
1 tablespoon vanilla extract
1 egg white, beaten to soft peaks

Place ¼ cup of the apple juice concentrate in a mixing bowl. Add the gelatin and cornstarch, mixing well. Heat the remaining apple juice concentrate to a boil in a saucepan and stir in the gelatin-cornstarch mixture, dissolving well. In a double boiler, scald the milks and then stir in the apple juice mixture and vanilla extract. Add the egg white with a whisk; cook briefly, stirring constantly with the whisk. Pour the mixture into a blender and blend at high speed for several minutes.

Transfer the custard to ice cube trays and freeze until ice crystals begin to form on the outside. Empty the contents of the trays into a well-chilled bowl. Using a hand mixer, beat the custard at high speed until the custard is stiff and has doubled in volume. For best results, refreeze the custard only until it reaches a soft-frozen consistency (if custard freezes to a firm consistency, thaw slightly before serving).

If desired, serve with fresh cut fruit, either as a garnish or mixed into the custard.

Makes approximately 6 servings
Calories per serving: 98

BANANA WHIP

> 5 ripe bananas, peeled and cut lengthwise into halves
> ¼ cup nonfat dry milk
> ¼ teaspoon cinnamon
> ⅛ teaspoon unsweetened carob powder
> 3 tablespoons vanilla extract

Place the banana halves in plastic bags and freeze for at least 24 hours. To make the whip, cut the frozen bananas into 1-inch pieces. Sprinkle the dry milk, cinnamon, carob powder, and vanilla extract into the bottom of a food processor; add the banana pieces (a blender can be used instead of a food processor, but the processor gives better results). Using the processor's metal chopping blade, beat the mixture until light and fluffy. Serve at once.

NOTE: If a firmer consistency is desired, place the *BANANA WHIP* in the freezer for a short time. *BANANA WHIP* may be placed in molds (popsicle molds or ice-cube trays) for a frozen treat.

Makes 5–6 servings
Calories per serving (⅕ recipe): approximately 114

EASY FROZEN PINEAPPLE SLUSH

> *1 8-ounce can unsweetened crushed pineapple, juice-packed*

Place the can of crushed pineapple in the freezer and leave it until it is frozen. Remove the pineapple by opening both ends of the can and pushing out the frozen fruit. Place the fruit in a blender or food processor and blend at high speed until creamy. Pour the pineapple into individual serving dishes and refreeze to desired consistency.

Makes 3 servings
Calories per serving: 47

DESSERT QUICHE

Crust:
> *2 cups fine whole-wheat breadcrumbs (from acceptable bread)*
> *⅓ cup frozen apple juice concentrate*
> *1½ teaspoons cinnamon*

Filling:
> *½ cup nonfat milk*
> *3 cups crumbled hoop cheese or other uncreamed cottage cheese*
> *½ cup frozen orange juice concentrate*
> *1 teaspoon lemon extract*
> *4 egg whites*
> *2 bananas*

Meringue Topping:
> *2 egg whites*

Prepare the breadcrumbs by processing bread in a food processor or blender. Mix the breadcrumbs with the apple juice concentrate. Spread the moistened crumbs on bottom of a 9-inch pie pan, pressing down to form a ½-inch thick layer. Sprinkle the surface with cinnamon. Bake the crust at 350° for 15–20 minutes.
Pour the milk into a blender and add the cheese. Stir in the

orange juice concentrate and lemon extract and blend until smooth but thick; transfer blender contents to a mixing bowl. Beat the 4 egg whites until stiff peaks form, then gently fold into the cheese mixture. Slice the bananas lengthwise in thin slices and lay them over the crust. Fill the crust with the egg white–cheese mixture.

For the meringue topping, beat 2 egg whites until stiff peaks form; spread over the top of the filling. Bake the quiche at 350° for 20–25 minutes. Allow it to set at room temperature for about 15 minutes before serving (it may also be served chilled).

Makes 8 servings
Calories per serving: 173

CAROB COOKIES

    3 cups whole-wheat pastry flour
    3 tablespoons unsweetened carob powder
    2 tablespoons baking powder
    ⅛ teaspoon baking soda
    ½ cup frozen apple juice concentrate; additional as
      required for cookie tops
    3 tablespoons nonfat milk
    2 tablespoons vanilla extract
    4 egg whites

Combine the dry ingredients in a mixing bowl. In a separate bowl, combine the apple juice concentrate, nonfat milk, and vanilla extract. Stir the liquid ingredients into the dry ingredients. Beat the egg whites until soft peaks form. Using your hands, work the egg whites into the dough.

Sprinkle a little flour on a breadboard and place the dough on the board. Knead for 2–3 minutes. Using a rolling pin which has been floured, roll out the dough approximately ¼-inch thick. Flour the board and rolling pin as necessary to keep the dough from sticking. Cut the dough into diamond shapes or use cookie cutters.

Place the cookies on nonstick baking sheets. Dip a pastry brush in diluted apple juice concentrate and brush over the cookies to remove the excess flour. Bake at 350° for 20 minutes, or until the tops are browned.

Makes approximately 4 dozen cookies
Calories per cookie: 33

PITA TARTS

¾ cup frozen apple juice concentrate
1 tablespoon lemon juice
⅓ cup currants
1 apple, peeled, halved, and coarsely shredded
*1 8-ounce can pineapple slices in unsweetened pineap-
    ple juice, drained (reserve juice)*
1/16 teaspoon allspice
1½ teaspoons cinnamon
2 large pita breads
1 teaspoon arrowroot
*Garnish: tiny pieces of apple and/or canned unsweetened
    pineapple*

Filling: In a saucepan, heat ¼ cup of the apple juice concentrate, ½ cup water, the lemon juice, currants, apples, ½ cup of the sliced pineapple (cut into thin pieces), and allspice. Bring to a boil, then turn down the heat and simmer uncovered for 20–30 minutes. Cool.

Crust: In a bowl, mix together ¼ cup of the apple juice concentrate, ⅓ cup water, and the cinnamon. Cut each pita into 8 pie-shaped wedges. Dip the pita wedges in the juice mixture and arrange them on a nonstick baking sheet.

Fill each wedge with about 2 teaspoons filling. Bake at 350° for 10–15 minutes. While tarts are baking, prepare a glaze. Heat the remaining apple juice in a small saucepan. Mix the reserved pineapple juice with the arrowroot to a smooth paste. Add the arrowroot paste to the simmering apple juice; cook and stir until clear. Spread the glaze over the hot baking tarts, garnish each tart with a small piece of apple or pineapple, and dot with additional glaze. Continue baking another 10–15 minutes. Store covered.

Makes 16 tarts
Calories per tart: 82

CARROT CAKE

3½ cups whole-wheat pastry flour
½ cup unprocessed bran flakes
2 tablespoons baking powder
1 tablespoon baking soda
2 tablespoons cinnamon
½ teaspoon allspice
1 cup nonfat buttermilk
½ cup nonfat yogurt
1 cup frozen apple juice concentrate
1 tablespoon frozen orange juice concentrate
2 tablespoons vanilla extract
2 cups grated carrots
1 8-ounce can unsweetened crushed pineapple, juice-
  packed, drained
½ cup raisins or currants, soaked and drained
1 tablespoon grated lemon rind
6 egg whites
BANANA-GINGER TOPPING (optional)

Combine the dry ingredients in a large mixing bowl. Add the buttermilk, yogurt, fruit juices, and vanilla. Use an electric beater to stir, then switch to high setting and blend until smooth. Mix in the carrots, pineapple, raisins or currants, and lemon rind. Beat the egg whites until stiff peaks form and fold into the batter.

Use a large nonstick bundt pan or a nonstick rectangular pan. To assure easy cake removal, spread a dab of oil over the surface with a dampened towel, then flour the pan. Add the batter and cover with aluminum foil shaped into a dome. Bake at 350° for 1 hour, then remove the foil and bake 25 minutes longer. Cool the cake for several minutes, then remove from pan and wrap snugly with aluminum foil. For greater moistness, allow the wrapped cake to set for several hours or overnight. If desired, frost with *BANANA-GINGER TOPPING* before serving.

Makes 16 servings
Calories per serving: 175

PRITIKIN BREAD APPLE PUDDING-CAKE

This recipe was developed specifically for use with Pritikin Bread; other acceptable whole-wheat breads may also be used.

> 1¼ cups nonfat milk
> ½ cup frozen apple juice concentrate
> 1 tablespoon vanilla extract
> ½ cup raisins, chopped, or currants
> 7 slices Pritikin Bread, untrimmed, in ½-inch cubes
> 2 cups peeled, cored, and thinly sliced apples
> 1 tablespoon each grated orange rind and grated lemon rind
> 1 tablespoon cinnamon
> ½ teaspoon nutmeg
> ¼ teaspoon cloves
> 4 egg whites
> 5 tablespoons unprocessed bran flakes

Topping:
> 1 cup Pritikin Bread crumbs (prepare by processing bread in a food processor or blender)
> 2 tablespoons flour
> 2 teaspoons cinnamon
> 3 tablespoons frozen apple juice concentrate

In a small bowl, combine the milk, apple juice concentrate, vanilla, and chopped raisins. Set aside to allow the raisins to soften. In a large mixing bowl, combine the bread cubes, apples, orange and lemon rind, and spices. Stir thoroughly to distribute the apples and spices evenly. Pour the liquid ingredients and raisins from the previous step over the bread mixture, stirring well to moisten the bread evenly and soak up all the liquid. Set aside for several minutes, then stir again to soften and break down the bread. Beat the egg whites until stiff peaks form.

Carefully fold egg whites into the bread mixture, making sure the egg whites are well distributed.

Sprinkle the bran flakes evenly over the bottom of a 13 × 9 × 2 nonstick baking pan. Gently spoon the bread mixture over the bran layer, filling the pan evenly; smooth the top. In a small bowl, combine the topping ingredients and mix well.

Sprinkle the topping evenly over the top of the pudding-cake. Bake at 350° for 50 minutes. Remove from oven and cover with foil immediately, to preserve moistness. Let cool slightly before cutting.

This pudding-cake can be served hot or cold or at room temperature. It keeps well when refrigerated, but its moistness should be protected at all times by covering tightly with foil or plastic wrap.

Makes 12–15 servings
Calories per serving (¹/₁₅ recipe): 104

BANANA-RICE PUDDING

> 4 egg whites
> 1½ cups mashed bananas
> 1 teaspoon lemon juice
> 1¼ cups nonfat milk
> ½ cup frozen apple juice concentrate
> 1 tablespoon vanilla extract
> 1 teaspoon cinnamon
> ¼ teaspoon cardamom
> ⅛ teaspoon nutmeg
> 3 cups cold cooked short-grain brown rice
> 1 cup Grape-Nuts cereal

In a mixing bowl, beat the egg whites with a fork until foamy. Stir in the mashed bananas and lemon juice, and then add the milk, apple juice concentrate, vanilla extract, and spices. Mix well. Stir in the cooked rice.

Place the Grape-Nuts in a blender and process on "grind." Reserve some of the cereal crumbs for topping, and spread the remaining crumbs over the bottom of a nonstick pan. Pour in the pudding mixture and sprinkle reserved crumbs over the top. Refrigerate the pudding for about 15 minutes before baking to allow the bottom crumbs to absorb the pudding liquid. Bake at 325° for 50–60 minutes, or until set and nicely browned. Top individual servings of pudding with hot or cold nonfat milk if desired.

Makes 8 servings
Calories per serving (without added milk): 209

GARBANZO "NUTS"

Dried garbanzo beans
Onion and/or garlic powder to taste (optional)

Rinse the dried beans in a colander, then put them in a covered pot to soak in water for a few hours or overnight. The water level should be 3 to 4 inches above the beans, as the beans will absorb much water during the soaking process. Add more water if necessary during the soaking period to keep the beans under water.

When ready to cook, drain the beans, rinse, and cover with fresh water again to about 3 to 4 inches above the beans. Bring to a boil, then turn down the heat and simmer the beans, partially covered, until tender.

Drain the beans well, then place them on a nonstick baking pan in a single layer. While the beans are still damp, sprinkle on onion or garlic powder if desired. Bake at 350° until the beans are quite dry and browned, about 45 minutes. Shake the beans occasionally while baking to brown evenly.

NOTE: If a more tender, flaky texture is preferred, freeze the beans after cooking and bake later.

Calories per ½ cup: approximately 245

CORN TORTILLA CHIPS

1 package of 12 corn tortillas
½ teaspoon onion powder (optional)
½ teaspoon garlic powder (optional)

Arrange the tortillas in a stack. Cut all 12 in half at once and then into quarters. Lay the quarter wedges on a nonstick baking sheet, avoiding overlapping. Sprinkle with the onion and garlic powder, if desired. Bake in preheated 375–400° oven until crisp, stirring and turning the chips to brown evenly. Remove the wedges as they are done. (Another method is to lay each whole tortilla on the baking sheet or directly on the rack and bake until crisp, then break into random-sized pieces.)

VARIATION: For a barbecue flavor, mix a little onion powder, chili powder, and paprika together to make a barbecue seasoning. Spread spices on a flat platter and stir the tortilla wedges through the mixture. Bake as above.

Makes 4 dozen wedges
Calories per wedge: 14

Dips, Spreads, Toppings

PIMIENTO CHEESE

1 2-ounce jar pimientos, undrained
¼ teaspoon Sauternes
2 pepperoncini (peppers in vinegar), seeds and stems removed
¼ teaspoon pepperoncini liquid (from jar of peppers in vinegar)
1 cup crumbled hoop cheese or other uncreamed cottage cheese
1 teaspoon onion powder
Additional pimiento (optional)

Place the pimientos, Sauternes, 1 pepperoncini, and the pepperoncini liquid in a blender and blend. Add the cheese and onion powder and blend until very smooth, stirring as required. Finely chop the remaining pepperoncini and stir it into the cheese mixture.

If desired, additional chopped pimiento may be mixed in with the cheese or used as a garnish. Chill thoroughly before serving.

Makes ¾ cup
Calories per tablespoon (without optional pimiento): 13

CRAB DIP

¾ cup nonfat buttermilk, or more if required
2 cups crumbled hoop cheese or other uncreamed cottage cheese
1 cup drained finely chopped canned artichoke hearts, water-packed
3 tablespoons dried minced onion
1 teaspoon soy sauce or tamari
¼ teaspoon Tabasco (hot pepper sauce) or to taste
7 ounces cooked crab meat
1 4-ounce jar pimientos, rinsed and drained
¼ cup finely chopped green onions or chives
½ teaspoon dill weed (optional)

Blend the buttermilk, cheese, artichokes, dried minced onion, soy sauce or tamari, and Tabasco sauce in a blender until smooth. Add the crab meat to blender and process at low speed to keep bits of crab meat intact. Dice the pimiento and add to dip. Mix in the green onion or chives and sprinkle in dill weed to taste. Cover and refrigerate at least 30 minutes.

Makes approximately 3⅓ cups
Calories per tablespoon: 12

SALMON PÂTÉ

1 7¾-ounce can pink salmon
½ cup canned water-packed artichoke hearts, drained
½ cup cooked green beans
⅓ cup canned green chili salsa
⅓ cup crumbled hoop cheese or other uncreamed cottage cheese
3 tablespoons diced canned pimiento
1 tablespoon onion powder
1½ teaspoons garlic powder
1½ teaspoons dill weed
⅛ teaspoon Tabasco (hot pepper sauce)

Remove skin and bones from the salmon and defat the salmon liquid by pouring it through cheesecloth. Place the salmon and its liquid in a blender with all the other ingredients; blend well. Chill for several hours to heighten flavor. Serve cold with raw vegetables or crackers.

Makes approximately 2 cups
Calories per tablespoon: 14

MOCK GUACAMOLE DIP

1 eggplant
3 tablespoons chopped fresh parsley
1 tablespoon chopped green onion
1 clove garlic
1 tablespoon lemon juice
1 large pepperoncini (pepper in vinegar), seeds and
    stem removed
1 teaspoon cumin
1 teaspoon dried parsley
½ teaspoon onion powder
⅛ teaspoon cayenne pepper
½ cup nonfat buttermilk
⅔ cup crumbled hoop cheese or other uncreamed cot-
    tage cheese
Dash salt (optional)

Pierce the eggplant skin in several places with a fork. Put the eggplant in a baking dish and bake in a 400° oven until tender, about 25 minutes. When cool, peel the eggplant and press the excess liquid from it. Place the eggplant in a blender with the parsley, green onion, garlic, lemon juice, pepperoncini, and spices; blend until smooth and pour into another container. Add the buttermilk and hoop cheese to the blender and blend until very smooth. Return eggplant mixture to blender and blend all.

Makes approximately 2½ cups
Calories per tablespoon: 8

CAPONATA

1 eggplant
2–3 tomatoes (Italian tomatoes, if available)
2 red or green bell peppers
1 white onion
3 tablespoons red wine vinegar
Oregano to taste

Pierce the eggplant skin in several places with a fork. Put the eggplant in a baking dish and bake at 400° until tender, about 25 minutes. When cool, peel and chop the eggplant. Chop the tomatoes, peppers, and onion and mix them with the eggplant. Add the vinegar and oregano. Serve as a relish or as a dip with *CHAPATIS* (whole-wheat tortillas) or pita bread.

Makes 6–8 servings
Calories per serving (⅙ recipe): 51

SALSA

4 cups peeled and diced tomatoes, fresh or canned
1 cup chopped onions
2 diced canned green chilies
2 tablespoons tomato paste
1 tablespoon red wine vinegar
2 teaspoons lemon juice
1 teaspoon garlic powder
Dash cayenne pepper

If using fresh tomatoes, place the whole tomatoes in boiling water for about one minute; then cool, peel, and dice.

Mix all the ingredients together, chill, and serve as a relish or dip, or as a topping for salads, hot vegetables, baked potatoes, or rice.

Makes approximately 1 quart
Calories per ¼ cup: 21

HORSERADISH

½ cup canned beets, drained (reserve some of the liquid)
2 teaspoons liquid from canned beets
2 teaspoons powdered horseradish
½ teaspoon vinegar
⅛ teaspoon onion powder
⅛ teaspoon garlic powder
⅛ teaspoon dry mustard

Put all the ingredients in a blender and blend until smooth.
Makes ½ cup
Calories per tablespoon: approximately 5

FISH DRESSING

1 15-ounce can tomato sauce
¼ cup water
1 tablespoon lemon or lime juice
1 cup crumbled hoop cheese or other uncreamed cottage cheese
1 tablespoon dried minced onion
1 teaspoon Dijon mustard
1 teaspoon powdered horseradish
½ teaspoon basil
⅛ teaspoon Tabasco (hot pepper sauce)

Place all the ingredients in a blender and blend until smooth, stirring as required. Chill before serving.

Makes 2⅓ cups
Calories per tablespoon: 8

CARROT SPREAD

6 carrots, quartered
1 onion, quartered
2⅓ cups crumbled hoop cheese or other uncreamed cottage cheese
¼ teaspoon cinnamon
½ teaspoon basil (optional)

Place the carrots and onion in a steamer basket or pot with a little boiling water. Steam, covered, for about 20 minutes or until vegetables are tender. Blend the carrots, onion, cheese, and seasonings in a food processor (or blender) until smooth. Spread on crackers or raw vegetables, or squeeze through a pastry tube for canapé decoration.

Makes approximately 3 cups
Calories per ¼ cup: 43

BEET SPREAD

4 beets
1 tablespoon dry white wine
2⅓ cups crumbled hoop cheese or other uncreamed
  cottage cheese

Place the beets in a steamer basket or pot with boiling water. Steam, covered, for 20–30 minutes or until almost tender. Peel and cut into quarters and steam again, using fresh boiling water, for about 10 minutes or until tender. Blend the beets, wine, and cheese in a food processor (or blender) until smooth. Spread on crackers or raw vegetables, or squeeze through a pastry tube for canapé decoration.

Makes approximately 3 cups
Calories per ¼ cup: 30

MOCK SOUR CREAM

½–¾ cup nonfat buttermilk
1 cup crumbled hoop cheese or other uncreamed cot-
  tage cheese
½–1 teaspoon vinegar or lemon juice (optional)

Pour ½ cup of the nonfat buttermilk into a blender and add the cheese a little at a time, blending and stirring as required to mix well. Add more buttermilk if necessary and blend until smooth. If a more sour flavor is desired, add a little vinegar or lemon juice and blend again.

NOTE: MOCK SOUR CREAM is a basic preparation useful as a topping for baked potatoes, salad, vegetables, fruit, enchiladas, and other dishes. It is also a versatile base for dips, spreads, and salad dressings, and can often be used in place of yogurt. It is practical to make this recipe in larger quantities for freezing. To use after freezing, thaw and stir vigorously. If the consistency needs thinning, stir in a little more buttermilk; if a thicker consistency is desired, blend in more cheese.

Makes approximately 1½ cups
Calories per ¼ cup: approximately 35

GREEN GODDESS TOPPING

    1 cup nonfat buttermilk
    2 cups crumbled hoop cheese or other uncreamed
        cottage cheese
    ½ cup chopped green onions
    2 pepperoncinis (peppers in vinegar), stems and seeds
        removed
    1 tablespoon prepared green taco sauce
    1 teaspoon basil
    1 teaspoon garlic powder
    1 teaspoon dried minced onion

Blend all ingredients together in a blender until smooth.
NOTE: A thinner topping may be made by adding a little more buttermilk, a thicker one by adding a little more cheese.
Makes approximately 2¼ cups
Calories per ¼ cup: 43

NONFAT YOGURT

    1 quart nonfat fluid milk
    ⅓ cup nonfat dry milk
    2 tablespoons low-fat yogurt or nonfat yogurt from
        previously made batch
    1½ teaspoons agar for added smoothness (optional)

Combine the milks, stirring to dissolve the dry milk thoroughly. Heat the mixture in a saucepan until it is almost boiling; it should just start to bubble slightly. Pour the hot milk into a container (glass, crockery, or stainless steel) and allow it to cool until about room temperature. Remove about ½ cup of the cooled milk and stir into it the low-fat or nonfat yogurt and agar if used. Stir the mixture back into the milk in the container. Place the container inside a larger vessel filled with warm water and cover with a towel. Set inside an oven overnight that has been preheated to 150° and then turned off. If you have an electric oven, turn the light on to provide warmth; in a gas oven, the pilot light is sufficient.

NOTE: Commercial yogurt up to 1 percent fat by weight may be used as a substitute for nonfat yogurt. Calories will be slightly increased.

Makes approximately 1 quart
Calories per ½ cup: 56

YOGURT "CREAM CHEESE"

3 cups nonfat yogurt

Place a cheesecloth-lined colander in a bowl. Pour in the yogurt, then gather the edges of the cheesecloth and tie. Set the entire assembly in the refrigerator and allow to drain overnight. Discard the liquid in the bowl (or use it in cooking).

VARIATION: Blend *YOGURT "CREAM CHEESE"* with 3 tablespoons chopped chives and 1 teaspoon each garlic powder and basil.

Makes approximately 1½ cups
Calories per tablespoon: approximately 18

YOGURT-HORSERADISH TOPPING

1 cup nonfat yogurt
1 teaspoon powdered horseradish
2 small green onions, chopped

Place the yogurt in a bowl. Add the horseradish and beat vigorously to blend flavor through. Stir in the green onions.

NOTE: This topping is good on fish, baked potatoes, and some vegetables, such as asparagus.

Makes approximately 1⅓ cups
Calories per tablespoon: 6

IRISH "CHOPPED LIVER"

1 large onion, coarsely diced
Defatted stock of choice (see recipes for stocks) or
*   water, as required*
1 16-ounce can French-style green beans, drained
4 hard-boiled egg whites (discard yolks)
Cayenne pepper to taste

Sauté the onion in a skillet in a small amount of stock or water until tender. Place the onion and the remaining ingredients in a food processor or blender and purée until smooth. Chill and serve as a dip or spread.

Makes 1¾ cups
Calories per ¼ cup: 36

Appendix

WALKING PROGRESSION PLAN

Begin at any level that is comfortable for you; if you haven't exercised in several years, it is best to start at Level 1. As you progress you may shorten the time spent at any level if you feel ready to do so.

	Days	Walking Sessions	Times per Day
LEVEL 1			
Weeks 1–2	Monday–Friday	10 min casual walking	3 × per day
	Saturday	10 min casual walking	4–6 × per day
	Sunday	Rest	
Weeks 3–4	Monday–Friday	15 min casual walking	3 × per day
	Saturday	15 min casual walking	4 × per day
	Sunday	Rest	
LEVEL 2			
Weeks 1–2	Monday–Friday	20 min casual walking	3 × per day
	Saturday	30 min casual walking	2 × per day
	Sunday	Rest	
Weeks 3–4	Monday–Friday	20 min brisk walking	3 × per day
	Saturday	30 min brisk walking	1 × per day
		30 min casual walking	1 × per day
	Sunday	Rest	
LEVEL 3			
Weeks 1–2	Monday–Friday	25 min casual walking	1 × per day
		25 min brisk walking	1 × per day
	Saturday	40 min casual walking	1 × per day
		20 min casual walking	1 × per day
	Sunday	Rest	
Weeks 3–4	Monday–Friday	30 min brisk walking	2 × per day
	Saturday	45 min casual walking	1 × per day
		20 min casual walking	1 × per day
	Sunday	Rest	
LEVEL 4			
Weeks 1–2	Monday–Friday	35 min brisk walking	2 × per day
	Saturday	60 min casual walking	1 × per day
	Sunday	Rest	
Weeks 3–4	Monday–Friday	40 min brisk walking	2 × per day
	Saturday	60 min casual walking	1 × per day
	Sunday	Rest	
LEVEL 5			
Weeks 1–2	Monday–Friday	30 min brisk walking	1 × per day
		45 min brisk walking	1 × per day
	Saturday	60 min casual walking	1 × per day
	Sunday	Rest	
Weeks 3–4	Monday–Friday	45 min brisk walking	2 × per day
	Saturday	75 min casual walking	1 × per day
	Sunday	Rest	
LEVEL 6			
Weeks 1–2	Monday–Friday	20 min brisk walking	1 × per day
		50 min brisk walking	1 × per day
	Saturday	90 min casual walking	1 × per day
	Sunday	Rest	
Weeks 3–4	Monday–Friday	60 min brisk walking	1 × per day
	Saturday	1½–2 hrs casual walking	1 × per day
	Sunday	Rest	

WALK/JOG PROGRESSION PLAN

If you can walk briskly for an hour and your health permits, you can start jogging. Most people will stay at each level for about a month; you can progress a little faster, or remain at the same level longer, if that's more comfortable.

LEVEL 1		TOTAL TIME: 40 min
Warmup	5 min	
Walk	20 min	
Alternate:		
Jog 30 sec		
Walk 2 min	10 min	
Cooldown	5 min	

LEVEL 2		TOTAL TIME: 55 min
Warmup	5 min	
Walk	30 min	
Alternate:		
Jog 45 sec		
Walk 1½ min	15 min	
Cooldown	5 min	

LEVEL 3		TOTAL TIME: 60 min
Warmup	5 min	
Walk	35 min	
Alternate:		
Jog 1 min		
Walk 1 min	15 min	
Cooldown	5 min	

LEVEL 4		TOTAL TIME: 60 min
Warmup	5 min	
Walk	30 min	
Alternate:		
Jog 1½ min		
Walk 1 min	20 min	
Cooldown	5 min	

LEVEL 5		TOTAL TIME: 60 min
Warmup	5 min	
Walk	30 min	
Alternate:		
Jog 2 min		
Walk 1 min	20 min	
Cooldown	5 min	

LEVEL 6		TOTAL TIME: 60 min
Warmup	5 min	
Walk	25 min	
Alternate:		
Jog 2½ min		
Walk 1 min	25 min	
Cooldown	5 min	

LEVEL 7		TOTAL TIME: 55 min
Warmup	5 min	
Walk	20 min	
Alternate:		
Jog 2½ min		
Walk 30 sec	25 min	
Cooldown	5 min	

LEVEL 8		TOTAL TIME: 50 min
Warmup	5 min	
Walk	15 min	
Alternate:		
Jog 3 min		
Walk 30 sec	25 min	
Cooldown	5 min	

LEVEL 9		TOTAL TIME: 50 min
Warmup	5 min	
Walk	10 min	
Alternate:		
Jog 3 min		
Walk 30 sec	20 min	
Jog continuously	10 min	
Cooldown	5 min	

LEVEL 10		TOTAL TIME: 50 min
Warmup	5 min	
Walk	10 min	
Alternate:		
Jog 3 min Walk 30 sec	15 min	
Jog continuously	15 min	
Cooldown	5 min	

LEVEL 11		TOTAL TIME: 50 min
Warmup	5 min	
Walk	5 min	
Alternate:		
Jog 5 min Walk 30 sec	15 min	
Jog continuously	20 min	
Cooldown	5 min	

LEVEL 12		TOTAL TIME: 50 min
Warmup	5 min	
Alternate:		
Jog 5 min Walk 30 sec	15 min	
Jog continuously	25 min	
Cooldown	5 min	

MAINTENANCE LEVEL		TOTAL TIME: 50–60 min
Warmup	5 min	
Jog continuously	40–50 min	
Cooldown	5 min	

TYPICAL MENU PLAN FOR NUTRITIONAL ANALYSIS

	700 kcal	850 kcal	1000 kcal	1200 kcal
BREAKFAST	½ cup HOT OATMEAL ¼ medium banana, sliced ½ cup nonfat milk, hot or cold ½ grapefruit	¾ cup HOT OATMEAL ½ medium banana, sliced ½ cup nonfat milk, hot or cold ½ grapefruit	1 cup HOT OATMEAL ½ medium banana, sliced ¾ cup nonfat milk, hot or cold ½ grapefruit	1½ cups HOT OATMEAL ½ medium banana, sliced ¾ cup nonfat milk, hot or cold ½ grapefruit
LUNCH	¾ cup CREAM OF CAULIFLOWER SOUP 1 cup MUSTARD GREENS, cooked RAW VEGETABLE SALAD No.1 (1 serving) 3 Tbsp. SPICY TOMATO DRESSING	¾ cup CREAM OF CAULIFLOWER SOUP 1 cup MUSTARD GREENS, cooked RAW VEGETABLE SALAD No.1 (1 serving) 3 Tbsp. SPICY TOMATO DRESSING 2 triple Rye Crisp crackers, unseasoned	1 cup CREAM OF CAULIFLOWER SOUP RAW VEGETABLE SALAD No.1 (1 serving) 3 Tbsp. SPICY TOMATO DRESSING 2 triple Rye Crisp crackers, unseasoned	1 cup CREAM OF CAULIFLOWER SOUP RAW VEGETABLE SALAD No. 1 (1 serving) in a whole-wheat pita-bread with SALSA (¼ cup) as dressing for sandwich 2 triple Rye Crisp crackers, unseasoned
DINNER	CHICKEN RATATOUILLE (1 serving) ½ cup cooked broccoli RAW VEGETABLE SALAD No. 1 (1 serving) 2 Tbsp. ITALIAN DRESSING 1 cup air-popped popcorn	CHICKEN RATATOUILLE (1 serving) ¾ cup cooked broccoli RAW VEGETABLE SALAD No. 1 (1 serving) 3 Tbsp. ITALIAN DRESSING 2 cups air-popped popcorn	CHICKEN RATATOUILLE (1 serving) ½ cup whole wheat noodles RAW VEGETABLE SALAD No. 1 (1 serving) 3 Tbsp. ITALIAN DRESSING 3 cups air-popped popcorn	CHICKEN RATATOUILLE (1 serving) ½ cup whole wheat noodles RAW VEGETABLE SALAD No. 1 (1 serving) 3 Tbsp. ITALIAN DRESSING 3 cups air-popped popcorn

NUTRITIONAL ANALYSIS OF A TYPICAL MENU WITH COMPARISON TO THE 1980 RDAs AND THE AVERAGE AMERICAN NUTRIENT INTAKES
(700 kcal/day)

FOOD	AMOUNT	CALO-RIES	PRO-TEIN	FAT	CARBO-HYDRATE
Oatmeal, cooked	½ cup	66	2.4	1.2	11.7
Banana	¼ med.	25.3	.3	.1	6.6
Nonfat milk	½ cup	44	4.4	.1	6.3
Grapefruit	½	40	.5	.1	10.3
CREAM OF CAULIFLOWER SOUP	6 oz.	81.5	6.9	.5	14.9
SALAD	1 recipe	53.4	3.8	.6	10.9
SPICY TOMATO DRESSING	3 Tbsp.	10.8	.45	—	2.7
Mustard greens, cooked	1 cup	32	3.1	.6	5.6
CHICKEN RATATOUILLE	1 serving	240.2	27	3	37.1
Broccoli, cooked	½ cup	20	2.4	.3	3.5
SALAD	1 recipe	53.4	3.8	.6	10.9
ITALIAN DRESSING	2 Tbsp.	12.4	.2	.2	3.2
Popcorn	1 cup	23	.8	.3	4.6
TOTAL		**702**	**56.1**	**7.6**	**128.2**

1980 RDAs:
( ) INDICATES AVERAGE AMERICAN INTAKES WHEN BELOW RDA LEVELS;
[ ] AMERICAN CALORIE INTAKES*

Men, 23–50 years of age		[2381]	56	—	—
Men. 51+ years of age		[2057]	—	—	—
Women, 23–50 years of age		[1565]	44	—	—
Women, 51+ years of age		[1436]	44	—	—

*U.S. Department of Agriculture, *Nationwide Food Consumption Survey 1977–78,* Preliminary Report No. 2

					MILLIGRAMS				
Ca	P	Fe	Na	K	VITA-MIN A (I.U.)	THIA-MIN	RIBO-FLAVIN	NIA-CIN	VITA-MIN C
11	68.5	.7	Tr	73	0	.1	Tr	.1	0
2.5	7.8	.2	.3	110	57.5	.02	.02	.2	3
148	116.5	.05	63.5	117.5	5	.05	.22	.1	1
16	16	.4	1	132	80	.04	.02	.2	37
138.4	155.8	1.5	74.2	525.4	898.4	.17	.25	1.2	91.5
101.9	76.5	2.8	42.6	615.9	4055.1	.16	.18	1.2	68.3
4.5	9.9	.36	3.0	97.5	318	.018	—	.24	7.5
193	45	2.5	25	308	8120	.11	.2	.8	67
149.2	332.8	5.9	74.2	1615.7	3638.9	.42	.4	11.6	141.7
68	48	.6	8	207	1940	.07	.16	.6	70
101.9	76.5	2.8	42.6	615.9	4055.1	.16	.18	1.2	68.3
6.6	7.6	.4	.6	47.2	117	.02	.04	.04	5
1	17	.2	Tr	—	—	—	.01	.1	0
942	977.9	18.42	335	4525	23,285	1.31	1.68	17.58	560.3
800 (720–800)	800	10			5000	1.4	1.6	18	60
800 (640–712)	800	10			5000	1.2	1.4	16	60
800 (<560–632)	800	18 (<12.6)			4000	1.0	1.2	13	60
800 (<560–632)	800	10			4000	1.0	1.2	13	60

NUTRITIONAL ANALYSIS OF A TYPICAL MENU WITH COMPARISON TO THE 1980 RDAs AND THE AVERAGE AMERICAN NUTRIENT INTAKES
(850 kcal/day)

				GRAMS	
FOOD	AMOUNT	CALO-RIES	PRO-TEIN	FAT	CARBO-HYDRATE
Oatmeal, cooked	¾ cup	99	3.6	1.8	17.6
Banana	½ med.	50.5	.7	.1	13.2
Nonfat milk	½ cup	44	4.4	.1	6.3
Grapefruit	½	40	.5	.1	10.3
CREAM OF CAULIFLOWER SOUP	6 oz.	81.5	6.9	.5	14.9
SALAD	1 recipe	53.4	3.8	.6	10.9
SPICY TOMATO DRESSING	3 Tbsp.	10.8	.45	—	2.7
Mustard greens, cooked	1 cup	32	3.1	.6	5.6
Rye crackers	2	50	2	0	10
CHICKEN RATATOUILLE	1 serving	240.2	27	3	37.1
Broccoli, cooked	¾ cup	30	3.6	.45	5.3
SALAD	1 recipe	53.4	3.8	.6	10.9
ITALIAN DRESSING	3 Tbsp.	18.6	.3	.3	4.8
Popcorn	2 cups	46	1.6	.6	9.2
TOTAL		849.4	61.8	8.8	158.8

1980 RDAs:
( ) INDICATES AVERAGE AMERICAN INTAKES WHEN BELOW RDA LEVELS;
[ ] AMERICAN CALORIE INTAKES*

Men, 23–50 years of age		[2381]	56	—	—
Men, 51+ years of age		[2057]	—	—	—
Women, 23–50 years of age		[1565]	44	—	—
Women, 51+ years of age		[1436]	44	—	—

*U.S. Department of Agriculture, *Nationwide Food Consumption Survey 1977–78*, Preliminary Report No. 2

					MILLIGRAMS				
Ca	P	Fe	Na	K	VITA-MIN A (I.U.)	THIA-MIN	RIBO-FLAVIN	NIA-CIN	VITA-MIN C
16.5	102.8	1.1	Tr	109.5	0	.15	Tr	.15	0
5	15.5	.4	.5	220	115	.03	.04	.4	6
148	116.5	.05	63.5	177.5	5	.05	.22	.1	1
16	16	.4	1	132	80	.04	.02	.2	37
138.4	155.8	1.5	74.2	525.4	898.4	.17	.25	1.2	91.5
101.9	76.5	2.8	42.6	615.9	4055.1	.16	.18	1.2	68.3
4.5	9.9	.36	3.0	97.5	318	.018	—	.24	7.5
193	45	2.5	25	308	8120	.11	.2	.8	67
—	—	.7	120	0	—	.7	—	—	—
149.2	332.8	5.9	74.2	1615.7	3638.9	.42	.4	11.6	141.7
102	72	.9	12	310.5	2910	.11	.24	.9	105
101.9	76.5	2.8	42.6	615.9	4055.1	.16	.18	1.2	68.3
9.9	11.4	.6	.9	70.8	175.5	.03	.06	.06	7.5
1	34	.4	Tr	—	—	—	.01	.1	0
987.3	1064.7	20.4	459.5	4769	24,371	2.15	1.8	18.2	600.8
800 (720–800)	800	10			5000	1.4	1.6	18	60
800 (640–712)	800	10			5000	1.2	1.4	16	60
800 (<560–632)	800 (<12.6)	18			4000	1.0	1.2	13	60
800 (<560–632)	800	10			4000	1.0	1.2	13	60

NUTRITIONAL ANALYSIS OF A TYPICAL MENU WITH COMPARISON TO THE 1980 RDAs AND THE AVERAGE AMERICAN NUTRIENT INTAKES (1000 kcal/day)

				GRAMS	
FOOD	AMOUNT	CALO-RIES	PRO-TEIN	FAT	CARBO-HYDRATE
Oatmeal, cooked	1 cup	132	4.8	2.4	23.3
Banana	½ med.	50.5	.7	.1	13.2
Nonfat milk	¾ cup	66	6.6	.15	9.5
Grapefruit	½	40	.5	.1	10.3
CREAM OF CAULIFLOWER SOUP	8 oz.	108.2	9.2	.7	19.8
SALAD	1 recipe	53.4	3.8	.6	10.9
SPICY TOMATO DRESSING	3 Tbsp.	10.8	.45	—	2.7
Rye crackers	2	50	2	0	10
CHICKEN RATATOUILLE	1 serving	240.2	27	3	37.1
Whole-wheat noodles	½ cup	100	3.3	1.2	18.7
SALAD	1 recipe	53.4	3.8	.6	10.9
ITALIAN DRESSING	3 Tbsp.	18.6	.3	.3	4.8
Popcorn	3 cups	69	2.4	.9	13.8
TOTAL		992.1	64.9	10.1	185

1980 RDAs:
( ) INDICATES AVERAGE
AMERICAN INTAKES WHEN
BELOW RDA LEVELS;
[ ] AMERICAN CALORIE
INTAKES*

Men, 23–50 years of age	[2381]	56	—	—
Men, 51+ years of age	[2057]	—	—	—
Women, 23–50 years of age	[1565]	44	—	—
Women, 51+ years of age	[1436]	44	—	—

*U.S. Department of Agriculture, *Nationwide Food Consumption Survey 1977–78*, Preliminary Report No. 2

MILLIGRAMS

Ca	P	Fe	Na	K	VITA-MIN A (I.U.)	THIA-MIN	RIBO-FLAVIN	NIA-CIN	VITA-MIN C
22	137	1.4	523	146	0	.19	.05	.2	0
5	15.5	.4	.5	220	115	.03	.04	.4	6
222	174.8	.08	95.3	266.3	7.5	.08	.33	.15	1.5
16	16	.4	1	132	80	.04	.02	.2	37
184.5	207.7	2.0	99	700.5	1197.9	.22	.33	1.6	122
101.9	76.5	2.8	42.6	615.9	4055.1	.16	.18	1.2	68.3
4.5	9.9	.36	3.0	97.5	318	.018	—	.24	7.5
—	—	.7	120	0	—	.7	—	—	—
149.2	332.8	5.9	74.2	1615.7	3638.9	.42	.4	11.6	141.7
8	47	.7	1.5	35	55	.11	.07	1	0
101.9	76.5	2.8	42.6	615.9	4055.1	.16	.18	1.2	68.3
9.9	11.4	.6	.9	70.8	175.5	.03	.06	.06	7.5
3	51	.6	Tr	—	—	—	.03	.3	0
827.9	1156.1	18.74	1003.6	4485.9	13,698	2.16	1.69	18.2	459.8

800 (720–800)	800	10			5000	1.4	1.6	18	60
800 (640–712)	800	10			5000	1.2	1.4	16	60
800 (<560–632)	800	18 (<12.6)			4000	1.0	1.2	13	60
800 (<560–632)	800	10			4000	1.0	1.2	13	60

NUTRITIONAL ANALYSIS OF A TYPICAL MENU WITH COMPARISON TO THE 1980 RDAs AND THE AVERAGE AMERICAN NUTRIENT INTAKES (1200 kcal/day)

FOOD	AMOUNT	CALORIES	PROTEIN	FAT	GRAMS CARBOHYDRATE
Oatmeal, cooked	1½ cup	198	7.2	3.6	35
Banana	½ med.	50.5	.7	.1	13.2
Nonfat milk	¾ cup	66	6.6	.15	9.5
Grapefruit	½	40	.5	.1	10.3
CREAM OF CAULIFLOWER SOUP	8 oz.	108.6	9.2	.7	19.8
Raw vegetables		53.4	3.8	.6	10.9
Whole-wheat pita, small	1	135	4.9	.4	23.5
SALSA	¼ cup	21.5	1	.2	4.8
Rye crackers	2	50	2	0	10
CHICKEN RATATOUILLE	1 serving	240.2	27	3	37.1
Whole-wheat noodles	½ cup	100	3.3	1.2	18.7
SALAD	1 recipe	53.4	3.8	.6	10.9
ITALIAN DRESSING	3 Tbsp.	18.6	.3	.3	4.8
Popcorn	3 cups	69	2.4	.9	13.8
TOTAL		1204.2	72.7	11.9	222.3

1980 RDAs:
( ) INDICATES AVERAGE
AMERICAN INTAKES WHEN
BELOW RDA LEVELS;
[ ] AMERICAN CALORIE
INTAKES*

Men, 23–50 years of age		[2381]	56	—	—
Men, 51+ years of age		[2057]	—	—	—
Women, 23–50 years of age		[1565]	44	—	—
Women, 51+ years of age		[1436]	44	—	—

*U.S. Department of Agriculture, *Nationwide Food Consumption Survey 1977–78*, Preliminary Report No. 2

				MILLIGRAMS					
Ca	P	Fe	Na	K	VITA-MIN A (I.U.)	THIA-MIN	RIBO-FLAVIN	NIA-CIN	VITA-MIN C
33	205.5	2.1	784.5	219	0	.29	.08	.3	0
5	15.5	.4	.5	220	115	.03	.04	.4	6
222	174.8	.08	95.3	266.3	7.5	.08	.33	.15	1.5
16	16	.4	1	132	80	.04	.02	.2	37
184.5	207.7	2.0	99	700.5	1197.9	.22	.33	1.6	122
101.9	76.5	2.8	42.6	615.9	4055.1	.16	.18	1.2	68.3
48	142	1.6	256	144	Tr	.18	.06	1.6	Tr
12.8	26.4	.5	3.2	240	880	Tr	Tr	.6	22.4
—	—	.7	120	0	—	.7	—	—	—
149.2	332.8	5.9	74.2	1615.7	3638.9	.42	.4	11.6	141.7
8	47	.7	1.5	35	55	.11	.07	1	0
101.9	76.5	2.8	42.6	615.9	4055.1	.16	.18	1.2	68.3
9.9	11.4	.6	.9	70.8	175.5	.03	.06	.06	7.5
3	51	.6	Tr	—	—	—	.03	.03	0
895.2	1383.1	21.2	1521.3	4875.1	14,268	2.42	1.78	20.2	474.7

Ca	P	Fe	Na	K	VITA-MIN A (I.U.)	THIA-MIN	RIBO-FLAVIN	NIA-CIN	VITA-MIN C
800 (720–800)	800	10			5000	1.4	1.6	18	60
800 (640–712)	800	10			5000	1.2	1.4	16	60
800 (<560–632)	800	18 (<12.6)			4000	1.0	1.2	13	60
800 (<560–632)	800	10			4000	1.0	1.2	13	60

CALORIC DENSITY TABLES

Table A lists foods in ascending order of number of calories per 8-ounce cup. Table B lists the same foods by food group, and Table C lists them alphabetically. Values are given for *cooked* vegetables, whole grains, legumes, and meats, and for *raw* fresh fruit, unless otherwise specified. Foods marked with a dagger (†) are to be avoided no matter what their caloric density because they are high in fat or cholesterol.

CALORIC DENSITY TABLE A

Food Item	Calories in 8-ounce Cup
Use Freely **(*0–64 calories in 8-ounce cup)**	
*Lettuce, Boston and Bibb (varieties of butter lettuce)	8
*Lettuce, romaine	10
*Cucumbers, raw	16
*Mushrooms, raw	20
*Celery, raw	20
*Cabbage	24
*Bok choy	24
*Cauliflower	28
*Squash, summer	29
*Turnip greens	29
*Green beans	31
*Mustard greens	32
*Bell peppers, green, raw	33
*Asparagus	36
*Broccoli	40
*Spinach	41
*Tomatoes, raw	45
*Carrots, raw	46
*Bell peppers, red, raw	47
*Beets	54
*Brussels sprouts	56
*Collard greens	63
*Artichokes[1]	—

[1]The caloric value of artichokes varies widely, but they are a low-calorie food.

Use in Moderation
(**65–144 calories in 8-ounce cup)

**Grapes	70
**Peaches	70
**Apples	73
**Apricots	79
**Bread	81
**Oranges	81
**Pineapples	81
**Milk, skim	88
**Squash, winter	93
**Pears	101
**Peas, frozen	109
**Orange juice	112
**Plums	112
**Apple juice	117
**Potatoes, white, boiled in skin	118
**Cornmeal	120
**Yogurt, part skim	123
**Egg whites, boiled	124
**Corn grits	125
**Cottage cheese, uncreamed	125
**Oatmeal	132

Restrict
(***145–249 calories in 8-ounce cup)

***Milk, low-fat	145
***Shrimp	148
***Yogurt, regular	152
***Milk, whole	159
***Clams, raw	170
***Oysters, raw (depending on variety)	±188
***Bananas	191
***Milk, chocolate	213
***Eggs, whole, boiled (whites may be used in moderation)	222
***Beans, most varieties	224
***Rice, brown, long grain	232
***Chicken, light meat without skin	232
***Soybeans	234

†***Cottage cheese, regular	239
***Chicken, dark meat without skin	246
***Turkey, light meat without skin	246

Avoid
(****250 + calories in 8-ounce cup)

****Turkey, dark meat without skin	284
****Catsup	289
****Potatoes, sweet, boiled in skin (depending on variety)	±291
****Tuna, packed in oil and drained	315
****Ice cream, 16 percent fat	329
****Milk, whole, evaporated	345
****Avocados	384
****McDonald's Quarter Pounder	420
****Cheese, cheddar	450
****Potatoes, white, fried	456
****Hamburger, 21 percent fat	648
****Chocolate, baking	667
****Sugar, white, granulated	770
****Walnuts	781
****Cashews	785
****Maple syrup	794
****Pecans	811
****Sunflower seeds	812
****Sugar, brown	821
****Almonds	849
****Milk, condensed	982
****Peanut butter	1520
****Butter	1625
****Margarine	1634
****Corn oil	1927

CALORIC DENSITY TABLE B

*0–64 calories in 8-ounce cup   Use Freely
**65–144 calories in 8-ounce cup   Use in Moderation
***145–249 calories in 8-ounce cup   Restrict
****250+ calories in 8-ounce cup   Avoid

Food Item	*Calories in 8-ounce Cup*
Vegetables	
*Lettuce, Boston and Bibb (varieties of butter lettuce)	8
*Lettuce, romaine	10
*Cucumbers, raw	16
*Mushrooms, raw	20
*Celery, raw	20
*Cabbage	24
*Bok choy	24
*Cauliflower	28
*Squash, summer	29
*Turnip greens	29
*Green beans	31
*Mustard greens	32
*Bell peppers, green, raw	33
*Asparagus	36
*Broccoli	40
*Spinach	41
*Tomatoes, raw	45
*Carrots, raw	46
*Bell peppers, red, raw	47
*Beets	54
*Brussels sprouts	56
*Collard greens	63
*Artichokes[1]	—
**Squash, winter	93
**Peas, frozen	109
**Potatoes, white, boiled in skin	118
**Corn	137
****Potatoes, sweet, boiled in skin (depending on variety)	±291
****Avocados	384
****Potatoes, white, fried	456

[1]The caloric value of artichokes varies widely, but they are a low-calorie food.

Food Item	*Calories in 8-ounce Cup*

Fruits

**Grapes	70
**Peaches	70
**Apples	73
**Apricots	79
**Oranges	81
**Pineapples	81
**Pears	101
**Plums	112
**Orange juice	112
**Apple juice	117
***Bananas	191

Grains

**Bread	81
**Cornmeal	120
**Corn grits	125
**Oatmeal	132
***Rice, brown, long grain	232

Dairy Products

**Milk, skim	88
**Yogurt, part skim	123
**Cottage cheese, uncreamed	125
***Milk, low-fat	145
†***Yogurt, regular	152
†***Milk, whole	159
†***Milk, chocolate	213
†***Cottage cheese, regular	239
****Milk, whole, evaporated	345
****Cheese, cheddar	450
****Milk, condensed	982

Food Item	Calories in 8-ounce Cup

Legumes

***Beans, most varieties	224
***Soybeans	234

Meat, Poultry, Seafood, and Eggs

**Egg whites, boiled	124
***Shrimp	148
***Clams, raw	170
***Oysters, raw (depending on variety)	±188
†***Eggs, whole, boiled (whites may be used in moderation)	222
***Chicken, light meat without skin	232
***Chicken, dark meat without skin	246
***Turkey, light meat without skin	246
***Turkey, dark meat without skin	284
****Tuna, packed in oil and drained	315
****McDonald's Quarter Pounder	420
****Hamburger, 21 percent fat	648

Desserts, Sweets, and Condiments

****Catsup	289
****Ice cream, 16 percent fat	329
****Chocolate, baking	667
****Sugar, white, granulated	770
****Maple syrup	794
****Sugar, brown	821

Nuts and Seeds

****Walnuts	781
****Cashews	785
****Pecans	811

Food Item	Calories in 8-ounce Cup
****Sunflower seeds	812
****Almonds	849
****Peanut butter	1520

Fats and Oils

****Butter	1625
****Margarine	1634
****Corn oil	1927

CALORIC DENSITY TABLE C

*0–64 calories in 8-ounce cup	Use Freely
**65–144 calories in 8-ounce cup	Use in Moderation
***145–249 calories in 8-ounce cup	Restrict
****250 + calories in 8-ounce cup	Avoid

Food Item	Calories in 8-ounce Cup
****Almonds	849
**Apple juice	117
**Apples	73
**Apricots	79
*Artichokes[1]	—
*Asparagus	36
****Avocados	384
***Bananas	191
***Beans, most varieties	224
*Beets	54
*Bell peppers, green, raw	33
*Bell peppers, red, raw	47
*Bok choy	24

[1]The caloric value of artichokes varies widely, but they are a low-calorie food.

**Bread	81
*Broccoli	40
*Brussels sprouts	56
****Butter	1625
*Cabbage	24
*Carrots, raw	46
****Cashews	785
****Catsup	289
*Cauliflower	28
*Celery, raw	20
****Cheese, cheddar	450
***Chicken, dark meat without skin	246
***Chicken, light meat without skin	232
****Chocolate, baking	667
***Clams, raw	170
*Collard greens	63
**Corn	127
**Corn grits	125
**Cornmeal	120
****Corn oil	1927
†***Cottage cheese, regular	239
**Cottage cheese, uncreamed	125
*Cucumbers, raw	16
†***Eggs, whole, boiled (whites may be used in moderation)	222
**Egg whites, boiled	120
**Grapes	70
*Green beans	31
****Hamburger, 21 percent fat	648
****Ice cream, 16 percent fat	329
*Lettuce, Boston and Bibb (varieties of butter lettuce)	8
*Lettuce, romaine	10
****McDonald's Quarter Pounder	420
****Maple syrup	794
****Margarine	1634
†***Milk, chocolate	213
****Milk, condensed	982
****Milk, whole, evaporated	345
***Milk, low-fat	145
**Milk, skim	88
†***Milk, whole	159
*Mushrooms, raw	20

*Mustard greens	32
**Oatmeal	132
**Orange juice	112
**Oranges	81
***Oysters, raw (depending on variety)	±188
**Peaches	70
****Peanut Butter	1520
**Pears	101
**Peas, frozen	109
****Pecans	811
**Pineapples	81
**Plums	112
****Potatoes, sweet, boiled in skin (depending on variety)	±291
**Potatoes, white, boiled in skin	118
****Potatoes, white, fried	456
***Rice, brown, long grain	232
**Shrimp	148
***Soybeans	234
*Spinach	41
*Squash, summer	29
**Squash, winter	93
****Sugar, brown	821
****Sugar, white, granulated	770
****Sunflower seeds	812
*Tomatoes, raw	45
****Tuna, packed in oil and drained	315
****Turkey, dark meat without skin	284
***Turkey, light meat without skin	246
*Turnip greens	29
****Walnuts	781
**Yogurt, part skim	123
†****Yogurt, regular	152

Recipe Index

381

General Index

A SPECIAL NOTE TO THE READER

After you have reached your proper weight, it is important to continue with the weight-maintenance program so that you will remain at your optimum weight. The maintenance program is described in greater detail in *The Pritikin Program for Diet and Exercise*. Recipes for weight maintenance are included in this book.

Of course, many meals are consumed away from home, and there is a small but growing number of restaurants offering Pritikin menus and meals. The Pritikin staff welcomes inquiries from restaurants wishing to offer Pritikin food and exhibit our identification stating that their dishes meet Pritikin guidelines. Please let us know of restaurants in your area that claim to offer Pritikin-approved menus so that we can make sure they subscribe to our guidelines.

We hope that the vast majority of people will find the ideas expressed in this book of substantial help. For others, the residence programs under medical supervision at our East and West Coast Centers may be advantageous. Here we offer a two-week (or longer) program for those who wish to lose weight or who may be on some prescription drugs and wish to learn a new way of living and eating. A 26-day program is also provided for those on substantial medication and who require more intensive medical supervision. Still others, who do not require medical supervision and who would find a residence program not practical for them, may wish to participate in the group-support educational Pritikin Better Health Program in neighborhood communities.

Almost daily, new research in nutrition and degenerative diseases confirms our basic program. Choosing the Pritikin way of life will put you years ahead of current diet and health recommendations. To assist those who need help in preparing meals for the weight-loss or maintenance programs, the Pritikin staff conducts ongoing research and development of food products. We have developed a Pritikin bread, and are in the process of developing other food products, including soups and entrées suitable for the 700–1200 calories-per-day weight-loss diets. For further information, or to be put on our mailing list and kept abreast of new developments, please write to Pritikin Programs, P.O. Box 5335, Santa Barbara, California 93108.

ABOUT THE AUTHOR

NATHAN PRITIKIN was the founder and director of the Longevity Center and the Pritikin Research Foundation. For over twenty years he conducted research in worldwide literature in the fields of nutrition, exercise and degenerative diseases, followed by clinical studies that corroborated the concepts he had developed. Mr. Pritikin, who held more than two dozen patents (U.S. and foreign) in chemistry, physics and electronics, was an Honorary Fellow of the International Academy of Preventive Medicine and coauthor of the bestselling *Live Longer Now*. Mr. Pritikin died in 1985.

We Deliver!
And So Do These Bestsellers.